AUTHORS

AUTHORS

KARL MILLER

Oxford   New York

OXFORD UNIVERSITY PRESS

1990

Oxford University Press, Walton Street, Oxford OX2 6DP
Oxford New York Toronto
Delhi Bombay Calcutta Madras Karachi
Petaling Jaya Singapore Hong Kong Tokyo
Nairobi Dar es Salaam Cape Town
Melbourne Auckland
and associated companies in
Berlin Ibadan

Oxford is a trade mark of Oxford University Press

First published 1989
First issued as an Oxford University Press paperback 1990

British Library Cataloguing in Publication Data
Miller, Karl 1931–
Authors
1. Authorship. I. Title
808.02
ISBN 0–19–212277–0

Library of Congress Cataloging in Publication Data
Miller, Karl, 1931–
Authors / Karl Miller.
p. cm.
Reprint. Originally published: Oxford : Clarendon Press, 1989. Includes index.
1. Authorship. I. Title.
809—dc20   [PN145.M487 1990]   90–38689
ISBN 0–19–212277–0

Printed in Great Britain by
Biddles Ltd.
Guildford and King's Lynn

PREFACE

For many years now we have been accustomed to speak of
authors in terms of intrusion. We intrude on their privacy, and
discover their intrusion into the books they write. They should
keep out of there, or should hide there. The concern with intrusion, with artistic impersonality, was a feature of Modernist programmes early in this century. Later in the century
we have been told by experts that authors are absent, or unimportant, that the power of their individuality has been
removed, and that the intending, responsible self of our
working assumptions is a delusion. This is a century in which
the self has survived, but in which it has not always been
allowed to write books.

In the chapters that follow there is no claim that authors
should be denied a private capacity, or prevented—if they wish
it, and so far as their occupation permits it—from keeping
themselves to themselves. Nor is there meant to be any idea
that art and autobiography can never be usefully distinguished.
But it is as well to say here that I believe, with the uninstructed,
that authors have personal lives which they communicate—but
which, as on many occasions in their private capacity, they
may not obtrude or display and may even dissemble—in the
various kinds of writing that they produce. The personal life of
a given writer is seen as continuous with his or her works and
the whole show is seen as exposed to a play of influence and
resemblance, to an activity of other works and other lives,
which nowhere justifies the presumption of any abrogation or
transcendence of personality. It seems to me a mistake to
suppose that there are works which escape what has been
spoken of as the limitations of the personal.

These are among the matters treated in the present book. It
has essays on writers, for the most part living novelists, whom
I have enjoyed reading in recent years, and several of the books
which come under discussion have seemed to me to raise points
of interpretation which directly relate to the by now somewhat
bewildering question of what authors are for those who read

them. Two of these authors could be called amateurs, and in this context amateurs are of interest. What are they, that other writers are not? Could it be said of them that, while not especially intrusive, they rarely attempt the impersonal? The first, Louisa Stuart, is a British author of the past, who wrote copiously, but hoped never to see her name in print: on the face of it, the *ne plus ultra* of authorial privacy. Stuart's 'memoirs' are—though more restricted in purview—fit company for the 'memorials' of her contemporary, the Whig lawyer Henry Cockburn, about whom I have written previously: their worlds seldom met, their politics collided, but there is a distinct affinity of talent and of temperament. The second of these authors is the Italian Primo Levi, whose name has been much in print, and who began his writing career with the intention of recording what had happened in the concentration camps of Nazi Germany. There is no difficulty about discovering him in his books.

The book consists of pieces which have been written—or, in the case of the one on V. S. Naipaul, revised—since 1985, when I published a book entitled *Doubles*. *Doubles* was about the literature of an experience which can be declared both hypothetical and historical: that of finding yourself the same but different, of finding within yourself a someone else, of wanting to say, as a boy of whom I have heard is given to saying about some objectionable act of his, that 'Jack did it'. This literature says that to be on your own, and under threat, may divide you; and the stories told of you are stories in which the victim of hostility may prove hostile. There is a sense both of exclusion and of escape. In the course of referring to literary works which pre-date Romanticism, where the debut of the modern double is usually located, the present book has remarks to make about the origins of romantic duality—which are considered with reference to the language and practice of alchemy, and to certain passages in the fiction and family life of eighteenth-century England; and it has romantic duality in mind, at times, when it refers to the question of authorship, and to the factor of resemblance in authorship. This is a factor which can be brought into relation with experiences suggestive of duplication, division and ambivalence: one writer can be like another in something like the way in which one person can be two. With their simultaneous displays of dependence and independence, resemblance and idiosyncrasy, authors are the same but different—like the human beings of whom they continue to be constituted.

To speak of authorship in terms of resemblance, in terms of the imitations that pursue it, and may never reach it, and may wander very far away from it, and in terms of the self that is different from others and dependent on others—to speak in this way is to do what, from time to time, has long been done. The Renaissance debate concerning *imitatio*, in which a Classical Roman debate was resumed, produced versions of this idea of sameness and difference, with Erasmus contending for an inventive and ingestive copying of the ancients. We find Erasmus writing in eloquent praise of the self-expressive individual author. To the dialogue presented by him in the *Ciceronianus* there succeeded the essays of Montaigne; to the power and authority of precedent, both men enable us to think, there succeeds and responds, in the manner of a dialogue, the power of the self-portrait. The observations on this subject which have been derived for the present book from a reading of later texts could at times, as I have suggested, be thought to repeat some part of what was said then. I should be so lucky as to be thought, in this respect, a pale shadow. It is impossible not to be impressed by the richness of the Humanist debate, and by that of the scholarship which has construed it over the past twenty-five years.

Some authors are more imitative than others, and we like to point out the resemblers among them, just as we like to point out the intruders. Both the resembling and the idiosyncratic author have to be seen as formed, determined; neither is 'free'. And yet there are those who are moved to treat the latter, to treat authorial uniqueness, and to treat what they think of as gift, or genius, in terms of an exemption from the thought of conditioning, as from the perception of resemblance and aggregation among writers: idiosyncrasy is said to owe nothing. The essays in this book are not so moved. They are meant to convey that authors can be told apart, that authorial uniqueness is likely to be valued by readers—by the reader who values his own uniqueness, willing though he may also be to share it with others, and indeed with authors: but that no author is ever in any interesting way alone.

It's not controversial to assert that literature haunts itself. A character in a book may be like the character in some earlier or later book. One writer may copy another, and may or may not mean to do so. Hamlet creates Hamlets, and his father's ghost was to set a style for later visitations. Don Quixote rides again, and again. Richardson's Lovelace leads to Laclos's Valmont, to Byron's Byron, and to Lermontov's Pechorin. A sisterhood of afflicted women spans the literature and historical record of the eighteenth century. Poor boys of various denominations may resemble one another, and there are ways of writing about them which were prominent during the Romantic period, but which pre-date it, and which recur over long intervals of time.

Meanwhile, from time to time, a cult of individuality, originality, of the unprecedented, has come and gone. It is not at present in good heart. Leavis's teaching enjoined the detection of 'unconscious reminiscence': but the hunt for culprits and flagrancies of this kind has been called off, and we can often appear now to belong to an age of imitation and intertextuality. Peter Ackroyd's fictions and biographies are appreciations of the art that alludes to art and repeats it, that tries conclusions with the foregone. These books of his are praised and opposed in this book of mine. His celebration of imitations is celebrated, and in a sense imitated, by a discussion which has doubts about it. Ackroyd and I are the same but different. We belong to a world in which renewal and rebuttal are apt to coincide.

This is a world made up of items which are different, incomparable, but which is full of resemblances, in which the study of literature has pursued the one-and-onlyness of certain authors while also pursuing comparison, provenance, coincidence, influence, reminiscence and cultural formation. And there has been an invidious modern tendency for the pursuit of resemblance to be directed at the 'lower' levels of literature, where sociological enquiries are allowed to do what they can, and for incomparability to serve in some devout way as a mark of excellence—as in the case of the parodist, the inimitable imitator, Beerbohm.

One of the essays in this book refers to Samuel Richardson's novel *Clarissa*, published in 1748. Laclos's novel *Les Liaisons dangereuses*, which was published in 1782, has often been compared with it. Difference and coincidence are present here. Determination, and imitation, are present. Each work could be thought to exhibit a divided purpose which may in part have eluded its author, and which may have tended in some degree to subdue or subvert him: but the sense of an author takes control of this affinity, as it takes control of others. No one would regard the works as clones, as peas in a pod, or as sharing an author.

Both of these works are based on letters that pass between the characters—a literary form which expedited the rise of the novel in the modern world. From *La Princesse de Clèves* onwards, the novel had taken an interest in the violation of pious women, and both works tell the story of an attempt upon virtue. Both are disapprovingly aware of an established libertinage while lending themselves to the sexual freedoms which were to be associated with certain sections of eighteenth-century society. Clarissa is attempted by Lovelace; Madame de Tourvel by the Vicomte de Valmont, who is a less compelling and a less individual Lovelace. Lovelace is of better birth than his victim. Both seducers are of better birth than the writers who thought them up. Laclos has been credited with the thwarted ambitions of an army officer, and with a reformer's concern with the position and education of women, a concern which may be judged to answer to Richardson's missionary interest in the correction of manners, opportunities for self-improvement on the part of the lower classes, and the inculcation of severities in the matter of conscience and religious observance. Both reformers risked the blunting of these purposes by suffering themselves to be violated by the successful depiction of successful and powerful libertine patricians.

Laclos states his awareness of Richardson, whose novels had brought about by then a world-wide dependence and resemblance. Valmont's letters boast of his intention to seduce Madame de Tourvel—in view of her renowned piety, an outlandishly difficult capture, which is conducted along the lines of a military manual—and, in particular, to cause her knowingly to submit to him, against her principles. This is to be his *gloire*. And this is what has become of the *gloire* spoken of by Madame de Lafayette and by Corneille. Madame de Tourvel sobs and swoons, then presses his hand at the door of her apartment: an

'almost involuntary' pressure, and 'one more proof of my
domination'. He is now confident that she would 'run after me
if I ceased to run after her'. He sends his valet to spy on her at
her reading: she is reckoned to be engaged on the first volume
of *Clarissa*. The valet adds: 'Monsieur will perhaps know it.'
Valmont knows the novel well enough to write of what it would
be to 'make a new Clarissa' of Madame de Tourvel by drugging
her and subjecting her to rape. But 'it is not enough for me to
possess her, I want her to yield to me.'

When Madame de Tourvel is possessed, however, it is
when, like Clarissa, she has lost consciousness—during one of
her swoons. Valmont's glory now requires that he insult her,
and she dies of grief and shame, in a further transport. Clarissa,
too, dies after her violation. But there is a difference. She *wants*
to die; she affirms her death; it will take her to a better world,
where she will be rewarded for her ordeal and steadfastness.
Richardson voluminously imparts that for those who live as
they should it is better to be dead. Clarissa has not yielded, and
is not defeated. Madame de Tourvel has been coerced, but she
has also yielded. Hers is not a happy death: and this could be
connected with the sense we occasionally have in the Laclos,
but never in the Richardson, that there can sometimes be a
happiness, a heaven, in sexual relations.

Both works sympathise with the woman who is the target of
the wicked intrigues: and yet they are both capable of arousing
a sympathy with their seducers. Richardson was sorry to meet
readers who preferred Lovelace to Clarissa, and we can take it
that a *goût de Valmont* was to prevail in France. These tastes
conflict with the willingness of both writers to educate and
reform. Richardson's religion is inscribed in his novel, together
with a solicitude for women which accepts their subordination.
Laclos, whose willingness is less palpable, is none the less a
transmitter of sentiments concerning the education of women,
and the exercise of privilege which insults them and which
subordinates army officers. At the same time, both books show
an exercise of aristocratic self-will, tempered by authorial
intent and by the conflicting loyalties inherent in the epistolary
form.

The Laclos has both a wicked man and a wicked woman.
Madame de Meurteuil is Valmont's superior, in wit and in

the energy of her inventions. She teaches the lesson that well-born women are under-educated, and is then punished for her accession to power by being disfigured with smallpox and banished from Paris—a fate worse, we may be meant to feel, than that of her co-conspirator, who meets Lovelace's dignified death in a duel. She is allowed at moments to suggest that sex may be pursued as a desirable experience in its own right, and not simply as a means of domination. It could be said of both books, however, that domination is their dominant concern and the source and limitation of much of the eroticism they contain: an equivocally regarded domination of women by men which is also the domination exercised by a ruling class.

All books are different, and not just those that are taken into the canon, where these two have never been entirely welcome. The battle of the books which is now being fought in certain quarters, and in which a victory for resemblance is being claimed, will not put an end to the telling of differences. But it is also true that these are two different books which are especially available to those who wish to build on literature's likenesses in order to argue for the existence, in relation to it, of fields of force, processes of change, factors of influence—among which can be classified, in the case of the new *Clarissa*, the old *Clarissa*. During the Romantic period, and at times thereafter, with the spread of the various romantic sexualities, the *Clarissas* could be read, or misread, as convergent texts of an erotic kind, as evidence of a phase of expansion or transgression in the sphere of sexual relations, of a time during which Lovelace could be preferred: and such readings may well have paid very little attention to the way in which, in both books, sexuality is, as we have learnt to think of it, displaced by, or subsumed in, a preoccupation with power and with the divine power that bestows salvation. There seem to have been Victorians for whom Richardson's *Clarissa*, with its freedom of speech and fearful subject, was the work of a kind of libertine. In this sense among others, the French novel's resembling of *Clarissa* can be found as engrossing as its transformational properties, idiosyncrasy and divergence.

Clarissa and *Les Liaisons dangereuses* have been treated as lesser works by canonical standards, and *Clarissa* has been treated as a lesser work than *Les Liaisons dangereuses*. Richardson's reputation has been the target of compounded snobberies. His religion has not appealed to successive literary cultures; he was seen as doctrinal at times when art and doctrine had been uncoupled. The disparagement of Laclos—as cynical, commercial, rational —has been more relenting, I think, and there has indeed been a wish to canonise his novel. For Baudelaire, this was *un livre essentiellement Français*, and so it was for Martin Turnell in his canon-conscious *The Novel in France*, which came out in 1950. While giving the impression that he does not like the way the novel is written, Turnell concludes that it makes its 'English counterpart' appear 'crude and immature'.

That is not how *Clarissa* appears to me. It appears to me that there has never been a book like it—much as one may also want to say that it is like *Pamela*, and like *Les Liaisons dangereuses*. Its hugeness and perseverance, the proliferating 'moments' of its tragic drama of conflicting wills—all this can more readily be seen as *sui generis* than as repeatable or programmatic, and has, indeed, more in common with Proust than with its French counterpart. There are none of the *longueurs* that occur in Laclos's concise yet eventful account, which is also an altogether less inward account. The Laclos is theatrical in a way that the Richardson is not. It is on the stage in London as I write, has been there for a long time, and looks as if it would require a military intervention to drive it off, and it has recently been made by Stephen Frears into a dynamic film. The drama to be found in Richardson's novel lies in the closets where the solitaries Clarissa and Lovelace plot and ponder— though there are doors which open on to a stage where sentiment and declamation perform their opera, or Restoration tragedy, and windows through which peers an England of rising expectations. Both the inwardness and the outwardness of the book carry the reader back into the past. *Clarissa* persuades you that the author and his characters are representative and resembling, while just as much persuading you of the individuality both of the author and of each of the characters who severally resemble him. I hope that when I come to talk about the novel again later in this book, and to link it with other events and testimonies of the past to which it carries us, it will be clear how much its incomparability is loved and prized.

Some of these chapters are based on material published in the *London Review of Books*. The chapter which deals with literary journalism draws on a lecture I gave at a conference on the subject held in Canberra, at the Australian National University, in May 1987. I am very grateful to my friends Susannah Clapp and Kathryn Metzenthin for the advice and assistance I have received from them. I have also benefited from discussions with Alison Thorne and Ian Hamilton.

CONTENTS

I · Things

GHOSTS did not go out when electric light came in, though it could be felt at the time that this was bound to happen. They can look like a trick of the moonlight and candlelight of the past: and yet most of the pieces in the *Oxford Book of English Ghost Stories*[1] are taken from the well-lighted last quarter of the last century and first quarter of this one. Readers of the book could be excused for thinking that ghosts have been turned on by the mechanisms which have produced the illuminations of the modern world, that they are a relief from the exactions of reason. Ghost stories can look like a nostalgic game, played when it was no longer widely held, by readers of books, that the spirits of the dead return to the land of the living—mopping, mowing, gibbering, giving their owl's cries, causing the tapers to burn blue, sheeted, but never in any circumstances nude. The last of these superstitions is commemorated in a story by A. E. Coppard, chosen for the *Oxford Book*, in which a dressy female *revenant* performs a more than usually disappointing strip-tease. She is also taking part in a literary *jeu d'esprit*.

The editors claim, oddly, that 'the working class and those in trade are generally too busy to concern themselves with ghosts'. But it is certainly true that, over the last hundred and fifty years, it is those relatively wealthy people who prefer to live in old houses who have been said to see ghosts, that many of the stories have less to say about ghosts than about old houses, and that many of their authors are the sort of people who live in them—in the old houses, for example, of Oxford and Cambridge. The stories could also be thought to belong to a modern world in which ghosts need to be explained, and in which they may be explained as symptoms of a disordered mind, of 'nerves' and exhaustion. 'He had been working very hard lately.' This man, in 1911, a painter haunted by a model knocked down in the Fulham Road, had been expecting something, and 'was enough of a psychologist to know that in that state you are especially likely to see what you expect to see'. The story is by Barry Pain.

Despite the impression which the *Oxford Book* imparts, ghost
stories go back a long way before the nineteenth century. And
so does their authorial explanation. Ghosts are creatures of
habit, and of *Hamlet*: Shakespeare's play is a ghost story which
is affected by the ghost stories of previous times, and which has
affected the habits of ghosts in later times. Some of these later
times were, for some people, quiet and sedentary. At the end of
the last century M. R. James's head lay easy, pillowed on Eton
and King's. In the introduction to a recent reissue,[2] 'Monty's'
stories are made, by one of the *Oxford Book* editors, to look like
a game which registers a displacement of the erotic. 'Even the
deepest friendship of his life, with James McBryde, stopped
well short of what we should now glibly class as homosexual
involvement', we are told. We are also told that the author
would read his stories to gatherings of male friends, and
that the golden undergraduate McBryde drew pictures for
the stories. 'Monty disappeared into his bedroom', recalled
another friend. 'We sat and waited in the candlelight . . .
Monty emerged from the bedroom, manuscript in hand, at
last, and blew out all the candles but one, by which he seated
himself.' In the excitements of M. R. James's golden time,
which was also that of Henry James, the ghost of Hamlet's
father, all the way from a remote and violent past, was to
participate.

In the first scene of the first act of *Hamlet*, this ghost is
awaited on the 'platform' of the castle of Elsinore. The platform is a feature, not of Elsinore's battlements, but of a gun-
bearing terrace in front of the castle. 'I think I hear' Horatio
and Marcellus, says Francisco. Marcellus tells Horatio that the
Ghost walks 'jump at this dead hour'—exactly at this point in
what Horatio is to term 'the dead waste and middle of the
night'. When the Ghost eventually appears to Hamlet it informs him that 'upon my secure hour thy uncle stole', and
Hamlet has responded to the news of the murder with 'O my
prophetic soul!' He had suspected some foul thing of this kind.
Others besides him see the Ghost, though his mother is sub-
sequently to fail to see it when *he* does. Barnardo says in the
first act that, on that night, he has 'seen nothing'. But Barnardo has seen the Ghost on other nights. At the very start
of the play Marcellus remarks of what he and Barnardo have

seen: 'Horatio says 'tis but our fantasy.' Horatio has explained.

A number of explanations of the Ghost are current in *Hamlet*. There is the suggestion that beholders are imagining it. People think they hear or see things in the play, and are often thought to imagine things. But then this may be the ghost of Hamlet's father, loosed from Purgatory in order to purge his sins, and still sufficiently sinful, as some might think, to nerve Hamlet to take revenge. Then again it may be some other sort of spirit, good or evil. The Ghost may be the Devil, or a 'goblin' set on by the Devil to play on Hamlet's nerves.

> The spirit I have seen
> May be a devil, and the devil hath power
> T'assume a pleasing shape, yea, and perhaps,
> Out of my weakness and my melancholy,
> As he is very potent with such spirits,
> Abuses me to damn me.

Spirits come to those in low spirits. Hamlet has already addressed the Ghost in Act One with the words, 'Be thou a spirit of health or goblin damn'd', and he proceeds in this soliloquy to speak of putting his uncle to the test by means of a piece of theatre in which the murder of a king by a usurper—which is also that of an uncle by a nephew—is played before the court. If his uncle passes the test, why then:

> It is a damned ghost that we have seen,
> And my imaginations are as foul
> As Vulcan's stithy.

But the uncle fails the test. Hamlet's mischief works, the strong imagination of this weak man proves true. It is hard not to see this as pinning the poor fellow to some course of redress, if not revenge. Having seen something, and proved it, he now has to do something. At the same time, the play has thrown doubt on what it is that he has seen, and subverts what he finds to do, souring his revenge, and causing his imaginations to be as foul as some of his actions. At the start of the play Hamlet teases Horatio: 'Methinks I see my father'—but it is only in his 'mind's eye'. And when Horatio replies, 'I think I saw him yesternight', the exchange is enough to make one wonder for a moment whether he, too, may have been imagining it.

In the middle of the play Hamlet says to himself—using a metaphor which could well have been familiar, we are told, to the readers of books among Shakespeare's contemporaries—that no one comes back from the dead. But this does not seem to mean that spirits may not pay visits. The matter is treated, with reference to Hell, in Book One, Canto Five, of *The Faerie Queene*:

> there creature never past
> That backe returned without heavenly grace;
> But dreadfull *Furies*, which their chaines have brast,
> And damned sprights sent forth to make ill men aghast.

And in Canto Two of the same Book, with reference to Limbo, Spenser writes:

> What voyce of damned Ghost from *Limbo* lake,
> Or guillfull spright wandring in empty aire,
> Both which fraile men do oftentimes mistake,
> Sends to my doubtfull eares these speaches rare,
> And ruefull plaints, me bidding guiltlesse bloud to spare?

It would appear that some part of *Hamlet*'s supernatural significance, with its compacting of bloodshed and guilt, weakness and uncertainty, is prefigured in these passages of Spenser, where ghosts are known to walk and wail and to cause mistakes, and where Shakespeare's words are used.[3]

In 1967 Eleanor Prosser published a book designed to show that, in Shakespeare's time, revenge was seen as sinful by those who published opinions, and relayed a common knowledge, about this, and about the abuse of melancholics by demons. Bacon saw revenge as 'a kind of wild justice'—a description which could well have added to its appeal for certain readers of later times: but he also saw it as a bad thing, a thing which weakened the rule of law. The rule of law which sees to the redressing of wrongs and the defeat of usurpers. Prosser has it that 'we sense instinctively that the desire to effect private vengeance is an evil'. But we also sense that it affords a kind of wild justice. Revenge is a 'double business'—which is what Claudius calls his repentance, soured by a conflict in which 'my stronger guilt defeats my strong intent'. The reader of the play is likely to reflect that revengers become killers, and to reflect, too, that revenge is a complex thing, and an imaginative thing—apt to make mistakes, and to commit its own crimes. The enigma of *Hamlet* can appear to lie in its sometimes seeming to be a play in which the hero sees things, sees a suitable ghost and makes up a murder, while remaining a play in which the ghost is seen by other people and in which we have to believe in the uncle's guilt. This, too, is a double business, and it is linked to the duality which is inherent in revenge. The uncertainty of the superstitious content of the play expresses the uncertainty of the revenge it contemplates, of the course of action enjoined by 'this thing' that appears to Hamlet.

Hamlet's marked ability to mean different things to different people is bound up with this. These different things are present in the play, and it is no less necessary to see him as a murderer than as a paragon. Shakespeare's tragedies often concern the humanity of a murderer, who may see things that speak to a prophetic soul, and they have in them the thought of murder as misreading. The signs may be either outlandish or mundane. In *The Elizabethan Hamlet* of 1987, Arthur McGee insists with Prosser that revenge was unequivocally forbidden in Shakespeare's time, arguing that the Ghost is a demon, and Elsinore a repugnant Catholic court, and that Hamlet resembles a Vice from the Morality Plays: he becomes 'the Devil's fool, his Vice / jester'. McGee's author is replicative, traditional. It is hard to read about this hellish Hamlet without feeling all the while that there is more to the play, and that the more there is, the paragon there is, produces, in relation to what McGee uncovers, a fundamental indeterminacy. Whether this makes the play what T. S. Eliot made it, an 'artistic failure', I would doubt. It has certainly made it interesting.

When the Governess in Henry James's *The Turn of the Screw* sees her first ghost, that of the wicked valet Peter Quint, the words she uses to describe the event—which initially persuades her that her 'imagination' has 'turned real', in the person of her handsome employer—are words in which *Hamlet* is remembered. 'It was plump, one afternoon, in the middle of my very hour'—the hour when she was in the habit of taking strolls. In the words of Hamlet's father's ghost, to which, as to other words in the play, James seems, consciously or unconsciously, to have been attending, it was her 'custom always of the afternoon'. 'Plump' could be reckoned a mistake for 'plumb', given James's nervous way with the vernacular—except that this is a mistake which the language encourages us to make and which is frequently heard, to expressive effect, in speech. But it also appears to be a recollection of *Hamlet*'s 'jump at this dead hour', in the 'dead waste and middle of the night', when the Ghost is in the habit of walking. When Quint is seen at Bly, moreover, it is at the top of one of the house's two crenellated towers, on a 'platform'. 'Platform' seems a possible word for the horizontal space at the top of a tower, but it is equally a word in *Hamlet* for the bottom of a tower, for the terrace where ordnance is placed, and James's use of it is a further reason to suppose that he had the play in his mind's eye. In staging his apparition, James was guided, I think, by the opening sequence, in which imagination, fantasy, is immediately and pointedly mentioned as an explanation of the something, or nothing, untoward which is being witnessed on this terrace, at a dizzy height overlooking the sea. James's text, no less than Shakespeare's, contemplates a need to explain the supernatural in terms of human frailty, whose name in certain contexts, for Hamlet and for many others, is woman. In dealing with a charge of rape not long ago, a British judge declared, with the delicate touch of his profession, that women imagine things.

One text leads to another, in the ordinary way of literature. In this case, one text has returned to haunt another, and to determine the presentation and explanation of a ghost. In writing his story, Henry James displays an interest in the work of a predecessor interested in the misreading imagination. The thought might help us to decide what kind of text it is that James produced. This has been a matter of dispute; critics have conducted a running battle on the subject for many years. Is the Governess meant to be seen as mad, and are the ghosts she sees, Quint and Miss Jessel, the projections of an inflamed imagination? And does she thereby violate the innocence of her charges, poor beautiful Miles and Flora? Or is the Governess a trustworthy witness to phenomena that a reader might expect to meet in the sort of ghost story where sceptical explanations are absent? Edmund Wilson advanced a version of the projective view, while F. R. Leavis—in the course of a 'disagreement' with Marius Bewley on the subject which is contained in

Bewley's book *The Complex Fate*—came out on the other side.

Leavis thinks of the tale as a trivial piece of mystification and writes of it in a peremptory manner: 'We are to accept her in unquestioning good faith as a wholly credible witness—a final authority.' This is a lot to ask of anyone, about anything. In discussing the tale, James, too, remarks that the Governess 'has "authority"', in relation to apparitions which he refers to as 'goblins'—Shakespeare's word in *Hamlet* for bad ghosts— and which must, he thinks, be distinguished from the sightings investigated by psychical researchers. But he also refers to the tale as 'an *amusette* to catch those not easily caught'. The catch, presumably, could consist in James's making the tale accessible to both of those opposed interpretations. Another double business. To command us to trust the Governess might imply that there are such things as ghosts: were it not that such commanders clearly do not believe this, or believe that James believed it. It is then difficult to avoid the suggestion that the tale is just an amusement, and that James could on occasion be minded to offer nothing more. To suppose that he is offering something more on this occasion is to suppose him interested in imagination, and in delusion.

Leavis's reading of the story is an impatient one. It is hard not to suspect that the narrative is meant to be suspicious, and the latent use of *Hamlet*, Act One, Scene One, with its stress on 'fantasy', makes it that much harder. This is a tale which is like other tales of the supernatural, and like other works by the middle James, such as *The Spoils of Poynton*, in that a central testimony arouses, and seems intended to arouse, suspicion. The Governess positively demands that we suspect her account of what it was for her to seek to 'plumb' the housekeeper at Bly and take the measure of its mysteries.

She is that romantic thing, a lonely sufferer whose weakness exerts a claim upon the reader. Like the central witness in *The Spoils of Poynton*, Fleda Vetch, she is, in James's prefatory words about Fleda, more than 'a mere little flurried bundle of petticoats'. The Governess in *The Turn of the Screw* is 'a fluttered, anxious girl out of a Hampshire vicarage' who dreams of a handsome man: but her testimony is to display her as both weak and strong. She is also a resolute psychical researcher endowed with the authority and composure of James's prose.

On her arrival at Bly, the house and its people are thought to be like 'a great drifting ship'. 'Well', she goes on, 'I was strangely at the helm.' She tells a strange story of a traditional sort, the story of a 'queer affair', and her experience, like Fleda's, is one of flights and drops, of nerves, and of having to summon the 'nerve' to steer the ship. She harps on 'the state of my nerves', and fairly warns us of 'my dreadful liability to impressions'.

Quint impresses her very much, with the 'matters in his life—strange passages and perils, secret disorders, vices more than suspected'. And perhaps less. 'The strange steps of my obsession' take her to the knowledge that her truth depends on proving Miles a liar. Of Quint's ghost she says: 'He was there or was not there: not there if I didn't see him.' She thinks she sees him: but if he was never there she has been corrupting her charges. She feels 'a perverse horror of what I was doing. To do it in *any* way was an act of violence.' On the last pages, however, she rejoices in the impression that she has managed an exorcism of Quint, and speaks of possessing Miles herself. She calls him 'my own'—an expression that does more to evoke the work of devils than to confirm the authority of a witness.

One incident which has been cited as evidence that James wants his readers to believe the Governess, for the sake of a tall tale, is the detailed description she gives of Quint to the homely, solid housekeeper—a description which enables Mrs Grose to recognise the valet, whose death had preceded the Governess's arrival. How did the Governess know what the bad man, with the bad name, looked like? It may be that James put this in to amuse, or to confuse, those readers who would be impressed by the Governess's liability to impressions. But she could surely have picked up details of Quint's appearance from the gossip about him that she had listened to at Bly. 'Haven't I to absolute satiety heard her described? I'll describe her for you in every particular.' This is an explanation which comes, not from *The Turn of the Screw*, but from another ghost story by James, 'The Friends of the Friends', chosen for the *Oxford Book*, a story in which a man is captured by a woman whom he was always to meet in life, and whom he is thought— by a female narrator we distrust—to meet after her death. But it is an explanation which is also applicable to the ghost of Quint.

The *Oxford Book* supplies a further aid to the appreciation of James's supernatural mode and of its attendant spirits within the literary tradition. It prints a story by Algernon Blackwood published in 1906, 'The Empty House'. In an English seaside town, a pair of researchers, a man and his intrepid aunt, tiptoe round the disagreeable rooms of a haunted house where, by one of those wicked servants of the age, a girl had once been thrown down the stairwell to her death, and where the crime is now re-enacted for the researchers. Two years later, James published 'The Jolly Corner', in which this stealthy tiptoeing was re-enacted. A James-like cosmopolitan returns to New York to haunt the family mansion, where he encounters his might-have-been, a sinister, wounded American businessman. Perhaps it is his weakness which sees the ghost. Seeing it, at all events, he swoons: and when he recovers it is to the prospect of a happier life. He is in the lap of a woman who has in her something of a mother, or a sister, or for that matter an aunt, a woman who has liked him and could even have liked his alter ego. Blackwood's piece is a 'mere' ghost story; James's is not— occasioned by the Blackwood though it seems to have been. We are in a world in which ghosts are usually thought to be imagined, and in which the imagining of them is, at times, the imagining of something else. James's story yields the inner conflicts of the perceiver, and the family life of the author.

The two stories contain features which had come to dominate the genre when it was elaborated in the course of the nineteenth century. The *Oxford Book* items transmit a horror of old houses which could also be called a form of approval. Old houses repel their boarders, conquering them, converting them. Their boarders will often be people of independent means, and of a scholarly or progressive turn. They are not afraid of theft or murder, but of the survival of a criminal past. And yet the past will often be seen as superior to the present, with its dreary rationalism and materialism. The ghost stories of the modern world declare themselves the testimony of the overworked, the ill, the mad: but this is a madness which expounds a metaphysics. 'I am not a very imaginative man, nor have I any sympathy with the modern craze for spooks and spectres.' The dull hero of this Hugh Walpole story in the *Oxford Book* never-theless sees ghosts—those of an orphan girl and of a beloved male friend of the hero's—which intimate that love triumphs over death.

Two stories here about grand old houses came out together at the end of the 1920s, and are alike in seeming to celebrate the life that can still be led there by the right people. In John Buchan's, dear old glamorous Fullcircle wins over what he presents as a bloody awful married couple—'Hampstead' pro-gressives—to a pagan-Catholic frame of mind, while Edith Wharton's house, Bells (nearest post-office Thudeney-Blazes), tries the strength of the sensible grand lady who inherits it. '"Fudge!" muttered Lady Jane', who is 'interested in old houses' and in travel, like Wharton herself, and who finds out that a Regency ancestor has ill-treated his deaf-and-dumb wife, and sequestered her at Bells, with the help of an agent. The agent has triumphed over death, and now goes so far as to strangle the housekeeper Mrs Clemm (the name, by the way, of Edgar Allan Poe's mother-in-law, who earned herself a living from the writer's posthumous reputation while proclaiming his immortality) for betraying the records of the crime. We are not told whether this exposure of an original sin, and of a male malevolence, forces Lady Jane to quit her house and garden and move to fresh pastures.

On occasions when the ghosts in ghost stories can be read as well as seen, when there's something there, when the frighten-ing thing is also an interesting thing, the interest may have to do with literature, with its recurrences and resemblances—with *Hamlet*, for instance, as I have been claiming. On one occasion in the *Oxford Book* the resemblance is with T. S. Eliot: the apparition or 'thing' of the mere ghost story is here made over into what could almost be read as a few bars of the *Four Quartets*. Charles Williams's 'Et in sempiternum pereant' relates: 'The thing itself, a wasted flicker of pallid movement, danced and gyrated in white flame before him.' This thing—the invention of a writer whom Eliot admired—has to do with a hideous, eternally punishable sinfulness: 'greedy loves and greedy hates.'

Hamlet walks in the *Supernatural Tales*[4] of Vernon Lee, alias Violet Paget, a friend of James, and of friends of his including

Edith Wharton. Her supernatural vein would appear to be an embellishment and burlesque of the eighteenth-century Italy imagined by this pioneer art historian (and pacifist). One of the tales also figures in the *Oxford Book*: a Norwegian composer is pursued through Venice by the trills of a ravishing-revolting male soprano. In 'Amour Dure', a delirious Polish scholar, a 'melancholy wretch, whom they called Hamlet', sees, and woos, a fatal aristocratic female of previous times. 'Why should there not be ghosts to such as can see them?' his diary enquires, and suggests that 'our vaunted science of today' may eventually be seen as just 'another superstition'.

Women imagine things. And they have been able to imagine and describe what it is that women imagine, what their weakness is, and to say how it could be defended. Enter the feminist ghost story. Edith Wharton and Vernon Lee belong to a ghostly sisterhood which, from the 1880s onwards, was to be responsible for much of the most interesting terror fiction. Among the women writers in question are E. Nesbit and the Americans Charlotte Gilman and Mary Wilkins. 'The Little Ghost' by Mary Wilkins, which evokes an abused child, another orphan-ghost, is arguably the most moving ghost story in the *Oxford Book of English Ghost Stories*, which cheerfully prints American writing on the grounds that such specimens inhabit an English literary tradition, and which is for long stretches, to be sure, quite unmoving. Both Charlotte Gilman and Edith Wharton were patients of Weir Mitchell, a famous 'nerve specialist' (and novelist) of the time in America: but in Gilman's *The Yellow Wallpaper* of 1892 the female narrator expresses an unwillingness to attend this doctor, when 'John says if I don't pick up faster he shall send me to Weir Mitchell in the fall'. The narrator suffers the cruel kindness of a patronising husband (himself a doctor) and founders in hallucination: and her brief confessions are now prominent in the feminist canon. John warns her against giving way to 'fancy': 'He says that with my imaginative power and habit of story-making, a nervous weakness like mine is sure to lead to all manner of excited fancies.'

Jack Matthews's collection of stories, *Ghostly Populations*,[5] contributes to the study of these questions; an earlier collection was entitled *Dubious Persuasions*. Matthews also contributes, as does Peter Taylor, to an excellent American fiction of the present time which seems to be virtually unknown in Britain, where feelings of respectful inferiority are a common response to some other varieties of American writing: this is a fiction which tends to be regional and reclusive in character, and which runs to stories rather than novels. His opening story tells of a prophetic captain who had dreamt that his ferry-boat would come to grief: 'Like Prince Hamlet, he was apparently visited by bad dreams.' And in July 1874 his boat had duly exploded on its Midwestern lake. The story takes the form of an address to tourists of a century later who have gone in a glass-bottomed craft to stare down at the remains of the ferry-boat—a vessel as sturdy, the speaker remarks, as the one they're travelling in now. His sententious courtesy would be enough to chill most sightseers, but it begins to cast a spell on the reader. He admonishes his passengers:

Consider the tragedy of that bright July day a century ago: it was a secret fulcrum, real and horrible, upon which those terrible dreams and our sober reflections today pivot in ceremonious directions. But it has been scarcely more real, in our long and untroubled retrospect, than those dreams that prefigured it. And who is to say which picture of the three (yes, I include the 'real', the historical event) is more real, more abiding?

Like *Hamlet*, this is a story about perception. The waters of the lake are made to seem like the waters of the past, in which all of these three pictures will be drowned. It is a story in which the dead are beautifully remembered, and which is memorably mysterious. If it is a ghost story, it can certainly be said to be about something. It reminds the reader that a place that is dreamt of, or thought about, can pass, in the course of a life-time, into the condition of places that have been visited in the flesh. And then they will all, in their imagined homogeneity, be gone for good.

II · Andante Capriccioso

THE fame of Don Quixote and Sancho Panza became known to the work in which they appear. In discussing itself as it goes along, Cervantes's novel examines the question of their fame, and in the second of its two parts it even takes avoiding action in respect of its own apocrypha. Their fame has lasted from that day—Hamlet's day, the first years of the seventeenth century—to this. Quixote, his squire, his adventures and enchanters, still matter; they are one of the legends of the romantic modern world.

The literature of Romanticism seized on the work in order to discuss itself. Smollett's translation of 1755, which was reissued in 1986,[1] pre-dated this capture, and perhaps it may be said that the translation assisted a romantic reading of Cervantes which it was also equipped to avert. His opinion of the work, expressed a little earlier in the Preface to *Roderick Random*, was 'classical' enough: Cervantes's 'inimitable piece of ridicule' was held to have 'reformed the taste of mankind, representing chivalry in the right point of view'. Smollett thought that a conversion of romance had been effected by Cervantes, which had allowed it to make itself useful by pointing out 'the follies of ordinary life'. Sancho's common sense and creature comforts are shown to advantage in this translation: the scene where he fouls himself in his master's presence, adding 'a new affair', a new terror, to the mysterious reverberations of the fulling mill, is very well told. But then few translators could do much to prevent such a showing, and Smollett is no less alive to the behaviour of the master, the lean, lank, long-faced first of the fogeys, panoplied in kitchenware as he goes about righting his wrongs and wronging his passers-by. Quixote's lucid intervals contain the wisdom of Cervantes, and he ends in an odour of pious good sense, having shed his illusions: this last lucidity, and all sense of the follies of chivalric romance, are keenly rendered by Smollett, whose efforts were to be succeeded by a special sympathy for this hero in his hour of illusion. Smollett was, in fact, to imitate the inimitable Cervantes for the rest of his life. He translated him, then re-translated him in a novel, *Sir Launcelot Greaves*,[2] which sets a mad knight amid the asylums and coaching inns of his own time; and Quixote's ghost can be found to flit through other fictions of his. Humphry Clinker and, in the same novel, the Scotch curmudgeon Lismahago can be caught in the acts of a Quixote. Good men are seen to be mistaken and to take tumbles, to be pursued by farce. Such were the Cervanticks which British writers had taken to copying. Rowlandson was to illustrate the scene in which Lismahago, fleeing a fire reported by a joker, descends a ladder from a first-floor window, with bystanders looking up his nightie, in their eighteenth-century way, at his 'long lank limbs and posteriors'—the plight of the heiress who flees, in another Rowlandson, the confinements of family life. The adventures of William Combe's Dr Syntax, for which Rowlandson did drawings, can also be classed as Cervanticks.

A scholar has said that Smollett is now 'discredited' as a translator from the Spanish, and it seems likely that there was cribbing and that the work was assisted. Smollett's version does not read as pointedly or as intelligibly as Walter Starkie's of 1957. But it has great gusto, and it is funnier; it is none the worse for being the work of an accomplished comic novelist with a fellow-feeling for the right-thinking and for the satirical and knockabout sides of Cervantes. 'Some new affair', when Sancho fouls himself, is very funny, and so is the reference to the 'under-hermit' left behind by the anchorite to mind a solitude visited by the wanderers, who also address each other, at one point, as follows:

'The cause of that pain', said Don Quixote, 'must doubtless be this; as the pole or staff by which you have suffered was long and large, it extended over thy whole back, comprehending all those parts which now give you pain; and if it had reached still farther, the pain would have been more extensive.' ' 'Fore God', cried Sancho, 'your worship has taken me out of a huge uncertainty, and resolved the doubt in delicate terms. Body o' me! was the cause of my pain so mysterious, that there was a necessity for telling me, I feel pain in those parts that were cudgelled?'[3]

This is not a passage which proves the point made in the book about translations—that they are poor things, like the turning inside out of a tapestry, with the figure in the carpet more or less preserved, but with all the knots and threads on display. The joke about being beaten up is matched in *Sir Launcelot Greaves*, when the squire says of an assault upon himself by his master that 'it was as common as duck-weed in his country for a man to complain when his bones were broke'. Whereupon the knight thrashes him with a horse-whip. There is too much in the way of grievous bodily harm in *Don Quixote*. There is a lot more in *Launcelot Greaves*.

Don Quixote is a comedy of errors not all of which are made by Don Quixote. The knight-errant makes errors, and there is a novelist-errant who makes errors, some of which he corrects. His commentators err in placing their permissible and forced constructions, and in correcting some of his errors. Smollett makes errors too. And André Deutsch did so in 1986—in reissuing this erroneous work. No notes, save Smollett's perfunctory few. No errata. 'I am resolved to seize occasion by the forelock, which she now so complaisantly prevents': a misreading here of 'presents' turns the meaning inside out. The eighteenth-century letter 's' has proved a trap which opens in the opening paragraph, where a prison is called (rather wonderfully) a 'feat of inconvenience'. A strange cart later becomes 'a fort of wagon'.

Mistakes are magic in a work which can readily be taken, or mistaken, for a fathoming of the human subjectivity which involves the possession of a point of view. Smollett had felt that on the subject of chivalry there was only the one 'right' point of view in the Cervantes, and here we touch again on what happened to the reading of Cervantes's novel after Smollett— when it became natural to think of rival points of view within this work among others, and within the one person. Is *Don Quixote* unprecedented, modern, by virtue of its capacity to interest people in points of view? Those who have read Chaucer might not think so. But those of the modern world who notice that—in the words of a novel of Ivy Compton-Burnett's—the truth is different in different minds, that one man's windmills are another man's giants, that one man's joke, trick, punishment, penance or revenge is another man's grievous bodily harm, are indebted to the story of Quixote's errors and impostures and enchantments. The epistolary novel of the English eighteenth century drew heavily on Cervantes while pursuing its concern with the different constructions that can be placed on the same events. 'People of experience and infirmity' see the Vauxhall Gardens 'with very different eyes' from the healthy young, according to a nubile correspondent in *Humphry Clinker*, where, two pages on, in a further letter, party politicians are said to see the affairs of Westminster, Westminster's Westlands, through an 'exaggerating medium' which others may find 'incomprehensible'.

There is very little reason to suppose that it took a historical turning-point, located in the writings of Cervantes and Shakespeare, for an interest in the placing of constructions to find favour: but constructions seem to have mattered a good deal in the course of the eighteenth century, and the interest is sure to have contributed to the romantic sense of a sovereign subjectivity. Quixote came to resemble the English Cavaliers of the seventeenth century in being, as the old joke has it, 'wrong but romantic'. He could be seen—to a degree that was foreign to Smollett—as in some sense right. Error is error: but there came a time when it could also be seen as enabling, as what people do, in living on, in going on with what there was before, in inventing something different.

The 'magnanimous' knight goes about righting wrongs—preferably those endured by persons of rank—and inflicting harm on those whom our own world has grown accustomed, with failing spirits, to call innocent bystanders. Sancho has resolved to 'avoid being hurt myself', but 'also to refrain from hurting any person whatsoever'. His master hurts any person whatsoever whom he perceives as an oppressor. I may be wrong, but it seems to me that Cervantes exhibits little feeling for these hurts: they are amusements, and they are symptoms of Quixote's deluded condition. During one of his lucid intervals Quixote casts a doubt on the righting of wrongs. Recourse to arms, he explains,

for childish trifles, and things that are rather subjects of laughter and diversion than of serious revenge, seems to denote a total defect of reason and discretion; especially as unjust vengeance (and surely no vengeance can be just) is diametrically opposite to that holy law we profess, by which we are enjoined to do good to our enemies, and love those by whom we are abhorred.[4]

But the doubt that is cast here is neither lucid nor unanimous, and it scarcely has the force of an apology for the hurts he inflicts. The passage could be thought to link the novel with Shakespeare's *Hamlet*, in which another comedy of errors can be perceived, and in which vengeance, as it is here for Quixote, is a double business. Hamlet is a madman of sorts, a disastrous revenger of sorts, and is in some degree Quixotic. A connection between the two heroes is made in *Launcelot Greaves*, where the knight's emergence from his initiatory vigil is compared to the port of the stalking ghost in *Hamlet*, which a bystander 'had seen acted in Drury Lane'.

Quixote's behaviour may or may not approximate to that to be found in an earlier work—to the Erasmian folly or simplicity which is capable of wisdom. But it can certainly be said that his behaviour is that of a divided man who is off his head for much of the book while also, for much of the book, capable of the grave, conservative good sense which is content to live off the produce of its gentleman's estates, which is seen in Don Diego de Miranda, and which Smollett was given to admiring. Quixote is presented as a compound; he is, as Humphry Clinker is said to be, a 'surprising compound of genius and simplicity', and his being so was to serve to endear him to romantics. His discourse is deemed a 'medley of sense and madness'—and Sancho has learned from it in a way which contributes to his own reputation as a 'mixture' of 'acuteness and simplicity'. Don Diego regards Don Quixote as a man whose Don Diego-like good sense is blended with a 'strange sort of madness': Don Diego 'was at times divided in his opinion, sometimes believing him in his senses, and at other times thinking him frantic; because, what he spoke was sensible, consistent, and genteelly expressed, but, his actions discovered all the symptoms of wildness, folly, and temerity.' Don Diego here commends the consistency of Quixote's speech, madly though he has just behaved in confronting his (sleepy) lion: but when Quixote speaks again it is to observe that such challenges are 'consistent' with the duties of a knight-errant. Sense and simplicity are blended in the aftermath of this particular exploit.

On such occasions Quixote can appear to belong with the strange, unstable compounds of the Early Modern world which

were to cast a spell on its successor. In writing about these
human specimens in their eighteenth-century embodiments,
Smollett used a notation of the past—the psychology of humours and elements—which had remained persuasive, and which
had developed as a concomitant of alchemy, the alchemy
derided in *Launcelot Greaves*. Despite this derision, a character in
the novel is called 'a strange composition of rapacity and pro-
fusion', the difficulties suffered by this character being 'the
natural consequences of an error in the first concoction'. This
was a psychology in which erroneous concoctions caused difficulties, but were capable of imagination and invention.

The God of the Middle Ages was no compound. For certain theologians, as I understand it, God could be known as
Simplicissimus—as simple in the sense, among others, of
single, one-and-the-same. Quixote is not that simple. But there
is, of course, something heavenly about him, and Erasmus
might have recognised in him an imitation of Christ.

Later times have seen a succession of Quixotes, in one form
or another. The *caballero andante* has kept going. Perhaps the
greatest, and the most faithful, of all such translations is
Daumier's painting of the two adventurers. Recent responses
include Erich Auerbach's chapter in *Mimesis*, where a historically scrupulous reading of the text is attempted, and that
free translation of Cervantes which accompanies a search for
symbolic meanings is reproved. No *sancta simplicitas* or praise of
folly is detected in the book; Quixote's madness is madness,
and its projects do not indicate that Cervantes felt there was
anything rotten in the state of Spain. To conceive of his insanity
'in symbolic and tragic terms seems to me forced. That can be
read into the text; it is not there of itself.' So Cervantes is an
entertainer, and we may suppose that his hero is not, let us say,
like the significant madman in Pirandello's *Henry IV*. Auerbach's version of Quixote and of Cervantes is far from incomprehensible: all the same, entertainers have their own way of
making judgements and suggestions, and Cervantes makes
some that are acknowledged by Auerbach himself. Symbolic,
quixotic conceptions based on this text have continued to
appear since 1946, when Auerbach's book on 'the representation
of reality in Western literature' was published, and Cervantes's
'gaiety' had come to seem irrecoverable. It has since become

difficult to believe that there is a reality to be represented.

The gaiety and games which suspend or challenge stock conceptions of reality, and of rationality, form part of the alternative fictional tradition for which the Czech writer Milan Kundera speaks, and which includes *Jacques le fataliste*, by Smollett's contemporary, Diderot. Here again are an argumentative master and servant, in an exercise of the self-examining picaresque; here again is a work which affirms its own fictionality. Diderot's novel is Cervantean (and Rabelaisian, and Shandean), and Kundera puts it with the work which it imitates, which it translates—with *Don Quixote*; he also puts it with Joyce's *Ulysses*. Distinctions between the fiction of fantasy and the fiction of reality have seemed to become more urgent than before with the success, in recent times, of the Hispanic fabulation which has crawled from Cervantes's overcoat to flourish, especially, in Latin America. But the distinctions aren't always easy to operate. Does Kundera write fantasy? Or does he digress into it? Smollett's *Launcelot Greaves* is not so much a fantasy as a comedy in which a young gentleman who is thwarted in love despairs and goes mad, and in which reality hits him, and hits the reader, in the face.

This magnanimous knight—his character 'dashed with extravagance' both before and after the recovery of his wits—actually rights some wrongs, while attacking his fair share of plebeians, and he is even an efficient fighter. This makes him different from Cervantes's hidalgo; but his adventures are otherwise patterned on the hidalgo's, with the tendency to physical violence greatly overdone. Here is the laughter which howls at broken bones and bloody noses. The deluded sea-dog's bruises leave him looking like a Negro, conveys Smollett, who had a dislike for Jews, and for the widespread fraudulence of the medical profession to which he was apprenticed in his youth. Nature knows best, he felt. Medicinal compounds are abhorred in his Quixote novel, just as, in *Humphry Clinker*, London's artificially whitened bread and other adulterations are a scandal. When Sir Launcelot is sprung from the private asylum where he has discovered that his beloved Aurelia is a fellow prisoner, he is so pleased that he forgets to let her out along with him, and has to go clumping back. Smollett does not seem to be suggesting that this is the kind of thing that Dulcineas must have learned to expect.

The series of adaptive, alternative, other-self *Quixotes* which Smollett helped to swell has shown two remarkable recent instances. In 1980, and again with revisions in 1985, there appeared a transposition and independent elaboration of one element of Cervantes's work into an idiom of the modern novel. This was *The Duchess's Diary* by Robin Chapman, whom I remember watching, many years ago, on the Cambridge undergraduate stage, in Jacobean doublet and hose. And now here he is with a Duke Jeronimo. It is as if he has yet to change back—such is his feeling for the ways of seventeenth-century Spain, for the plight, in particular, of a woman immured in a dynastic marriage of convenience. The novel takes an episode of *Don Quixote* which Chapman's duchess reckons 'inconsistent' with the whole: the episode is that of the amused and often unamusing entertainment of knight and squire by their duke and duchess, who play tricks on the guests and treat them in the fashion bestowed on Bottom and company by the court in *A Midsummer Night's Dream*. Chapman's duchess is drawn to the real Cervantes, whom she and her husband entertain in the course of the composition of his great work: certain occasions in Part Two of that work are thereby prefigured. After his departure she takes to her diary, then to her heels, and goes to Madrid, only to find him dead. She is seen as half-mad, nervous, anorexic, doting on her author while also fretting over his eventual representation of her in fiction. All this—her pining and exodus, her dealings with untrustworthy authorship, and with the 'chimera' of Cervantes—is subtly represented in Robin Chapman's satellite work. Chapman not only wrote his book, incidentally, but made the mistake, as some must have thought it, of publishing and selling it himself, Quixote-fashion. It sold out.

On looking into Chapman's Cervantes, I discovered that the romantic art of duality, much practised since Smollett, is invoked for *Don Quixote*, whose contradictions, mixtures and medleys may indeed be thought ancestral to this art. Madness in Chapman's novel is autoscopic, self-hallucinatory. It sees and hears itself. So does art. Quixote and Sancho are Cervantes—one flesh: and are also man and wife. An author 'contains his own opposites'. This Book of the Duchess is a learned invention, and yet a fully animate one; and it has a preface which enables us to measure the distance we have wandered, in the matter of point of view, since Smollett. What is now 'universally known' about Cervantes's masterpiece, according to the preface, is that 'imagination is as unreasonable as reality'.

A further translation of Cervantes was effected in 1986, in a piece by the American punk writer Kathy Acker. The piece, entitled 'Don Quixote', appeared in the *Fred*, a magazine published in London's Ladbroke Grove, and was later incorporated in a novel. For Acker, Don Quixote is a woman.

When she was finally crazy because she was about to have an abortion, she conceived of the most insane idea that any woman can think of. Which is to love. How can a woman love? By loving someone other than herself. She would love another person. By loving another person, she would right every manner of political, social, and individual wrong: she would put herself in those situations so perilous the glory of her name would resound.

The heroine has her abortion, having pledged herself to those adventures which give rise to abortions. Chivalry is exposed to the lives of women now, and is thus re-seen. The piece suggests that books drive you mad. But Kathy Acker writes them and reads them. She has written into her fiction the hostile French writer Jean Genet, godfather of punk, and it seems she was a reader of Smollett when she was at school. She writes of an anxious and dangerous sexual existence beside which the violence of the eighteenth-century comic novel pales. Chapman's Acker proved to be noticeably different from mine, when the novel appeared in which this piece was incorporated. He called it 'a dead-eyed romance, indebted to Burroughs rather than Cervantes. Acker's aborted, dog-escorted Quixote seeks love, but she gets the brush-off from Nixon's surreal Russo-America.'

Acker's, as it happens, is not the first female Quixote: three years before Smollett's translation came the extravaganza of that name by Charlotte Lennox.[5] This looks forward to the romantic dupes, the turned heads, of the turn of the century, to E. S. Barrett's *The Heroine*, to the terrors of Northanger. Arabella, Lennox's fair visionary, is fine: but perhaps too much of an unsisterly joke to count as evidence that the legend can accommodate what has happened to women and what they have made of it.

Cervantes's book takes much of its staying-power and trans-formative capacity from its appeal to a modern world in which it can be believed that madness is in everyone, having come out of the 'dark cote' where Chaucer found it imprisoned, and in which it has been seen both as a paradigm of subjectivity and as an exemplary state. One name for its ranging or errant behav-iour has been nerves, and *Launcelot Greaves* uses that name. Locked in his asylum, the knight, who has by then regained his sanity, quizzes the quack who has been hired to put him away.

'I should be glad to know your opinion of my disorder.'—'Oh! sir, as to that,' replied the physician, 'your disorder is a—kind of a—sir, 'tis very common in this country—a sort of a'—'Do you think my distemper is madness, doctor?'—'O Lord, sir,—not absolute madness—no—not madness—you have heard, no doubt, of what is called a weakness of the nerves, sir,—though that is a very inaccurate expression . . .'

Delivered among the malicious incarcerations for alleged insanity which were a worry at the time, for those with a mind to worry about such things, this medical opinion is mocked by the novelist. But perhaps it says something, accidentally or in error, which was and has remained true, and which was not very often said at the time. Who is not nervous? And the more nervous people there are, the more we may need spitting images, a comedy of hurt. It is a need which would appear to be very common in this country at present.

III · Louisa

BOOKS have their fates, and I would like to write about two books from the deep past whose fates have been very different. One of them has always been well known and the other was not known at all until the other day. One of them is very long and the other is very short. Each in its own way is a wonderful piece of work.

They stand at opposite ends of the century that runs from the 1740s to the 1840s, but they may be thought to bear each other out, in ways which affect an understanding of the family life of that time, and of its incorporation in the literature of Romanticism—that part of it, in particular, which is premissed on conceptions of the divided or multiple self. One of the books is fiction—of a kind, however, which is often investigated for its affinity to fact; while the other records the facts and feelings and constructions of the biographer of a friend. One is the more than a million words of Samuel Richardson's novel *Clarissa*, whose first edition was reissued in 1985, by Penguin, in the guise of a slab of gold bullion.[1] The other is by an admirer of Richardson's novels, two generations later—Lady Louisa Stuart, whose *Memoire* of Frances Scott, Lady Douglas as she became, was redeemed from the archives of the Border nobility, with the blessing of a former prime minister, Lord Home, and published[2] at the same time as the Penguin *Clarissa*. The memoir appears to have been written in the 1820s, and is addressed to Frances's daughter Caroline in order to acquaint her with certain passages in her mother's experience of a stressful early life. Frances died in 1817, the year before Scott's novel *The Heart of Midlothian* delivered its spectacle of an invincible female will. Louisa Stuart fancied that her friend Scott might have modelled his exemplary Jeanie Deans on her friend Frances. She seems to have been wrong: but it is never wrong to look for fact in fiction, and for fiction in fact.

The letters that make up *Clarissa* tell the story of an intelligent and beautiful girl who refuses a rich suitor and falls out with

her ambitious and hideous family, the Harlowes. She is tricked
into running away from her 'friends', as she calls them, by the
rake Lovelace. This man gloats over the items of her dress on
the day of her departure, items which indicate, what with the
sharpness in the air, that she had not intended to be gone with
him, for all that she had been drawn in that direction. He
gloats over her ruffles, her mob-cap with its sky-blue ribbon,
her apron of flowered lawn, her blue-satin braided shoes.

Her morning gown was a pale primrose-coloured paduasoy: the
cuffs and robings curiously embroidered by the fingers of this ever
charming Arachne in a running pattern of violets and their leaves; the
light in the flowers silver; gold in the leaves. A pair of diamond snaps
in her ears. A white handkerchief, wrought by the same inimitable
fingers, concealed—Oh Belford! what still more inimitable beauties
did it not conceal!—And I saw, all the way we rode, the bounding
heart; by its throbbing motions I saw it! dancing beneath the charming
umbrage.[3]

Lovelace spirits this Primavera, this Venus, to a London
brothel, where he eventually drugs and rapes her. We had been
brought to feel that she might have come to love him, in
attempting to reform him, while Lovelace has acted from
motives both of love and revenge—a teasing conspiratorial
revenge which has intended harm to her, to the Harlowes, and
to women. She is now in danger of the fate tersely ascribed to
a girl in Louisa Stuart's memoir: 'She lost her character,
married obscurely, and ceased to be talked of.' Clarissa had
been willing to be talked of as an old maid, which is how Louisa
Stuart was to talk of herself. After the rape it is open to her to
marry her attacker: but she refuses this orthodox course, to
which she is encouraged by those around her, and chooses
to die. She is a marriageable, marketable, impeccable Venus
who has turned into a nun. She sleeps beside the coffin on
which she has taken to writing her letters, and joyously awaits
her heavenly reward.

These are some of the events and some of the emotions of
Clarissa: a long story has been cut short, but it is a long story
which has practically no digressions. Richardson's reader
Louisa Stuart would not have felt at sea in pondering such
vicissitudes. She was the daughter of Lord Bute, another North

British prime minister, whose retreat to Luton Hoo, in the
sourness of political defeat, helped to embitter her youth. Her
choice of husband was cancelled by her father, and the friends
she made outside the family circle were dearer to her than those
friends who were her siblings. She had a gift for friendship, and
for literature, which lasted for almost a century—she was born
in 1757, ten years after the publication of the first two volumes
of *Clarissa*. And those who have come to know her from a study
of Scott's life and works will not be startled by the quality of her
memoir. Scott himself thought her the best literary critic he
knew, thought she had genius, and a 'perfect tact'. The memoir
is critical of romantic attitudes in a customary eighteenth-century
fashion—a fashion that can be found in Scott. 'Most people
addicted to romancing', she writes, 'are their own heroes.' But
it can also be said of her that she was herself given to romancing.
She was to be a traveller on the road taken by Scott which led to
the invention and enjoyment of a romantic literature, and the
vicissitudes of her life were such as to fit her for the journey.
Her memoir is admirable in its sensitive astuteness. It is a work
which is not discountenanced by the portrait of an afflicted and
virtuous female, and of an adulterous aristocracy, which is
conveyed in the celebrated novel by an earlier lady of quality,
Madame de Lafayette's *Princesse de Clèves*.

Louisa Stuart's memoir turns her friend Frances into a
Clarissa-like victim and paragon—no one on earth like her.
The theme of the persecuted maiden is treated—the theme
which Richardson did much to transmit to the literature of
Romanticism. Frances suffered the misfortune of incurring the
enmity of her mother, Lady Dalkeith, later Lady Greenwich,
one of the unruly Campbell connection and a 'wicked witch',
according to Louisa Stuart, herself a relative of the witch on her
father's side. There are commentators who have detected as
implausible, in Richardson's novel, not so much its postal
dimension, the 'ready scribbling' which exceeds the call of duty
and isn't always fully compatible with decency—not that so
much as the harshness of the Harlowes towards their paragon.
But I think it would be a mistake to make light of the plausibility
of this harshness for the novel's first readers. Lady Dalkeith,
at all events, was as harsh as any Harlowe. This passage
depicts her in her ordinary abrasiveness: when in London, she

sallied every morning at the earliest visiting hour, entered the first
house she found open, and there, in a voice rivalling the horn,
published all the matches, intrigues and divorces she had heard of;
predicted as many more; descanted on the shameful behaviour of the
women and the scandalous profligacy of the men; wondered what the
world would come to—than bawled a little on public events, made
war or peace; and, having emptied her whole budget, packed it afresh
to carry it to another door, and another, and another, until dinner-
time called her home. The rounds of the newspaper were not a bit
more regular or certain.[4]

Horace Walpole christened her the *Morning Post*, after the newspaper of that name, recently launched and eager for scandal.

She took as her second husband the rogue politician Charles
Townshend, who seems to have married her for money and influence, and has been thought to have gone in fear of her female
will. J. Steven Watson's Preface explains that Townshend's
customs duties occasioned the loss of America, and his death in
1767 brought to an end a series of dazzling Parliamentary feats
and turns. 'Those volatile salts are evaporated', ran one of the
tributes. Watson calls attention to the statement, in the biography of the politician by Lewis Namier and John Brooke,[5]
that Townshend needed his wit to shield a poverty of heart.
This might be held to be like Lovelace, and in each case the
wit is very brilliant. Each is a paragon in this respect. And
Townshend was also known for his easy success with women.

In 1767, Frances, the 17-year-old stepdaughter of this 'young
drunken epileptic', in Watson's words, witnessed the sudden
end of a relationship with him which had at one point threatened
to turn into a disastrous intimacy, but which may equally have
rested on Townshend's desire to protect her from her mother's
aversion. There is no evidence in the memoir of any poverty of
heart on Townshend's part. Nevertheless, for reasons that
included the threat of this dangerous liaison, she had been
forced, before that, into a 'flight' from her family: this is a
word that is used of what Clarissa did, and Watson applies it to
what Frances did. She later managed a happy marriage to
Archibald, Lord Douglas, the claimant in the notorious legal
imbroglio, to which Louisa Stuart awards only twelve words.
Her words do not ventilate the suspicion that Douglas may
have acceded to the 'gay world' of aristocratic England, with its

impostors and hangers-on, as a French gypsy child smuggled in
to secure a succession: as a changeling, no less.

Each of the texts I am discussing is the work of a fine feeler,
and Richardson's was to set patterns of sentiment for later
times. And yet he was also plain-spoken and shrewd. So was
Louisa Stuart, who seldom yields at all culpably to the cant of
fine feeling, and that only when the merits and miseries of her
heroine are at issue. Of Townshend's fondness for his step-
children she observes: 'the very desire of *playing amiable* (as it is
called) might insensibly lead him to imbibe true affection.'
This is somewhat damaging to Townshend, but does not make
him out to be empty: a poor heart does not so imbibe. Elsewhere, as both Louisa Stuart and Jane Austen cause us to be
aware, playing amiable was an attribute of the tyrannical male.

Here and there, the two texts coincide. The memoir says
that a daughter of Townshend's by Lady Dalkeith was seen to
step 'into a post-chaise with a gentleman, and came home no
more': another of the eighteenth century's runnings-away.
Miss Townshend came home no more, but was talked of, and
deplored. The gentleman in the chaise was no gentleman but
an Irish adventurer, or blackleg, evoked by Louisa Stuart with
the air of some sprightly marchioness: he was like the appren-
tice, 'a dirty ill-looking fellow not to be touched with a pair of
tongs', who was apt to arrive with tongs of his own, in place of
Monsieur le Blanc himself, to dress a lady's hair in time for a
ball. 'All his friends had ten thousand a year; he talked of his
horses and his carriages, his estate and his interest; and when
he addressed you as a lady, you could not help drawing back
for fear he should give you a kiss.' Miss Townshend, she
writes, was 'always vastly ill dressed', her figure 'what the
vulgar call *all of a heap*'. In Clarissa's letters that lady is 'struck
all of a heap' on encountering a solemnity of countenance
among her 'dear relations', as, in the knowledge of their
cruelty to her, she chooses to describe them.

Clarissa's use of 'all of a heap' might seem to direct her
author some way down towards the bottom of the heap,
towards the vulgar. In terms of rank, Richardson the printer
and writer stood below his hideous Harlowes, while they in
turn are below Lovelace, who is also able to look down on the
activities of politicians, on his uncle's House of Lords. He is a

great man, and the leader of a gang of gentlemen, but at times
he is like some member of the unemployed, a doleman—the
name, as it happens, of one of the gang. His own riotous
activities give off all the more of an infernal glow in seeming to
illuminate a desolation in which he and his friends have
nothing to do. He is free to invent his life, his plots, as a writer
might be; he is in certain respects marginal, as writers were
often to be in times to come. The same doleful impression can
be got from Restoration drama, to which—to its comedy as to
its heroic tragedy—Richardson was attentive.

Louisa Stuart was above both the novelist and his imagined
ladies and gentlemen, and it is of interest that, in 1802, she
perceived in Richardson's fiction 'a thousand traits worth
very great attention', as it is that her maternal grandmother
Lady Mary Wortley Montagu 'despised' this 'strange fellow',
thought him unable to reproduce the speech of real ladies and
gentlemen, but read him eagerly, sobbed over him, and thought
the Harlowe family of the first two tomes of *Clarissa* 'very
resembling to my maiden days'. Richardson's account of the
ruling class was faulted for vulgarities, but was not repudiated,
either by Lady Mary or by the vastly well-connected Lady
Louisa, who was courted, as was her friend Frances, by Pitt's
minister, the manager of Scotland, Henry Dundas, and who
valued the novel for its resemblance, imperfect though it was,
to the life that had been led by the elders of her class. But there
was another reason too—a reason to which I have already
referred, but to which she herself could hardly be expected to
refer—why she would have wished to pay great attention to
Clarissa. It appears that, in her girlhood, she wished to marry
her second cousin William Medows, a future Governor of
Madras, and that the marriage was forbidden by her father.

A further verbal coincidence deserves to be pursued. On a
visit to Edinburgh Townshend is slighted, while much is made
of his witch wife, who whines of a group of family retainers:
'Observe the attachment of these poor people—Affectionate
creatures! They are crying for joy to see me.' Townshend
rejoins: 'Don't be too sure of that, Lady Dalkeith. I believe,
if the truth were known, it's for sorrow to see *me*.' Not the
rejoinder of a man with a craven fear of his wife. A similar joke,
which could well have been the parent of other such jokes,

occurs in the novel, when Miss Howe exclaims: 'Hickman will cry for *joy* on my return; or he shall for *sorrow*.' The ambivalence of tears, which corresponds on this occasion to Miss Howe's hot-and-cold treatment of her suitor, is a notion in keeping with the way in which Richardson tells his story of Clarissa's quarrel with her kin.

This last coincidence is a stimulus to trying to say more about what the books have in common. They bear each other out in saying the same thing, and in taking it back, and, at times, in sharing an idiom—an idiom which may seem to be related, though usually indirectly, to this saying and unsaying, and which was subject like any other to the processes of historical change. Both writers show the life of the aristocracy and gentry as confining and cruel. Both question the 'imaginary prerogative', as Richardson calls it, of male supremacy. Both show women at risk, and men as the enemies of women, and as strangers to them. 'Such are men', sighs Louisa Stuart, in reporting an insulting allusion to Frances by Frances's brother. This might be thought a stock sigh of the sentimentalist, and compared with the insouciant 'what wretches you men are!' in Richardson's *Pamela*: it is enough to remind one that Louisa was a common name for the distressed romantic heroine, as Jane Austen was to point out. But this sigh is not, in context, inane, or far-fetched. We may assume that real distresses and constraints, suffered by women in a position to read books, were a reason for Richardson's prominence in eighteenth-century Europe. Pushkin remarks in *Eugene Onegin*, finished in 1831, that Tatyana's mother had never read, but had much admired, his novels in the days when she was being married off against her will: we take this to be the kind of joke which has some history in it.

> The lady's lasting admiration
> The novelist had long since won;
> She had not read with fascination
> Of Lovelace or of Grandison,
> But she had heard of them a dozen
> Or more times from her Moscow cousin,
> Princess Aline, when she was young,
> And when, besides, her heart was wrung:

She was affianced, but her mother
Had made the choice, 'twas not her own . . .[6]

Lovelace addresses his dear friend Jack Belford as 'thou',
while Clarissa does not be-thou her dear Miss Howe. Hers is
an eloquence which can often be read as a lesson to others,
to an emergent public. In *Clarissa* Richardson, a male, was to
produce a book whose real intimacies, as they may seem to a
modern eye, and whose humour, are male, and whose male
and female are at war: the uncertain evidence of its *tutoyer*
might seem to suggest as much. And yet this is also a book
which takes the side of its women. Elsewhere in Richardson the
mode of address is used in order to show what an exercise of
male supremacy is like. When Mr B. be-thous Pamela, on an
early occasion in the first novel, it is in order to reprimand her:
'thou strange medley of inconsistence!'

'God protect me from my friends—I can deal with my
enemies myself.' The saying was a favourite one of Louisa
Stuart's, and is attributed by Jill Rubenstein, editor of the
memoir, perhaps to Voltaire, perhaps to Maréchal Villars. It is
a saying which is relevant to *Clarissa*, and which was to be
deemed relevant—by Henry Dundas's dangerously ambiguous
dear relation Henry Cockburn—to the vagaries of late eighteenth-century kinship and political connection. In neither of
these books, however, does the attitude it implies, the warning
it delivers, escape suspension and retraction. Both are, in this
matter of the family and of the friends who belong to it and
surround it, medleys of inconsistence.

Richardson spoke out on behalf of the claims and merits of
women, but he was careful to bear witness, too, to the case for
order and deference within the family, and for the subordination of women. (He was to be gossiped about, incidentally, as a
remote father to his girls and a punctilious master of servants.)
Louisa Stuart has been credited with an acute grasp of contemporary politics, but she did not think that a female wisdom
on the subject should be made public. Nor did she think she
should publish her writings, or become a bluestocking. And
yet she speaks up for the women of her class. The view of
families and of females which is projected in both works is
complex and wide-open to partial representation. It is a view

which was bound to attract to itself ideas of contradiction and inconsistency. Contradiction and inconsistency were qualities of which the Augustan literary culture centrally disapproved, but which were often exhibited and enquired about there. They are qualities which have often been revealed in relation to those codes and submissions which have found a proving-ground in the context of family life, and they are revealed in Richardson's portrait of it here, and in the complication of mind which he ascribes to Clarissa and to Lovelace. Clarissa refuses to be restored to the family whose authority she ardently respects. Perhaps it could also be said that, in the matter of whether or not to marry her attacker, she gloriously refuses to do what Pamela gloriously does.

Clarissa and the Stuart memoir are the long and the short of a conception of family life which can be associated with the affective individualism claimed for the period. There are no pleas in Richardson for the sexual emancipation of women, and his opinions on education take account of an odious permissiveness among the better-off. It is nevertheless the case that this evangelical Christian, this enemy of the Enlightenment, devotes much of his energy in *Clarissa* to enabling us to understand profoundly how it could come about that a good young woman might move towards flying from her family. By the end of this interval of time permissiveness was on the way to abrogation. In the 1820s Louisa Stuart mentions a recent remark by a woman friend whose girls had 'never heard of adultery in their lives', which causes her to add that 'so opposite was *F.*'s training that she heard of little else'. While granting that Byron's training had a good deal in common with Lovelace's, and that Lovelace can be awarded a measure of parental responsibility for Byron, most readers now suppose that times had changed by the 1820s, and there were soon to be Victorians who objected to Richardson's indecency. And yet the indecent Richardson was one of those who had been responsible for the change.

Family life was a subject which warranted the language of duality, and which was suitably accommodated by the dualistic epistolary novel, where authors refrain from exposition, and opposite points of view are sequentially presented. As the successive editions of *Clarissa* indicate, its author was keen to extract from his readers the right view, the improving view, of the behaviour of its principals; the novel grew, moreover, from the ethos of conduct books, and is itself a conduct book. But it could be said that even the decent and decorous Richardson was plunged into ambivalence by his use of letters.

One of the letters in *Clarissa* gives a blunt and unqualified account of filial duty. This happens when Mrs Howe apologises to the heroine's mother for the unfortunate interferences of her daughter Anna Howe, Clarissa's bosom friend. Mrs Howe is all for a 'due authority in parents', and Clarissa is portrayed as a 'fallen angel' who has suffered the consequences of the fault she has committed in disobeying her family. 'These young creatures', she writes, 'have such romantic notions, some of *love*, some of *friendship*, that there is no governing them in either.' Clarissa's ill-treatment at the hands of Lovelace was 'what everybody expected', just as everybody now expects her to marry her rapist. Clarissa herself thinks that children should obey their parents, but that parents should not coerce their children unjustly. She comes to concede that she has indeed been at fault in placing herself in a situation where it was possible for Lovelace to cheat her into running away. But she then goes against what many of her acquaintances expect of her when she refuses to marry him. And a view of parenthood very different from that of Mrs Howe, who is seen by some of the scribblers as greedy and foolish, is apparent throughout. At no point in the history of its reception can many readers have experienced the novel without assenting to the reproofs it directs at an ungoverned patriarchy, totalitarian fatherhood— without taking the force of Clarissa's words concerning her own father: 'a *good* man too!—But oh! this prerogative of manhood.' In other words, Mr Harlowe is an amiable patriarch who almost always behaves badly. Lovelace refers to Mr Harlowe's way with a wife who did not dispute 'the imaginary prerogative he was so unprecedentedly fond of asserting'. This is a prerogative which the heroine of the novel both regrets and accepts.

Anna Howe's interferences are a challenge to it—but a challenge which Richardson sometimes seems to overrate. Her egotistical and arrested relation to her friend's ordeal, when a few hours' ride might have saved the day, is a source of discomfort for the reader, though a great help to the postal dimension of the novel: the remote control which she chooses to exercise very nearly begins to look like a filial deference to her mother's wishes dissembled by cloying exclamations of love and friendship. The end of the novel appoints her to the undeserved role of honoured and shrilly censorious chief mourner.

The novel, then, says that patriarchy should neither be abused nor abolished, and in saying so sustains an element of uncertainty which has allowed it to be read and resorted to for a variety of reasons, which enabled it to be liked in the Romantic period and before for its exhibition of fine feelings, for its resistance to parents, while at the same time enabling it to appeal to believers in Christian duty and to believers like George Eliot in some secular equivalent. The novel as a whole is contradictory, and the picture it gives of the human mind is one that lays stress on contradiction.

The story of Clarissa versus Lovelace is told in a fashion which may have made it hard, for most people, to choose without hesitation between the two, for all Richardson's authorial and editorial efforts to obtain from his readership a severe condemnation of the latter. For all these efforts, he was obliged to regret that he met more people who sympathised with Lovelace than with Clarissa. While advancing—in what we might take to be a nineteenth-century way—the proposition that there were two sides to every question, Balzac was to ask: 'Who can decide between a Clarissa and a Lovelace?' Not only is the novel that Lovelace inhabits contradictory, moreover: Lovelace himself is. He is seen as inconsistent by the people of the novel, which was written at a time when it could readily be agreed that inconsistency was a bad thing. The readiness and robustness of that agreement were not destined to survive, and there are grounds for thinking that they are a little under siege in *Clarissa*. Richardson's picture of the mind can be examined in the hope of showing that it makes sense to think of his fiction as a bridge between Renaissance and Romantic duality.

In discussing the literary use of the double or *doppelgänger*, and of divided identity, from the Romantic period to the present, I have written in the past about a number of recurrent dualistic formulations: about the idea of inconsistency, of the strange case, of the 'strange compound' in the domain of personality or temperament (another word for 'compound' in former times), and about the figurative use of the verbs to 'soar' and to 'steal'. Such a use of the second word can be culled from Richardson's novel, where Clarissa writes to Anna, 'Oh that I were again in my father's house, stealing down with a letter to you' (and where she is later to deceive Lovelace by means of a heavenly *double-entendre* for the phrase 'my father's house'). In the fiction of Romanticism the image of the double is put with that of the orphan; nearby is the stock figure of Proteus, a name for the changeable self. Or so I tried to argue. And I tried to suggest that Romanticism offers versions and transformations of the confessional sentiment: 'I can't decide whether or not to break with my friends, whether or not to leave my father's house.' It is a sentiment which can appear to be linked to a rift within the self or to a repertoire of selves. But it is not a sentiment which the Romantics were the first to express.

In relation to Romanticism there is a prehistory of such terms, and they are important items among *Clarissa*'s million words. Clarissa herself is called an orphan and a 'romantic creature', and Lovelace, that creature of disguises, is called a Proteus, a thief, a 'strange wretch'. His mind is a 'strange mixture'. The word 'strange' is often used in the novel, where it bears the standard sense of someone or something from beyond the decorum of familiar and of family life—a sense which also appears in Lady Mary Wortley Montagu's reference to Richardson, that creature from another class, as a 'strange fellow'. Strangeness intrudes, and Richardson intruded on a decorum that could be breached from within. Pamela came as a strange creature to Mr B.—but reader, he married her! The novelist Fielding, Richardson's satirist, and a relative of Lady Mary Wortley Montagu's, and therefore of Louisa Stuart's, married his late wife's maid in the year in which the first two volumes of *Clarissa* appeared. Strangely enough. In her 'Introductory Anecdotes' concerning her grandmother—published anonymously but soon, to her displeasure, attributed to their author—Stuart provides this maid with a character, a favourable reference: 'few personal charms', but 'an excellent creature, devotedly attached to her mistress, and almost broken-hearted for her loss. In the first agonies of his own grief, which approached to frenzy, he found no relief but from weeping along with her.'[7]

Wretches are strange, strangers are wretches. And yet we are all strange in being wretchedly mixed-up. A standard, indeed perennial conception is expressed by Lovelace's friend Jack Belford: 'What wretched creatures are there in the world! What strangely mixed creatures!—So sensible and so foolish at the same time! What a *various*, what a *foolish* creature is man!' Similar statements are made in turn by Lovelace and Clarissa. Lovelace says: 'Everybody and everything had a black and a white side, as ill-wishers and well-wishers were pleased to report.' And Clarissa writes: 'with what intermixtures does everything come to me that has the appearance of good'—such as that good man, her father, one might reflect. Amiable is odious. And Lovelace himself is both amiable and odious—both simultaneously and successively so. Like Charles Townshend, he is volatile. Clarissa tells him: 'there is a strange mixture in your mind.' Lovelace responds to that opinion of hers by mentioning his 'inconsistency'. At this point in the novel Richardson inserts a footnote which observes that his character's actions have been consistent with a principle of inconsistency. Lovelace is black and white, loving and vengeful towards Clarissa, masterful and conspiratorial but also generous and witty, and alert to the life about him. Balzac's question is by no means inappropriate.

The Richardson scholar A. D. McKillop has said of the writer: 'He was aware that the "heroic total of great opposites" in this character made the ethical teaching of the story less unequivocal than his admirers expected.' Richardson's faith disposed him against equivocation, against duplication: his was a faith which held to 'the one thing needful'. And yet he seems to have felt that opposites could be great and an accumulation of opposites heroic. He did not give himself, or his admirers, what was expected. His novel is a mixed creature. Meanwhile Lovelace's, and the novel's, inconsistency is certain to have appealed to a romantic prejudice which was then in the process of formation—to the outlook of the author of *Don Juan*, for instance, with its dogmatic inconsistency. This is a poem in which 'consistent' is rhymed with and contrasted with 'existent', and writers are advised that they can't afford to be inflexible if they are to describe the way things are, the mixture of things.

The strange mixture of Lovelace's mind can be compared with the 'brittle compounds' that Belford says all minds consist of, male and female, and with Lovelace's remark to Belford: 'Different ways of working has passion in different bosoms, as humour and complexion induce.' Mixture, complexion, compound, humour—Richardson's picture of the mind has residues, and more, of the Elizabethan world picture. If Lovelace is a creature of shifts and disguises, he is also a sublunary creature who speaks of rising and flying, and of the black and white of an up and a down. He is not an atheist or a scientist, as Richardson took care to devise, and the old knowledge of a flight in the direction of the spheres of angelic intelligence, and of a drop to damnation, is repeated in him. Equally, it is Elizabethan of Miss Howe to mention a 'general scale of beings', with its high orders and low. Romanticism was sometimes to reiterate a pre-scientific cosmology and psychology, drawing on Shakespeare above all, and Richardson could well have been influential at an intermediate stage in the process of transmission and recall. He looks forward to the Romantics: in his dislike for the Enlightenment he also looks back, as the Romantics themselves were often to do.

Richardsonian inconsistency had recourse, therefore, to an old idea of the mind, to the doctrine of the elements or humours applied in the dualistic compoundings of alchemy. It did this at a time when such notions could be dismissed as magic, and when inconsistency was especially unpopular, when there was a righteous common knowledge of it, and a use of adages on the subject with which to scold an inferior, and when Samuel Johnson could assert that there are occasions when 'a poet may be allowed to be obscure, but inconsistency never can be right'.[8]

The Elizabethan words 'humour' and 'temperament' referred to a balance or imbalance between the four elements (earth, water, air and fire) or the four humours (melancholy, phlegm, blood and choler). Gold was produced, and the golden or perfect man was produced, when the elements were rightly proportioned. The idea of balance was crowned with the promise of endurance, and indeed of immortality: but since the Fall human beings had been imperfect—strange mixtures. It was an idea which appears to have held no strangeness for Richardson and his contemporaries. An equal mind—a name for composure which is used in *Clarissa*—was a balanced mind, and a thing to be desired. As of old, however, human life could also be seen as inherently or predominantly unequal, unstable, brittle.

These matters are treated in the poetry of Donne, which declares that all souls contain 'mixture of things, they know not what'. The souls of two lovers may become one, in a manner which is recalled when Miss Howe swears that Clarissa is the better 'half of the *one soul* that, it used to be said, animated *the pair of friends*, as we were called'. The souls of his lovers have been equally or harmoniously re-mixed, according to Donne, who also believed, or declared, that 'Whatever dies, was not mixed equally': so that this symbiosis of lovers might seem to be going to last for ever.

Here, then, was an outlook of the past which still meant something to Richardson: and perhaps it is not as implausible as it can seem in some of Donne's teases. We might well believe we are mixtures, and not know what the mixture is, or of what it is. It was an outlook which had not disappeared by the time of the Romantics, who were, in fact, to deepen and develop it, and to subject it to further teases. By this time the outlook had come to be ruled by the idea of the strange compound which denoted an identity dangerously divided, and there was to be a zealous and at least half-approving interest in persons, real or imaginary, who could be called by this name: James Hogg was described by a fellow dualistic writer as a 'strange compound of genius and imbecility'. These are matters which were never entirely to disappear from the spoken language, and they were to be features of the psychology of Jung, which relates the separation and integration of the alchemical process to the existence within the individual of psychic opposites and to the work of psychoanalysis.

In both of these books there are indications that the strange mixture was on its way to becoming the divided self of the Romantics, and in the vicinity of their authors there are some further indications. Diderot, an admirer of balance, and of Richardson, was to devise, in the 1760s, the intensely dialectical *Le Neveu de Rameau*, which relishes the thought that a man may be 'torn between two opposing forces', and in which it could be said that a work of integration is performed. And perhaps it could also be said that the United States of America —which was to become a stronghold of romantic literature, and of the divided mind—was an involuntary creation of the divided mind which evaporated in 1767, that of the romantic Townshend.

At this point it is worth consulting Louisa Stuart's memoir once again. Just before Frances's marriage, a scene is played out beneath the elms of Hyde Park, during which she reveals herself to Louisa Stuart as having been every bit as much of a strange mixture as Lovelace, every bit as volatile as Townshend. She, too, has been possessed by an unequal mind. But now at last, she says, she is in a fit state to marry her 'safe man'. The scene itself belongs to the 1780s, but the account of it[9] to the 1820s.

The inequality of her spirits which could not be disguised, the deep dejection which would succeed her greatest gayety, the efforts she often seemed making to employ and interest herself about odd trifles not worth her attention, the expressions she would drop (as if half in joke) fraught with some meaning more melancholy than met the ear—all this ought to have told me the tale beforehand—To give an instance; one morning when, sitting with us, she had been most transcendantly agreeable, flashing out brilliant wit, stringing together a thousand whimsical images, my mother quite charmed with her exclaimed—'What a happiness it is to have such an imagination as yours! You must enjoy a perpetual feast'—'Ah!' returned she—'So you may fancy, but I am afraid I know better. I often feel convinced I have two *Selves*: one of them rattles and laughs, and makes a noise, and would fain forget it is not alone—the other sits still, and says—Aye, aye! Chatter away, talk nonsense, do your utmost—but here I am all the while; don't hope you are ever to escape from ME'—

The tale is that for several years Frances had been the prey of a 'fixed, deep-rooted, torturing passion' for a certain unworthy man. This female affliction, as it is made to seem here, placed her in a quandary which brought about her inequality of spirits, these alternations of mood, the dejections which followed her flashes of wit—flashes in which, however, the memoir does not enable us to believe. The experience is taken to account for the 'two selves' to which she laid claim, and for which it seems that she was to be both pitied and admired. And it accounts for her saying, when she came to study the little stretching paws of her infant daughter Caroline, who was to be the recipient of the memoir: 'is not that exactly what we are all about throughout our whole lives; continually stretching and reaching at something, we hardly know what, and some other thing stronger than ourselves always pulling us back?' Back to 'common life', she means, back to those 'domestic feelings' which Louisa Stuart contrasts with the emotion of love. Frances says with Donne that we don't know what we are, what we are made of, and there were women who did not know what love was. It was rumoured of the Duchess of Buccleuch that 'she did not understand *that sort of thing*'. (Louisa's italics.)

Frances refused to accept this unworthy man, who makes one think of a second Townshend. The scene continues:

'I will not tell you, said *F*., that *he* ever felt what I did, nor perhaps is he capable of it; yet at one time I could not doubt that he was extremely inclined to make me his proposals, and would have done so on a very little encouragement. But no—Oh no, no!—I had just—only just enough of reason left to see that this must not be—that we must never marry—it would have been worse than madness to think of it—And I withstood the temptation like a famished wretch refraining from the food he knows to be mingled with poison.'

Having reported this strong image for the divided self, Louisa Stuart goes on to say that the wretch 'had suffered the torment of striving and striving without success to detach her affections from one whom her understanding and principles forbade her to approve, and would even have compelled her to reject', and to explain that a crisis was reached when the man

frankly avowed himself an unbeliever, almost to the extent of atheism. 'I could hardly bear up 'till I got home, said she; then I gave way at once and cried all night with a sensation of despair not to be described'—

Frances, who knew what it was to fly from home, had also refused to go off with a man whom her principles could not approve, a man who, unlike Lovelace, had strayed towards atheism.

Louisa Stuart suggests that she and her friend showed 'some self-command' in never again reverting to this subject. In writing about it as she does, we may feel that she is reliving torments of her own, a dilemma of her own.

Richardson's text and Stuart's are stations on a progress towards the subject-matter and appeal of romantic fiction—towards, let us say, James Hogg's *Confessions of a Justified Sinner*, which was written at about the same time as the memoir, and in which duality and family are mixed in a mysterious way—but in a way that can be investigated. With their dubious families, their principles, their patent good sense, their sentimental ardours, the two women of the memoir may be thought to stand in an ambivalent relation to the romanticism which arrived in the course of their later lives: such ambivalence is likely to accompany an interval of transition, and intervals of transition are likely to be propitious to the formation or intensification of a cult of ambivalence. All times are times of change, of course, and *Clarissa* can be accounted the changeable work of an earlier time of change, a work in which some of the same uncertainties can be noticed: but at a time when an important change is recognised to have occurred, it seems appropriate to look for evidence of the mentality which is both for and against family life, which both encounters and refuses the future. The memoir carries disparagements of the romantic, as we have seen; Frances did not run away with her unworthy man, what's more, and Louisa Stuart's sympathy with her friend's sternness in this respect is taken for granted. Nevertheless, the narrator plainly sympathises with the torment and division experienced by her friend, and this is a sympathy which accords with literary innovations of the earlier nineteenth century—with the novels of Scott, for instance, themselves compounded of reason and romance.

For Richardson, too, the word 'romantic' had a pejorative meaning: and yet his novel's disparagements of the romantic are assigned to ill-wishers. It is Clarissa's bad brother who speaks of her as a 'romantic young creature', filled with a perverse female 'tragedy-pride', who was of an age to be 'fond of a lover-like distress'. The novel powerfully displays the operations and indomitable purposes of a heroine who frequently appears to be quite the opposite of any romantic creature, and whose purposes have appeared strange and morbid to the readerships of later times. But it also served those of the generations that followed who would rather have read of a young woman running from her family than of a young woman who loses her chastity and wills her own death. There were then to be those who believed, or believed with a new intensity, in an individual psychology of opposing forces, contending sympathies, who believed in an interesting inconsistency, and in the kind of artist who takes equal pleasure in creating an Iago and an Imogen, a Lovelace and a Clarissa. Such readers, too, had reason to admire Richardson's novel.

He called it a 'history'. It is also a romance, and an example. He intended it to be a work of 'the Tragic Species', and it is that too. The work exacerbates the Christian confidence in a hereafter; it does not fit with the tragedies which are called by that name in academies of learning, and preferred to all other works, and which quite often lack a hereafter. But the contradictions of *Clarissa* can be compared with those of the canonical tragedies, and the novel should not be shut away from them and put with what specimens we are able to remember of the Restoration stage tragedies to which he attended. It is an aspect of Richardson's tragic work that it was to prove as capable of inviting as of precluding romantic sympathies, and that the history of its reception affords as much as it does in the way of contradiction and change. There are relatively single-minded works which have had a similar history. But it may be that, in the case of *Clarissa*'s relation to such a history, the element of cause and effect is more than usually decipherable.

There is a delicate, ghostly sketch of Louisa Stuart by John Hayter, dated 1837: a long, strong face, large mouth, large, lustrous eyes, set in a gossamer froth of cap, ribbons and ample lace collar. There are other pictures too: a Zoffany which shows the youngest of eleven children in early adolescence, stretching and reaching, a winsome portrait by Mrs Mee of the young woman, surmounted by a very fancy plumed hat, and a sketch of the dame by Sir George Hayter—at her studies, darkly clad, fiercely attached to her book. Fanny Burney thought her 'far from handsome': but 'understanding and vivacity' made up for that, and produced a 'pleasing' deportment and appearance. In writing in a comparative way about the memoir, I have been acutely conscious of the human being that she was and is, and conscious of the hope that her little book will be read, now that it has escaped from the muniment room, and that it will be read in conjunction with her previously published writings, to which I am about to turn. If the *Memoire of Frances, Lady Douglas* is the work of an amateur, it is also the work of a shrewd and clear-headed woman who was to display, in all of her writings from adolescence onwards, a narrative flair, an eye for human idiosyncrasy, and an ear for cadence that makes music of the least of her tales and tidings.

The conjunction with the biography of Townshend by Namier and Brooke, produced in Namier's old age, is bizarre. Theirs is a specialist study of a political career—utterly professional, but, as the portrait of a human being, highly unforthcoming. Perhaps there is an interest in the problem posed by the scabrous Townshend for these two distinguished historians of Parliament and of Parliament's rank and file—in their finding 'so often unaccountable' the actions of 'this seemingly protean personality', with the 'wonderful abilities, inordinate vanity, and poverty of heart'. Townshend spoke of his 'love of *consistency*', knowing that he was held to be 'inconstant', and these writers detect 'at least one curious consistency'—in his policy for America, grounded, they think, in his 'early impressions' of an unhappy family life. Horace Walpole told how on one occasion he had 'acted in his usual wild, romancing, indiscreet manner'. Fox thought him his own worst enemy. George III told Louisa Stuart's father, Lord Bute: 'I look on him as the worst man that lives.' Meanwhile this worst man said of Stuart's father, and of a choice between him and the Duke of Newcastle: 'Silly fellow for silly fellow, I think it is as well to be governed by my uncle with a blue ribband, as by my cousin with a green one.' *De haut en Bute*: but the worst man took 'great pains' while in office to relieve the suffering in private madhouses—great pains mentioned with a sneer by Walpole. Namier and Brooke do not seem to have had access to the manuscript of Louisa Stuart's memoir. They explain that, after years of mental stress and physical illness, of the triumphs, crises and offences that we associate with the brilliantly disturbed, marriage to Lady Dalkeith, a woman with 'little interest in politics', provided Townshend with a 'haven'.[10]

'I never yet saw my name in print, and hope I never shall', wrote Louisa Stuart, well on in her hundred years of life, in the early 1830s. She felt that for a woman in her situation to publish what she wrote misbecame both her petticoats and her rank. Asked by a woman of quality if it meant 'losing caste', she replied: 'Why—why—yes.' So much for her bluestocking grandmother. Before the nineteenth century was out, however, annals of hers, and collections of her letters, had been laid before the public,[11] and at the time when this hope was expressed, the secret of her writings, such as it had been, had already suffered the exposure which had finally overtaken the secret of Walter Scott's 'Waverley' authorship, a few months before. The secret was out, and the exposure was in part a self-exposure. When the identity of the author of the 'Introductory Anecdotes', published anonymously in 1837, was bruited about, she had long been known to be a writer by her equals and immediate inferiors. Worse, though, was to come. After her death, her name was to appear in print and to attract the attention of posterity's *profanum vulgus*. We may be said to know her now, against her will.

Cautious and constrained though the 'Anecdotes' may seem, they are a document critical to the understanding of Stuart's life. The quarrelsome, scandalous and gifted Lady Mary Wortley Montagu wrote romances, ran away in order to marry (it may be noted that both her mother and her grandmother eloped, and that Stuart herself stayed at home), ran to what she perceived as the 'romantic' East, and returned to England to save lives, and upset the clergy, by introducing inoculation for smallpox, by which she had herself been attacked. She was connected by marriage with a notorious 'romance' of the time, Lord Grange's marooning of his wife on St Kilda. She gave birth to a hostile son: this uncle of Stuart's is characterised in the 'Anecdotes' as 'singular', 'irregular', 'unstable' and 'inconsistent'. Elsewhere, Stuart speaks of a male relative as having escaped whatever may have been the 'evil influence' of Lady Mary, escaped the 'taint' of her blood: a violence of language which is absent from the 'Anecdotes'.[12] Lady Mary's letters were composed and distributed as literature, and in that respect resemble those of her granddaughter, where phrases are repeated and embellished from one epistle to the next and purple passages can be found which also figure in her memorial writings.

Among her posthumously published work is another memoir, also addressed to Frances's daughter Caroline and composed around 1827, in which Samuel Richardson and his view of marriage are strikingly discussed. The memoir concerns a forbear, John, second Duke of Argyll, and various females of the connection. The duke was seen by a brother as 'wrong-headed and romantic', and is seen by Louisa Stuart as a hero and a man of sense married to a country simpleton, a Jenny Warburton ill-suited to the Lady Jane, but 'quite free from any taint of the cunning which often attends weak understandings'. The centre-piece is an evocation of the high and mighty Lady Mary Coke, daughter of this duke and a woman of paranoid tendency, with the appearance of a fierce white cat, some of whose outrages were outrages and some fiction. She emerges as a replica both of Clarissa Harlowe and of Don Quixote. Louisa Stuart shows a tendency—familiar in her own age, as in others—to see resemblances to Don Quixote: she was also a reader of Spanish and a discriminating reader of Cervantes's novel, which Smollett, she thought, had coarsened in translation.

The white cat disliked the rake whom she did not decline to marry, and the wedding night was a humiliation designed and boasted of by Lord Coke, who 'found her ladyship, he said, in the mood of King Solomon's Egyptian captive—"Darting scorn and sorrow from her eyes"; prepared to become the wretched victim of abhorred compulsion. Therefore, coolly assuring her she was quite mistaken in apprehending any violence from him, he begged she would make herself easy, and wished her a very good-night.' There followed a regime of insult and incarceration. The unravished Lady Mary fought back with a writ of habeas corpus and a King's Bench divorce suit. The judges beheld a tragedy queen, but one who had difficulty in spelling out her grievances. It was settled that she should be allowed to live in the country 'unmolested, upon condition that she should withdraw her suit, pay its expenses herself, never set her foot in town, and have no separate maintenance but her pin-money'. Louisa Stuart observes that

neither bad husbands nor bad wives can be easily got rid of in our stiff, straitlaced country, whose austere old statutes invest the former with an authority which Lord Coke had taken care not to overstep,

save in a single instance, i.e. when he denied her mother the permis-
sion of seeing her. Had the doors been freely opened to the Duchess,
they might have continued fast closed upon Lady Mary for ever.[13]

A country, one might say, both straitlaced and Lovelaced.

Lady Mary's victim career had only just begun: further
persecutions were to have their fondly imagined grand designer
in none other than the Empress Maria Theresa in Vienna.
Real troubles this 'heroic sufferer' could manage: imaginary
ones were the very devil. In Paris, Horace Walpole was roused
in his nightcap to defend her against an Imperial scheme, an
episode which loses nothing in the 'humoursome' Walpole's
telling (elsewhere, Louisa Stuart tells what she reckons everybody once knew—that Walpole was no son of Sir Robert); nor
does that time when she missed the boat at Ostend—which 'she
believes was sent away on purpose', wrote Walpole, 'by a
codicil in the Empress Queen's will'.

The resemblance to Clarissa is implicit. The resemblance to
Don Quixote is pondered by Stuart several times over. Horace
Walpole, too, thought that Lady Mary was 'like Don Quixote,
who went in search of adventures, and when he found none
imagined them'. Louisa Stuart thought her more like Don
Quixote than anyone else on earth. Even so, the parallel was
imperfect. She was not insane. And perhaps we may add that
she was unlike Don Quixote in being 'nothing more than
simply and barely the person she was'. Lady Mary was consistent in her contrariness: 'Her character was thoroughly
singular, if not *unique*; but never contradictory: you always
knew in what direction to look for her . . .'. Whereas—in the
sense suggested earlier in this book—Don Quixote is plural in
his singularity. But the two were alike, and alike in 'lowering
the tone': Don Quixote 'overthrew the chivalrous spirit', while
elevated sentiments were repressed by those who did not wish
to be seen as doing a Lady Mary Coke.[14]

When she was a girl, Louisa Stuart felt overlooked (though
there is evidence that she was looked at) by a Lady Mary Coke
intent on her tales of woe, her presence minded 'no more than
that of the round-cheeked marble boys that supported the old-
fashioned chimney-piece', and we may scent an element of
revenge in this part of the memoir, and in the masquerade

which crowns it, where Louisa, incognita, quizzes her about
'our mutual friends' at the court of Maria Theresa. Lady Mary
—'Queen Mary', as Louisa used to call her—was delighted to
share her knowledge of the court with this expert, who went as
far as to ask about 'the conduct of Joseph', the Empress's son,
venturing

to say outright that I understood from good authority he had been so
captivated by a certain English lady, not far off, that nobody knew
what might have happened but for his mother's tyrannical inter-
ference. Lady Sackville, who was sitting by, opened her eyes very
wide and stole a fearful look at Lady Mary, concluding, I believe,
that she would rise in a fury and tear off my mask. No such matter,
indeed. She bridled, simpered, fanned herself, almost blushed, and, I
assure you, looked as prettily confused but as well pleased as ever was
boarding-school girl on hearing her charms had smitten the Captain
in quarters.[15]

By playing such tricks in her 'shyhood', and by being
'precisely the last person in London whom my nearest friends
could suspect of being the mask that teased them', she felt that
she had gained confidence in public (though we might think
that they are tricks which only the confident could play). She
learnt, in this way, to speak out. 'Hiding my face set my
tongue at liberty.' The letter to Scott of 1817 in which she looks
back at her disguises says of the self that had been in the
making: 'You see I have been in training for a conspirator.'
This narrowly anticipates what Jane Austen was to say about
the heroine of *Northanger Abbey*, published at long last the following year: Catherine had been 'in training for a heroine'. At
certain levels of the literary culture that came about in the
course of the centenarian Stuart's lifetime, to be a heroine was
to conspire. The letter then takes up a favourite subject—how
it felt for this conspirator to be privy to the secret of Scott's
authorship of the 'Waverley' novels, and we are led to think
that Scott, too, the Great Unknown, had set his tongue at
liberty by hiding his face.

Louisa Stuart insisted that she hated printing and publishing;
but among the women of consequence perched in their second
place at the apex of the Hanoverian state, she published herself
remarkably. She read aloud to them her Argyll memoir. One

piece of writing was printed by her for limited circulation among friends and interested parties—in response to a demand. Her letters were a work in themselves, and were written as one. Constantly conversable, she paid her visits and made her stays. She was never a power behind any throne; nor was she the kind of political spinster she despised. But by being the person she was, by doing a Lady Louisa Stuart, and by setting her tongue at liberty and doing some part of what she said she hated, by breaking her taboo, she would appear to have ruled her roost. She commanded a public of her peers.

Ambivalent herself in the matter of women's rights (the rights of man espoused by liberals were unequivocally opposed), she writes in the memoir about a comparable ambivalence in Samuel Richardson. The memoir fastens on an article of his, in the form of a letter contributed to Johnson's *Rambler*,[16] a piece of writing which helps to explain the ambivalence with which his artistic achievement has been regarded.

Richardson is recalling the good old days of the *Spectator*, when marriages had been made in church, on a basis of eye-contact and polite voyeurism—behaviour which Stuart elsewhere condemns as that of the ogling Lord Foppingtons of her youth, and which Leigh Hunt was later to thrill to in the line: 'Stolen looks are nice in chapels.' Richardson had formerly regretted that 'the better half of the human species' should contain 'Seekers' who went to church in the hope of a husband: but he now takes the habit to have been Arcadian compared with the barefaced publicity and flirting of balls and pleasure-gardens which have replaced it. 'With what ardour have I seen watched for, the rising of a kneeling beauty? and what additional charms has devotion given to her recommunicated features?' Whose ardour is this? A peeping Tom is shadowed by a peeping Sam. The suitor's friend on these occasions 'applies to those of the young lady, whose parents, if they approve his proposals, disclose them to their daughter. She perhaps is not an absolute stranger to the passion of the young gentleman.' The reader is then told that, 'thus applied to, she is all resignation to her parents. Charming resignation, which inclination opposes not.' Richardson's sermon dreams that the female could generally be expected to concur with her arranging family. It is as if *Clarissa*, which reads like the true story of a refusal, and which had appeared three years earlier, had never appeared at all.

Louisa Stuart had this to say:

Nor were marriages thus arranged among the great alone; the very proverb, framed, as all proverbs are, by and for the vulgar, 'Marry your daughter betimes, for fear she should marry herself,' is a convincing proof of the contrary. Consult, indeed, an author of much later date, one certainly not too well versed in the manners of high life, one whose theme and object it was to treat of love—Richardson, I mean, the great father of modern novels—Richardson himself cannot help betraying an evident predilection for matches thus soberly settled. In No 97 of the *Rambler* (written by him) you find his beau-idéal of a matrimonial transaction carried on exactly as it ought to be. The young man can see the young woman only at church, where her beauty and pious demeanour win his heart. He applies to her parents through a mutual friend; they acquaint her with his offer; she is all resignation to their will, for perhaps (mark the *perhaps*) she had seen him at church likewise. Then it proceeds: 'Her relations applaud her for her duty; friends meet, points are adjusted, delightful perturbations, hopes, and a few lovers' fears fill up the vacant space, *till an interview is granted.*' In plain English, the two persons concerned have never exchanged a single syllable in their lives till they meet as an affianced couple. And this he calls marrying for love![17]

These words might be called the plain English of bitter experience—by readers who have it in mind that Louisa Stuart's marriage for love was forbidden by her father. There is a story to the effect that, fourteen years before the words were written, she wore mourning dress for the deaths of her sister Lady Portarlington, of a dear friend of hers, Lady Ailesbury, and of the man whom she had wanted to marry, and with whom, after his marriage to someone else, she had remained friendly. It is a little like the sort of story which she herself used to refuse to believe. The text of her mourning clothes may at the time have been tantalisingly hard to read, and is no clearer now. Were these the 'quasi-widow's' weeds which have been attributed to her in later times?

Louisa Stuart wrote poems which tell of fairies and follies, of the Emperor's new clothes, of the vanity of human wishes, of reason's doubtful sway over 'Those yearnings of the soul that

secret swell'. Pope's playfulness, and Johnson's solemnity, are
attempted. There's a poem on growing old (the one with the
yearnings); another on growing older still; lines 'On approach-
ing Ninety' are reported but have not been recovered. Her
heroic couplets can seem crabbed and awkward, and are
outdone by the scatter of lays, ballads and burlesques. 'Ugly
Meg' is about a Border fright married off to a Scott of Harden:
they live happily ever after. And there's an interesting eldritch
poem—in a fairy-tale mode which makes use of the dactyllic
Scott—entitled 'The Cinder King', in which persons and pre-
dicaments of her life, and of other women's lives, are darkly
conjured. Betty has seen a bride led to the altar—'which bride
she was not'. Since she is not that bride, she decides to marry
for money—to woo the Cinder King. She sees pictures in the
fire, and out of it starts this demon, a relative of the Erl King.

'Come, Betty, my bride,' quoth, croaking, that thing,
'Come bless the fond arms of your true Cinder King;
Three more kings, my brothers, are waiting to greet ye,
Who—don't take it ill—must at three o'clock eat ye.

'My darling, it must be, so make up your mind,
We element-brothers, united and kind,
Have a feast and a wedding each night of our lives,
And we constantly sup on each other's new wives.'

Betty is smothered in ashes and lost for ever.[18]

It is in her memoirs, though, that she writes best—there and
in the memorial and story-telling episodes of her letters. Her
remembrance of the past has the soul of a novelist, one who
responded to the art of 'poor Miss Austen' (so-called shortly
after the writer's death), as well as to that of Walter Scott, the
subject of much of her practical criticism, and indeed it is in the
role of an elderly Emma that she can sometimes be found when
she writes to Louisa Clinton, who is at one point cast as
Emma's protégée Harriet Smith, and made aware of the
virtues of Mr Knightley. Louisa Clinton is scolded throughout
for being like the young Louisa Stuart in fancying herself
afflicted, or, as one might prefer to say, for resembling her
enduring alter ego, her afflicted half. Having trained as a
heroine, in other words, Louisa Stuart was never to outlive that

training. During her girlhood she was herself scolded and quizzed for the sensibility which she had begun both to indulge and to seek to control, while proving deficient in its exhibition, in the shedding of tears which featured in a heroine's instructions. For her reading and writing and reveries, her castles in the air, she was abused by siblings, eaten by brothers and sisters, charged by the family with resembling her grandmother, the tainted Lady Mary. She represents this as an 'anti-intellectual' kin among whom reading and writing, sensibility and *bel-esprit*, bore the ill-natured name of 'liter-a-pudding'. And yet her mother would appear to have been a cultivated woman, though one with an educated suspicion of cultivated women; and her father was not only a gloomy former minister, digesting his days of office, and of insult, of the rumours that made him the lover of George III's mother, and forever dosing himself with physick—not only that but a botanist of distinction, an Augustan virtuoso. 'Clearly she loved her family, but hated her home', wrote R. Brimley Johnson in 1926. This is not *very* clear: but then neither, in a sense, was she, and it is the kind of thing she sometimes makes one think.

The numerous letters which have been published, perhaps no more than a morsel, however, of her output, are a work of exceptional human interest—for all their consignments of news and gossip, for all their colds and coughs and gout, their deaths and declines of poor Lady This and poor Princess That, the 'ins and outs and hows and abouts' among relations, her franks and posts, the timetables of her progresses from one country seat to another. A sister, Lady Portarlington, told her, after their mother's death in 1794, that she was now free to do exactly as she pleased: there should be no more 'pining your life away'. Louisa portrays herself, in all her Richardsonian epistolariness, as an old maid who may have missed her Mr Knightley but whose life has nevertheless improved with the years. And yet 'something always comes in the way'. She has, in the past, done things, made nameless errors. Depressions sit beside her at her studies and on her progresses; castle-building, 'that secret *vice* of the mind', retains its seductions. For her friends, she afflictedly has us think, she has been, as it were, a Jonah, and one part of her remains the person she blames in Louisa Clinton.

She disliked the 'miftiness' of the patrician spinster with a taste for outrage, but was herself a detector of affronts from puppies and mountebanks. She is trenchant, in a manner that has been ascribed to old maids, about the presence in literature of *l'amour physique*, strangely supposing her forbear Fielding, in *Tom Jones*, to have been reticent in that respect. Both reading and making love could be construed by her in terms of killing and eating: but consumers of liter-a-pudding should be allowed to forget about some of its ingredients. 'The smallest grain of *amour physique* poisons the whole, renders it literally and positively *beastly*, for it is describing the sensations of a brute animal . . . I should say, as of my dinner, let me eat in peace, do not force me into the kitchen or the slaughter-house to see the nastiness which you say attends the best cookery.'[19] But if she was capable of exhibiting 'vartue' and 'narves'—her spirits were rated 'unequal', discomposed, during one of the bad times of her youth—she was also capable of smiling at them, and of employing these Fieldingesque forms in referring to them. Old maids have been dishonourably treated, and it can be said of her that she was like other old maids in possessing an unremitting power of mind.

A principal interest of her letters lies in what they reveal of her training in sensibility, in the entertainment of those violent, warm and tender feelings classed as romantic, and in what they also reveal of her strenuous training in their containment, and of a self-command exercised over the many years of her incontestable maturity. And there is a further interest in the degree to which this heroine resembles the readers and writers of the modern world. Her letters foretell a future in which reading was to be a way of life for people with a feeling for authorship who were fated never to publish, and for whom, as for authors too, literature could mean both an escape from the world and a passionate adherence to it.

The philosopher Hume spoke of the mind as a 'bundle' of impressions and ideas. The historian Macaulay spoke of Horace Walpole's mind as 'a bundle of inconsistent whims and affectations'.[20] Louisa Stuart's mind, in its romantic as in its other tendencies, was innocent, I think, of affectation: like her 'humoursome' Horace Walpole, however, she can be detected in inconsistency. These are inconsistencies which help to place her among the fascinating eighteenth-century bundles. It may seem a mistake to call her complications by a name that was then, and that was to remain, frequently opprobrious: they might once have been, and could still be, talked of as an aspect of 'sense', and in terms of the preservation of a balance. And it is true that the character of this writer of 'characters'—who did for her peers what her peers did for their footmen—sounds a note of paradox which can't always have been audible to her own ears. But it is also true that she *believed* in inconsistency—believed in the adages which continued to speak of it as inherent, believed that there was an 'order of things' to which there belonged a 'spirit of contradiction'.[21] It may be that, in believing what she did about division, she shows herself divided between the central eighteenth century, which portrayed it as morbid, and the nineteenth, which was often inclined to worship it.

At one point in the letters, conflicting reports of an Alpine holiday are deemed an 'instance of truth's abode in the well', and her attitude to the situation of women displays a comparable uncertainty, a similar exposure to the spirit of contradiction. She writes of an unshakable 'natural dependence' of women on men, while seizing opportunities to stand up for those of her sex whom she took to be her equals. It is in her attitude to the situation of women, and to matters of taste and manners, that her inconsistencies are at their most engrossing.

Her attitude towards the dynastic politics of her heyday is comparatively unequivocal. It is that of the *ancien régime*, of a dynast who believed that there was a 'right way of thinking', which incorporated the good sense that gave support to hereditary right, and made it right to scold her protégée. 'Far descended and highly allied'—in one of her own expressions—she can't be thought ever to have repudiated the political opinions of her resonantly-named connection, of the Stuarts, Scotts and Douglases she moved among, than whom, certainly for deferential people in the North, there could hardly have been anything grander, than whom there could hardly have been anything more like the history of Scotland in person. She looked up to Walter Scott, but was conscious of outranking him feudally, in the great game of gentle and simple, while Scott, for his part, was bashfully conscious of her royal blood. Of

James Hogg, the Ettrick Shepherd, she was conscious that, unlike Maria Edgeworth, he was the sort of person who could be forgiven for gaffes such as those that involved a choice between 'coloured clothes' and mourning (Hogg's gaffes were invariably more flagrant than that).

For her—as for Scott, and Hogg—Parliamentary Reform was 'mischief' and 'demolition'. Her straitlaced country should not be rashly eased. Her letters at the end of the 1820s say little about the extension of the franchise: they perceive a wider threat, a threat to the order of things, to the monarchy, the aristocracy and the Church. Faced with the Reform Bill, she added her voice to Scott's *Troja fuit*—the old world is gone. An old world of kings and clans and the words of Virgil, a world which went roving back to the Tory city of Troy. In an important letter to Louisa Clinton of 5 November 1830 she writes:

How abominable a thing is party! I have not the least doubt that the heads of the Whigs view such a reform with abhorrence in their hearts, and have only joined the cry in pure mischief, not dreaming it could ever come to anything. They know now that they have pledged themselves to pull out the corner stone of the building, and when they have done it, more reform, more, more, more! will ring in their ears ten times louder, till all is levelled, and themselves crushed down in the ruin.

On 11 November she warns her friend against the 'reading and writing day-schools', which favoured these skills at the expense of a training in 'habits of industry'. This last term was taken from a pamphleteer who had encouraged her to hold that education favoured Radicalism and crime—which did not spoil her pleasure in the Radical Cobbett's *English Grammar*. On 19 November she resumes her forebodings about Reform:

if the Whigs would now rally round the Constitution, steadily resist the Radicals, put down the mob with a strong hand, economise gradually and considerately, treat their sovereign civilly, and introduce the changes they have unfortunately tied themselves down to make as cautiously as the magnitude of the subject demands (I mean with regard to parliamentary representation), I myself should wish them a long and happy reign. But in the various short inroads of theirs that I have witnessed they have regularly done the very reverse of all this, ruined themselves by their own rashness, enraged others by insolence, and gratuitously affronted the king, whom it was their game to conciliate . . .

The letter draws to a close with two emotive sentences. The second alludes to Louisa Clinton's father, but she could well have been thinking also of her own—of Lord Bute and of his rough treatment at the hands of the mob and the press and the fearsome John Wilkes: 'I fear our hour is come. Tell me of your father, etc.'[22]

The crisis hugely excited her, and set her nerves on edge. And her political outlook was more complicated than these utterances suggest. Her sharp tongue was necessarily, one might say, as critical of certain of her family's friends as it was of that puppy, and reviewer, Lord Brougham.[23] Her grandmother Lady Mary, in the very different environment of George I's reign, was, Louisa said, 'Whig to the teeth—Whigissima': but 'Toryissima' would hardly suit herself. Neither of the parties pleases the Louisa Stuart of the letters, and she was against party anyway, linking the political, at times, with coldness of heart. She is likely to have known that there was no longer any alternative to party, and is unlikely to have had any secret desire to go back to a Stuart absolutism. In a sense, she had nowhere to go, and can give the impression of not knowing where she was—of insufficiently knowing that the world around her had indeed changed. New meanings were forming for the word 'industry', and for the word 'mob', and it may be that some of these new meanings were never to register with her. To others, however, she was especially sensitive. She was offended by the words used by both sides in the Parliamentary contest witnessed in her seventies, and the deteriorations of the nineteenth century were apparent in the way that '*slang* has superseded language'. It was the cant of progress, talk of the 'March of Intellect' and of a 'genuine spirit of freedom', that offended her most. At one point she associates it with a tale she has heard of insubordinate servants. She very much feared with her pamphleteer that delinquency would increase with 'what is vulgarly called the march of intellect'. 'I do hate', she wrote,

marches of ages and all that vile slang, as bad taste independent of its moral consequences. Nothing corrupts our language so much as using words in the French sense instead of the English one. *Marcher* means simply walking, to march. Something so different that the march of an age totally alters their metaphors; a *marche du siècle* being the quiet progression of the 'inaudible and noiseless foot of time' instead of its measured pompous strut.[24]

Firm as she was for birth and breeding, rooted as she was in a vantage-point that may have blinded her to much that was going on in England (Scots as she was, she thought of herself as English, and as caring for little more in Scotland than its landscapes), she could nevertheless see further than her caste. Her testimonies to the worth of her servant and friend, Mrs Cross, are evidence of this. Ever since her days with a mother distracted by 'so many trials, so many sorrows', she wrote in 1822, 'I have lived with my superiors in intellect and character'. She has done it 'whenever I could; God knows, I do it in my own house in the person of my own poor humble maid. I feel every day that she has far better sense than I.' The testimony may be set, in this context, beside her fear on one occasion that Scott might exhibit 'too partial a regard for aristocracy'. This, as it happens, is just what was said by James Hogg, whose claim that Scott had 'a too strong leaning to the old aristocracy of the country' may have been seen by Lockhart—Scott's biographer and son-in-law, whose wife was among Stuart's friends—as one of his terrible gaffes.[25]

Sharp as she was in her objections to male arrogance, to the behaviour of the lords of creation, she was no enthusiast for the forward march of women. The better education for females that she sometimes called for was the better education of far-descended and highly allied females. Politics were for men. 'Lady though I am', she wrote, she did not like to see ladies enter that arena, as they had offered to do over the regency question in revolutionary 1789. About the bluestocking sisterhood of her young days, ladies though they were, she tends to be gently satirical, as she is about a noted feminist of a time before, her grandmother's friend, the quaint but redoubtable Mary Astell. She used to attend meetings held by her bluestocking relative Mrs Montagu. 'We went at the hour appointed and took our stations in a vast half-moon, consisting of twenty or five-and-twenty women, where, placed between two grave faces unknown to me, I sate, hiding yawns with my fan and wondering at the unwonted exclusion of the superior sex.' But then in from the dining-room came a procession, a statehood, of eminent males, bishops and chancellors. 'They looked wistfully over our shoulders at a good fire', to which their way was barred. A stillness prevailed. 'We must all have died at our posts, if one lady had not luckily been called away, whose exit made a gap for the wise men to enter and take possession of the fireplace.' This is one of her finest narratives. Divided loyalties are beautifully expressed.

These bluestocking occasions were 'not always productive of what Pope describes, in a line which they were particularly fond of quoting, "The feast of reason and the flow of soul"'. She goes on to say:

For Reason, she might predominate, or might not; but you may judge how there could be any flow of soul, where most of the company came with a set purpose of shining, and all were aware that they could not pronounce a word which would pass unscrutinised. Mercy on the people who understood what they were about so ill as to vent the first whimsical thought that chanced to come into their heads![26]

There have often been attempts to separate matters of taste, including literary judgements and ways of feeling, flows of soul, from their moral consequences, and Stuart separates them, as we have seen, in her discussion of slang, while treating them on other occasions as inseparable. It may be said of her that she was both willing and unwilling to believe in a dimension of experience to which the rules of right thinking do not apply, and that her taste, in literature and in manners, enables one to recognise an aspect of her dividedness.

At the age of 17 she spoke of the ridicule directed against her for being 'romantic' and—the very word she would eventually use of her wicked and disinherited uncle—'singular'. In later life she was apt to explain that she had failed in the 'self-conquest' which she enjoined on others, and there were romantic tendencies of hers which she was never to conquer. She could be thought to have moved, in the course of her life, from romantic love to romantic friendship, with members of her own sex. But there seems no way of knowing whether she was ever seriously unmindful of the duty of self-conquest, and—in a manner to which we are accustomed—she was also to move, with age, to a greater severity in that respect. This singular being was plural, in the way that other singular beings were to be and had been before her. She was both regular and singular. Right-thinking and wrong. Candid and clandestine. Romantic and not. Her romantics were both a criticism of her class and an aspect of its manners, and were never to become the politics that could ensue among others of her class who wished, as she sometimes did, to behave as victims, and as the victim's friend. Her castles in the air enabled her to peer over the battlements of her social position. But they did not make a liberal of her.

The romantic Ladies of Llangollen were, for her, 'the very grossest flatterers and palaverers upon earth', members of the 'Genus Mountebankum'. And yet she shared the tastes of those who admired this pair—for the picturesque, for old houses and black mountains. She is, as her mother is not, 'partial to a wild scene'. She asks her dear sister, Lady Portarlington, parted from her by the Irish Sea, to join with her in gazing at the moon—a sentimental practice of the time, and, as she feels she has to admit, a 'silly' one. These are sentiments of the 17-year-old Louisa, who also writes: 'If you did but see me rambling over the rocks!' Lord Haddington's Tyninghame, visited in middle life in 1799, had once been a monastery, and was 'patched with apartments by its successive owners, so no regularity without or within, up steps and down steps, full of closets, passages, and staircases—a good place for a ghost to haunt'. Both in and out of her lady's chamber, this ghost from the past, as she herself became, was drawn to irregularity. On a later visit to filthy Scotland—her friends there fortunate in their palace of Dalkeith—she spies a Highland hill that had 'too even and dull a line for beauty'. Equal and equable were no longer beautiful.

A romantic, but withal a right thinker, who had no patience with the Gothic sublimities of Mary Shelley's fiction—very much the sort of stuff which boys and girls had gone for in her youth, she felt: 'Not a page but contains some sentence far beyond what Don Quixote went mad in trying to understand.' The poetry of Byron—an intriguing test for her divided state— she came round to in the end, but took a long time to do so.

She was also to change—but in a contrary direction, this time for severity's sake—her first opinion of *La Nouvelle Héloïse*. Rousseau's novel was 'the most interesting book I ever read in my life': 'I believe it might be very dangerous to people whose passions resemble those he describes. But I have nothing to do with love, so it is safe for me . . .'. She was, again, 17 when she wrote this, and her hopes of marriage to William Medows had very recently been destroyed. In the early 1830s she wrote: 'I believe no book ever did so much mischief.' It is made to seem as bad as the Reform Bill.

The romantic right-thinker was to persist, an unstable compound, throughout Stuart's life—a life sustained, one might add, by a Christian piety which would seem to have become less than secure. There, her heart was not right, and was not put right by the lectures and confidence of her sisters. She wrote poems which suggest that there may be a heaven to look forward to, that 'there may come a future better day', while persuading Jill Rubenstein, editor of the memoir of Lady Douglas, that 'she could never quite manage to believe in an afterlife'.

It would be fanciful to suppose that this judicious woman carried some trait or taint of her delinquent uncle. It is less fanciful to suppose that her experience embodied a strain of resentment and refusal, which helped to make her a reader and a writer, and a student of the romantic, and which may have owed something to her errant grandmother. Louisa Stuart was uneven—in the period sense which concurred with an old use of the word 'unequal'—at a time when unevenness, raggedness and ruggedness grew tall, when rocks and mountains, and human inconsistency, ceased to be unsightly. A process of change which began before she was born, and which is frequently interpreted as a matter of taste, as an episode in its history. A process which can sometimes appear to have no more to do with any march of intellect than with one of her rambles through Regent's Park, from her house nearby at 108 Gloucester Place. There is no doubt, however, that the process can be defined in terms of its intellectual and moral consequences, and no doubt that they continue to shape what we are, and what we say we are.

IV · Backwaters

IN the course of the 1970s V. S. Naipaul published two novels—
Guerrillas in 1975 and *A Bend in the River* in 1979—which address
the theme of alienation, marginality. The orphan modes apparent in the novels are those, respectively, of vengeance and
flight. And there are also orphan countries there—poor places,
backwaters, as it might seem, at opposite ends of the earth.

Early in 1972, two corpses were found in graves dug in the
garden of a house near Port of Spain, Trinidad. The house
belonged to a hustler called Michael de Freitas, latterly known
by his Black Muslim names, Michael X and Michael Abdul
Malik. In London, where he spent a number of years, he had
gained a reputation as a crook and as a threatener of whites and
defender of the coloured-immigrant population. One of the
corpses was that of a local youth, the other that of an English
girl, Gail Benson, who had come to the West Indies as the
slavish lover of an American Negro, Hakim Jamal, 'God' to
his friends, who was eventually to be shot dead in Boston. It
turned out that Gail Benson had been stabbed and buried alive.
De Freitas was tried, with others, for the Trinidad killings.
Kate Millett and William Kunstler went about the world protesting against the trial on the grounds that it was 'political'. In
May 1975, De Freitas was executed.

With these events in mind, Naipaul wrote a novel. He is of
Hindu stock, grew up amid the elaborate racial estrangements
of Trinidad, and now lives in England. He is a writer of rare
gifts, and among his gifts is a capacity to wound. He had previously written a journalistic piece about the killings, in which
De Freitas figured as shabby and contemptible, and Gail Benson
as a silly upper-class woman whose accessibility to the knife
might almost have been construed as a last desperate act of
Sixties modishness: an antic exported from Swinging London.
In a second article on the killings, Naipaul's wife Patricia used
the word 'antics' to characterise the behaviour of the De Freitas
set, which she firmly separated from the serious politics of the
Caribbean.

I knew Gail Benson slightly when she was a schoolgirl, and remember a pretty moon face, big eyes, a freckled complexion deepening to russet, dark hair parted down the middle—a nut-brown maid and modern miss who must have wanted to be away from the French Lycée in South Kensington, shy, uneasy, wound-up. I was curious to see what shrift she would receive in Naipaul's novel: the work of a man who has been spoken of by an old friend, the novelist Paul Theroux, as having in earlier times been 'merciless, solitary, and (one of his favourite words) unassailable'.[1] Well, it can be said that he does not allow his mercilessness to go undetected on this occasion. And yet the treatment of his characters is not exactly what that prefatory article of his might have led one to expect.

Guerrillas is set in an imaginary Caribbean country, whose capital city is by the sea. There are mountains nearby. Inland, a great plain. The landscape yields three centres of activity. First of all, outside the city, next to a growth of forest, there is Thrushcross Grange. Named after the mansion in *Wuthering Heights*, this is a desolate agricultural commune run by Jimmy Ahmed, back from London, where he has been in some vague way a celebrity. He has extracted land and money from business interests, but his revolutionary experiment has foundered from the start. Nathaniel Hawthorne spoke of the 'phantasmagorical antics' he had played in describing the socialist community which appears in *The Blithedale Romance*: the antics played in the commune conceived by Ahmed could also be called phantasmagorical. A nut-brown man by South Kensington standards, he is light-skinned in the West Indies: he is a Chinese Negro, who thinks of himself as a *hakwai* Chinee—*hakwai*, he explains, being 'Chinese for nigger'—and who has not failed to notice that Emily Brontë's Heathcliff is rumoured to be the Emperor of China. He is also a self-styled haji, or Muslim holy man. He has gathered about him a defecting company of slum boys, with one of whom, Bryant, of the distorted face, his hair done up in small Medusa pigtails, he sometimes makes love.

The polluted landscape, and the heat in which it languishes, are important to the novel. The heat, and the drought, have set this country on fire. The hills smoke, mounds of rubbish smoulder, the verges of the roads are charred. All this is felt to

testify, not just to a general rankness and decay, but to a con-
flagration of another kind—to what will happen if the political
and racial tensions of the island can no longer be contained.
Gangs and guerrillas are talked of. Wealthy people are talking
of escape from a Caribbean version of James Baldwin's 'the
fire next time'.

A white woman named Jane has come here from London,
drawn by the glamour of the Third World, supposing herself to
have arrived where the action is, where the 'doers' are. She
is, as she acknowledges, 'playing with fire'. For a while she
believes that Peter Roche is a doer. Tortured by the regime in
South Africa, Roche has written a book about it, and now, in
the Caribbean, has joined the firm of Sablich's as a welfare
worker, whose job is to define and to publicise the firm's good
intentions toward the community. It does not take long, however, for Jane to become disillusioned. She 'knew' that 'she
had come to a place at the end of the world', a backwater where
there was no action at all. She lives with Roche above the city
in a 'Californian' company house on the Ridge: this suburb,
barricaded, fireproof perhaps, but lived in by prospective quit-
ters of the country, supplies a further scene for the events of the
novel. Every so often, wild disordered men, with matted hair
and 'unseeing red eyes', are glimpsed 'tramping along old
paths, across gardens, between houses, and through what
remained of woodland, like aborigines recognising only an
ancestral landscape and insisting on some ancient right of way'.
One of them has taken up residence in a hut in Roche's garden.
When Jane has Roche inspect the hut, the wild man, with his
black face and his pigtails, has gone, leaving behind him 'only
a vague warm smell of old clothes, dead animals, grease and
marijuana'. Perhaps he will be back—next time.

The novel's third scene or zone is the city itself. The auto-
mobile has turned the city inside out, ranging new communities
around the periphery and letting the centre rot: not far from
the centre is an old slum district where the gangs operate. They
are a reality, whereas the guerrillas are only a dream—phantasmagorical. But they are a reality which Naipaul treats in
such a way that they, too, can at times seem phantasmagorical.
Everywhere, transistors give off the Reggae beat, making the
place a party that never stops, and that might catch fire.

A sense of mystery and futility is imparted by events at the Grange and on the Ridge, and that sense is heightened by what takes place in the city when the party catches fire and rioting breaks out. Politicians rush to the airport with their loot. Then American military helicopters drift about the sky: a show of strength which is meant to secure American interests on the island, to make it safe for the bauxite investment. Ahmed does not lead this revolution. No one does. It is not a revolution. It is a mystery. A journalist politician, Meredith Herbert, is made a minister—perhaps in order that he should be damaged by having to deal with the people on the streets; he is, perhaps, physically beaten up. His role in relation to the disturbances is never really clarified, nor is that of Stephens, an intelligent boy who deserts the Grange, is in touch with the gangs, and is murdered. The gangs exist as intimations of a power which cancels Ahmed's claim to be a revolutionary leader. That power is located in the slums, in the kinship and solidarity which prevail there, in sanctions which welfare workers will not be able to comprehend.

The angle from which the riots are studied makes them appear distant and unimportant, while also worrying. The same angle was conspicuous in the title story of Naipaul's previous book, *In a Free State*, where a coup in a new African country was studied, as it were, out of the corner of an eye; and it also occurs elsewhere in his work. On these occasions the eye discerns a kind of visibility in 'an area of darkness': this, in fact, is the title of the book which records Naipaul's 'experience of India'. Enthusiasts for explanation, however, might want to explain that this 'darkness visible' tends to obscure and diminish what deserves to be understood, and that, for him, there are important countries and unimportant countries, and that the coups and riots of the latter are severely diminishable. Here, he surrounds the politics of his imaginary country with darkness, distinguishes between its politics and what might be seen as the antics of bystanders, and concentrates on these bystanders. At the same time, the reader can be made to feel that, on closer inspection, the country's politics might prove to be antics too.

Naipaul may in consequence be open to the charge of trying to diminish both the Michael X murders and the politics of the

Caribbean. It can be said in his favour that the Michael X set seemed very like a fraud and a circus, and that these people had no deep connection with the politics of Trinidad. In that last respect, however, they were like practically everyone else on the island, which may in itself be a reason why we should not be quick to decide that their behaviour lacked political significance, and consisted of antics.

Guerrillas, then, is shaped in order to accommodate its three zones, and in accordance with a distinction between the political and the phantasmagorical, though there are moments when phantasmagoria, futility, threatens to envelop the island—Grange, Ridge, gangs, government, politics and all. It is shaped, besides, in accordance with a dramatic momentum which reaches successive peaks with the two sexual encounters between Jane and Jimmy Ahmed. The encounters are separated by the riots and the second is followed by Jane's death.

Jane is a disgruntled, mean and worldly woman who presents herself as the victim of the men she sets out to attract and soon sees through and rejects. For all her action-seeking, caring cosmopolitanism, she is imperial-insular in outlook, and soon sees through the Third World. When she goes to bed with Ahmed, it is a fiasco. He looks at her in fear: 'the cleft was like a dumb, stupid mouth.' Her kiss is hard and wild; it goes with her 'screaming' eyes. The later encounter is prefaced by advice from Jimmy, whose leadership pretensions are by now in ashes: 'Be calm. You're too greedy. You give yourself away when you kiss like that. A woman's whole life is in her kiss.' Whereupon he calmly buggers her. In Argentina, according to Naipaul's journalism, such an act belongs to the fantasies of machismo: here, at the end of the world, and of Ahmed's tether, it bears the mark of defeat. Sodomy is then compounded by a somnambulistic, almost involuntary murder, in which Bryant deals the blows.

The novel breathes a certain animus against Jane. In contrast, the portrait of Ahmed has none of the disdain which could be observed in the writer's article about Michael X. Ahmed's bluffs are called, but they are understood, and carefully related to his earlier life on the island. His words about kissing are worth hearing. The airmail letters which he exchanges with his liberal friends in England tell a worse story of them than they do of him, and hark back in fine style to that golden time when such friends used to kneel in London mosques with Michael X and other celebrities, squinting up at the Heavyweight Champion of the World's effulgent arse. Jane is unlikely to earn much sympathy by virtue of the attention given to the environment which produced her dabbling in eventfulness and her poor kiss, and yet the two environments have more in common than would once have been thought possible. It is a quite Caribbean Britain that has made her: a Britain at the end of the world which it used to rule.

Ahmed's revulsion from Jane sometimes seems to be shared by the writer. It is possible to think that this plebeian has been lent some part of Naipaul's aristocratic fastidiousness, some part of his hostility, while also suffering the consequences of an exposure to these qualities, and to recall that both Ahmed and the author of *An Area of Darkness* are preoccupied with the hanks of human shit that litter certain landscapes. Ahmed's revenge is too bad to be condemned by the writer, who condemns his taste in furniture, and who condemns Jane. The tragedies of miscegenation have never been simple—ever since Othello did what he had to do to Desdemona. But it seems clear that this one bears the marks of defeat and despair, and of a reprisal directed at the liberal England which has let the violator down.

Naipaul's Caribbean country has been looted and exploited in the past, and it is still being looted and exploited. Together with its stultifying racial enmities, this seems to have brought it to a halt, and placed it beyond history. The behaviour of Naipaul's hustler-hero, his greedy white woman, his pseudo-guerrillas and mysterious gangs, his grafting emergent politicians with their State of Emergency, can be divided into the phantasmagorical and the political. But these dimensions, as I have said, often appear to coincide. His leading characters are seen to be, in some sense, petty and peripheral: but peripheral to what? To standards of conduct attained in other countries, metropolitan standards, or to something on the island? The island's public affairs and significant politics can occasionally be seen, out of the corner of an eye, to be no less invaded by contingency and incomprehensibility and futility than the life and times of Jimmy Ahmed, to have the status of rumour, to be little more than a remote and indecipherable response to a ran-

dom outbreak of violence. There may be readers who object
that the novel makes a mystique of darkness and futility in the
course of saying that the whole island is peripheral, arrested.
This is a possibility to which an admirer of the novel keeps
having to revert.

Times have changed since Naipaul began to write about the
societies of the Caribbean: these are now less apt to seem, to
the outsider, petty and remote. His early comedies might have
been taken to represent an unheard-of civility from the back of
beyond. Then, in 1961, came *A House for Mr Biswas*: a rich,
spacious novel of emergence from backwardness, indeed from
slavery, an emergence which is invested with irony. Since then,
he has written, among other things, *The Mimic Men*: while
relatively unsuccessful, this is the novel which most resembles
Guerrillas, and it undoubtedly 'diminishes' the politics of
emergent countries by raising doubts about the character of
their independence and the motives of their leaders. Over the
intervening years, however, the West may be thought to have
let him down by declining, diminishing, to the condition of the
West Indies: by becoming a backwater, with its Watergate and
Ulster, its economic arrests and somnambulistic states of emergency. Naipaul's readers could well have become inclined to
ask why it is that his novels seem to say that there is nothing to
be done in, or with, the countries of their concern. What are
other countries doing?

Naipaul has long been a reader of Conrad, and *Guerrillas*
can make you think of *Nostromo*. The geographies are similar.
Conrad's novel is about a fire-prone seaside South American
republic, with foreign investors and their concessions: its silver
has its lightly rendered counterpart in Naipaul's bauxite. And
the Conrad cry of 'Inconceivable!' may be weighed against
Naipaul's insistence upon areas of darkness. Compared with
what we find in Naipaul's novel, however, Conrad's Costa-
guana is a country of the mind: it has the air of having been
built to accommodate his meanings. What we find in *Guerrillas*
is a narrative of unfailing fascination which delivers to the
senses of the reader a country very like the countries he knows
in the real world: equally, his experience of that country is very
like his experience of Naipaul's India, in being rarely subdued
by an awareness of the writer's more deliberate meanings. It is

characteristic of the novel that climate and vegetation should count for no less than its comedy of manners, in which the Jewish businessman Harry de Tunja plays an enjoyable part, and that neither of these two elements, so far as they can be distinguished from the rest of the novel, should count for less than the opinions which they help to convey.

This is a very different work from *Biswas*. It is brief and fast: it moves to the rhythms of a single drama, and the pace is perfectly judged. Either book could be considered the masterpiece of someone whom I think of as among the most gifted authors now at work in England. It might appear that the whole life of the later novel is in its sting, but there is more to it than sting. Conrad said of *The Secret Agent*, another book about revolutionaries, cranks, crooks, somnambulists, peripherals and phantasmagoricals, that it was written 'in scorn as well as in pity', and the same could be said of *Guerrillas*. But in passing, as they may be thought to have done, from journalism to fiction, Naipaul's feelings, and their objects, underwent a change. There is less scorn in the novel than there had been in the article, and a pity that must have come as a surprise to readers of his work. Some readers were upset by the hostility shown towards the murdered woman, and by the sympathy shown towards Jimmy —the sympathy of an author noted for his sceptical attitude towards revolutionaries, who had been hostile, in print, to all of the participants in the historical events which supplied part of his plot. There must also have been readers who were led to reflect on Othello's self-righteous murder of Desdemona, and to reflect that Shakespeare's play expresses a view of mixed marriages which is both encouraging and discouraging.

In both *Guerrillas* and *A Bend in the River* the description of a coup, of an emergent country's state of emergency, is put together with the description of a sexual relationship between people of different races: an affinity is suggested, also apparent in the novella *In a Free State*. In *Guerrillas*, the rebellion is mysterious, cryptic, while the sexual relationship is fully lit: a contrast also apparent, but somewhat different, in *A Bend in the River*. Both novels see the world in colonial colours—as determined by empires, in the furtherance of which races have defeated and enslaved each other, in which they have met and married, in which a black mercenary might marry a daughter of Venice. For much of its course, the later novel takes all this for granted. It is what is likely to occur. Races insult each other, and make war, and make love, and they may mix these activities up. At the same time, the novel finds more to object to in the less objectionable aspects of these activities than many readers might anticipate. It is the work of a writer for whom, in successive fictions, the theme of sexual dealings between people of different races has necessitated the representation of violence. Rapes and murders occur in this area, and may, of course, have to be treated. And the theme is obviously of high consequence for the portrayal of any society where race is a trouble and where one race has subdued another. The society may be symbolised by such dealings, and experienced through them. Hardship and discontent may declare themselves there, in a victim's revenge. In addressing itself to such possibilities, however, *A Bend in the River*, for all its air of simplicity, is never simple. Its narrator and chief human presence is by no means straightforwardly a victim, and the difference between oppressor and oppressed can be hard to identify.

The novel is narrated by a Moslem of Indian origin, whose family has been settled on the east coast of Africa, as traders. Salim leaves them, takes off on the first of a series of 'flights', and treks to the interior, to a country which appears to be compounded of the Congo and of Uganda, in order to earn a living from a store which he has acquired from a man whose daughter he is expected to marry one day. Reading Salim's palm, the man points out that he is 'faithful'. Salim can be designated a Kenya Asian: the name we give to those hard-working aliens who have been driven out of African countries, and who include the shopkeepers and merchants expropriated in Uganda by Amin. Kenya Asians are now working hard in the darkness and grime of British cities, where Patel is among the commonest names in the telephone directory.

Salim is bound by certain of the rules and assumptions of kinship. His kin are entrepreneurs, a wandering bourgeoisie: they have known what it is to be strangers in tight corners, as he himself is a stranger in this tight African town. At the same time, he has wandered some distance from his kin, in spirit. So he is both doubly an outcast and no outcast at all. Unlike many of the towns through which he has bribed his way in his Peugeot from the coast, this one isn't 'full of blood'. But it is between coups, or unrests, and has lately been smashed and looted. It is the sort of place which will always revive and rebuild, and in such a place Salim's part is to make good, carry on. The country, formerly a colony, now 'independent', is controlled by a black 'big man' in the capital down-river. An atavistic, tribal, magical resistance spreads about the bush: starveling rebels are hunted by an army, but magic bends the army's guns. There is far less of the mystification which can be attributed to the account of the troubles in *Guerrillas*: what we get is the mysterious politics·of forest and township as observed by an outsider, by an African Asian who understands a good deal of what is going on. Salim buries his valuables—from another point of view, his ill-gotten gains—and an ominous silence descends on the town:

Sometimes I thought I could hear the noise of the rapids. It was the eternal noise at that bend in the river, but on a normal day it couldn't be heard here. Now it seemed to come and go on the wind. At midday, when we shut the shop for lunch, and I drove through the streets, it was only the river, glittering in the hard light, that seemed alive. No dugouts, though; only the water hyacinths travelling up from the south, and floating away to the west, clump after clump, with the thick-stalked lilac flowers like masts.[2]

Outside the town, a polytechnic and seminar centre has been planted by Presidential fiat. It is headed by the big man's white man, the Belgian scholar Raymond, who has lost favour with his patron and is sinking into ceremonies of highly-placed sagacity. Salim has an affair with the white man's white woman, his stylish wife Yvette: radical chic persuades him that he 'never wanted to be ordinary again'. Hitherto a shameful brothel man, Salim is uplifted by their meetings in his flat: 'My wish for an adventure with Yvette was a wish to be taken up to the skies.'

Blood flows within the town; Raymond's work on a collection of the President's speeches, which could restore him to favour, languishes. Presently the affair ends in insult: Salim beats Yvette and spits on her, and flies to London, where he gets to know his intended bride. When he returns to the town, he is arrested, but is set free by Ferdinand, an African promoted from the bush whose patron he has once been. Salim makes good his escape on the steamer—bound, we take it, for his bride. The family slave boy, Metty (the name means half-caste), who had come to live with him, is firmly left behind. Salim is now homeless in the sense that he has shed an old tendency to nostalgia: 'the idea of going home, of leaving, the idea of the other place', he takes to be weakening and destructive. This feeling is added to a previous illumination, to a stoicism which believes in 'the unity of experience and the illusion of pain'.

Salim tells Salim's story. It is not Naipaul's; it does not constitute the author's testament or confession on the subject of race relations and the rest of it. The novel (or so I hope) signals a separation between author and narrator with its very first sentence: 'The World is what it is; men who are nothing, who allow themselves to become nothing, have no place in it.' An early passage[3] separates this man, who does not want to be nothing, from the trading elders of his family—pessimists who could take risks, and were consoled by their religion.

I could never rise so high. My own pessimism, my insecurity, was a more terrestrial affair. I was without the religious sense of my family. The insecurity I felt was due to my lack of true religion, and was like the small change of the exalted pessimism of our faith, the pessimism that can drive men on to do wonders. It was the price for my more materialist attitude, my seeking to occupy the middle ground, between absorption in life and soaring above the cares of the earth.

Elsewhere Salim separates himself from the doers and makers of the big world beyond him, of whom it is said: 'They're making cars that will run on water.' Such people are 'impartial, up in the clouds, like good gods'. The men in the bush are watched by gods who are barely a jump above their heads: these white gods are more remote. Salim reads about their doings in his magazines of popular science, and letting Ferdinand into the secret of his interest, he feels he is revealing his 'true self'. But if his 'true nature' is to be romantically on the rise, and to have 'ideas', it is also his nature to occupy the middle ground. It isn't lost on him that his reading matter—popular science, pornography—is 'junk'. For much of the time, he is the achiever who tries for a reasonable percentage return.

Salim presents himself in a light which requires the reader to be told that, although he himself has been making good, he is grieved, or affects to be, by the discovery that the slavish Metty has been getting on: 'You've been very much getting on as though you're your own man.' Their relationship has tenderness in it, and treachery. Metty betrays his master and is then left in the lurch, predicting a future whose likelihood the novel does not lead us to discount: 'They're going to kill and kill.' Metty is a misfit, as Golding's Matty is in *Darkness Visible*, a novel which appeared at the same time as Naipaul's. English fiction loves such people; it never tires of the lurch, of such areas of darkness.

Salim's outlook incorporates a version of that of his friend Indar, who teaches in the polytechnic for a while, and lends himself to the philanthropic white-liberal cultivation of the African experience, where some of the best comedy in the book is located. At one point Indar recounts his struggles and illuminations. 'Raised' from the ruck, originally, by his family's wealth, he doesn't want to 'sink', and rejects 'the idea of defeat' that prevails in the Third World: 'I'm tired of being on the losing side. I don't want to pass. I know exactly who I am and where I stand in the world. But now I want to win and win and win.' Salim, too, wants to win, and his affair with Yvette is a victory: 'All my energy and mind were devoted to that new end of winning the person.' In possessing her, he is both taken out of, and placed in possession of, himself: 'She gave me the idea of my manliness I had grown to need.' When the friendship begins to fail, he says: 'What she drew out of me remained extraordinary to me.' The affair seems to him to belong to the town, to have no future, and they are parted when the town comes under fear and hazard. He finds himself 'considering the idea of flight', and the idea of defeat: 'I suppose that, thinking of my own harassment and Raymond's defeat, I had begun to consider Yvette a defeated person as well, trapped in the town, as sick of herself and the wasting asset of her body as I was sick of myself and my anxieties.' But the fit of jealousy in which he beats her would appear to mean something more than these words of explanation enable one to understand. This jealousy may be felt to be like Othello's in having more to do with difference of race, and with the jealousies of race, than the jealous man, or than the work he belongs to, seems disposed to state.

Three of literature's myths underlie the narrative. They are myths of the foreign woman, which bring together achievement and betrayal, achievement and desertion. Of the stories I have in mind, Othello and Desdemona, Samson and Delilah, Dido and Aeneas, only the third is spoken of, and it is spoken of oracularly.[4] The town has two Classical mottoes, one of which consists of

Latin words carved on the ruined monument near the dock gates: *Miscerique probat populos, et foedera jungi*. 'He approves of the mingling of the peoples and their bonds of union': that was what the words meant, and again they were very old words, from the days of ancient Rome. They came from a poem about the founding of Rome. The very first Roman hero, travelling to Italy to found his city, lands on the coast of Africa. The local queen falls in love with him, and it seems that the journey to Italy might be called off. But then the watching gods take a hand; and one of them says that the great Roman god might not approve of a settlement in Africa, of a mingling of peoples there, of treaties of union between Africans and Romans. That was how the words occurred in the old Latin poem. In the motto, though, three words were altered to reverse the meaning. According to the motto, the words carved in granite outside our dock gates, a settlement in Africa raises no doubts: the great Roman god approves of the mingling of peoples and the making of treaties in Africa.

There is irony here. We are made to feel that the reversed meaning is wrong. This is a book which takes for granted, and which has doubts about, the mingling of peoples, and it is a book which takes pride in its chosen people—Salim's people and, in some measure, Naipaul's. Virgil's Aeneas leaves a burning Troy to go on his adventures, effect his betrayal, and arrive at the Tiber, where an empire is to rise. Salim is an Aeneas who makes it to London, where those of his blood are founding a way of life, and he has his Dido both in Yvette and in Metty. Perhaps this much can be said without suggesting that the book is an epic for Kenya Asians, which tells of a people threatened by nobodies, nothings, and managing to survive. Nor is it a one-sided account of the injustices suffered by this people, or a defence of the energetic stranger.

The myths are not all equally available to the novel, and they are not enough to explain it. This lucid and candid prose, strong in the detail of a particular time and place, often ignores, and can on occasion seem to depart from, the sense of the literature it embodies. The offended looks of the muzzy black *citoyen* who is put in to own Salim's store when trade is politicised are funny, and important, and owe nothing to the *Aeneid*. But those who would prefer to explain the book as a comedy of manners, or as current affairs, might have difficulty in explaining the prominence given to the love affair. The plot states that an attachment to a strange woman, a woman who does not belong to this.community of strangers, is succeeded by a return to the community, and by the dispersal, and survival, of the community. Salim states that he was having a rough time, and was tired and suspicious of Yvette: he does not say that a tribal god commanded him to leave her. It may be that neither statement need be held to subtract from the other, but there could well be some dispute as to which of the two is the more deeply entrenched in the novel. Salim gets out of Africa, and as he does so, there seem to be allusions to the journey up-river in Conrad's *Heart of Darkness*, which also ends (though by no means hopefully) with an Intended.

When his steamer quits the town, it is attacked by rebels, but manages to fight clear. Meanwhile, in this closing scene, the water hyacinths proceed towards the sea, as they have been doing throughout the action. They keep coming, like immigrants, or refugees, like the South-East Asian boat people subsequent to the novel. Salim's flight to whatever is to become of him can be compared to the movement of these flowers, and to the Romeward journey in Virgil. His fortunes are those of a solitary who is due to return to his people and to chance it with them in a further foreign place. And they are those of a hero, as well as a drifting hyacinth. He is a hero, with a hero's faults: an achiever and an adventurer who is also a victim and an outcast, a shameful man and a faithful family man. Subtly mythic and ethnocentric, the novel is one of Naipaul's most rewarding. It speaks of the separation of races, and of a world which mixes them up. But if it sometimes seems to be saying, on Salim's behalf, that race or kinship wins, it is also the case that it is full of losers, that it has a lively feeling for the Africans of market and bush, and for their African troubles, and for the situation of Salim as someone evolved or emerged from a tribal narrowness to an experience of sexual love which is liberating and dramatic, and that it does justice to Metty's last state, left behind in the dangerous town at the bend in the river.

V · Poor Boys

RONALD Fraser's *In Search of a Past* was published in 1984, and Ralph Glasser's *Growing up in the Gorbals* in 1986. These are books by middle-aged semi-Scots who have chosen to publish accounts of their early lives which lay stress on the troubles they experienced, on the troubles inflicted, within their respective environments, by poverty and servitude, and on the responsibility of relatives for some of what the writers had to suffer. The question could be thought to arise of whether they are seeking revenge. Authors are not supposed to avenge themselves in their writings, but they do, and if they were to be prevented, there would be far fewer books. I am not confident that either book may be said to be well-written; that question, too, could be thought to arise. *In Search of a Past* affects not to be written at all—so much as researched, recorded and compiled. But the editorial method which is applied to the data has much to display that is well-spoken. They are both interesting books because they tell interesting stories, and are arranged to dramatic effect in interesting ways. Juliet Mitchell has called Fraser's book 'a miniature masterpiece', while, according to Chatto, Glasser's 'may well become a classic of modern autobiography'.

Both men made for the Mediterranean eventually, for reasons which may have involved a respite from British miseries and injustice. These were located, in Fraser's early life, amid the flatlands, and the privileged high ground, of Southern England, and, in Glasser's, amid the antique squalor and grimness of the Gorbals district of Glasgow, now erased by developers and replaced by the squalor of the high-rise estate. Fraser was to be the author of *Blood of Spain*, an oral history of the Civil War.[1] Glasser was to be the author of a study of a Calabrian village, and the Spanish war bears a bleak meaning in the story he tells here. His adult life has been spent as a psychologist and economist, engaged on problems of development in the Third World. He has published a second volume of autobiography, in which he deals with his years as a student at

Oxford before and after the world war, and is now bursar of one of the colleges there.

Ronald Fraser's book arranges a marriage between Freud and Marx. One law for the rich and another for the poor, as the two systems can be made to seem, are laid down together in a book which commemorates a desertion, on the author's part, of the rich for the poor. He had hit on the 'aim of combining two different modes of enquiry—oral history and psychoanalysis—to uncover the past in as many of its layers as possible'. He is saying this—outlining the aim—to his analyst in the course of the therapeutic sessions whose speech forms part of the oral record that constitutes almost all of the book. He is to learn about the troubles of his early life by interviewing the servants of the family and by submitting to the interviews of psycho-analysis. The analyst had previously referred to their sessions as a 'voyage of inner discovery': Fraser thinks that his tape-recordings make possible a 'voyage into the social past'. The latter trip may enable him to discover the 'external objects', the analyst thinks: 'now, through analysis, you're seeking the internal objects.' 'And the two don't always coincide', Fraser replies: 'That's my split vision. Formed by the past, a person is also deformed by it.' The exchange has roused the analyst to contributions that are firmer and more energy-consuming than those he generally vouchsafes: 'it's not the past but what we make of the past that shapes our future and present.' Fraser observes that 'analysis is more limiting because it recreates the past only in the forms in which it was internalised or repressed'.

Not every reader of his book can have come to it believing the chauvinistic claims that have sometimes been issued on behalf both of psychoanalysis and of oral history, or prepared to believe that these pursuits could be successfully combined. But it does not take long to decide that the experiment is being conducted with skill, and that the pursuits have at least a little in common. A piece of oral history may be meant to do without a presiding historian in much the same way in which an ana-lytic session may be meant to do without a presiding analyst; theoretical presuppositions are subject in each case to a show of suspension, though it is clear that the theories of Freud and others will be present in the consulting-room, and that oral his-torians may be sympathetic to socialism and to the methods of

Marxist historiography. Fraser's book is not without its evident presuppositions, and not every reader will feel that this auto-biographer, having perused and digested his tape-recordings, talked to his analyst and completed his inner and outer voyages, knew something radically different about his past from what he had known before: that something had been found, or proved. He had lived with his past for the best part of fifty years, and his book tells what he had come to know of it over that interval of time, with help from the theories of Marx and Freud. And in so doing it can often convey that a past is not a thing to be dis-covered. As the analyst said, it is not discovered but made.

Ronald Fraser was not trying to determine, like certain historians of former times, what his past 'really was'. But there is some question of a pathogenic secret, of the recovery of material hitherto repressed which influenced his perception of his mother: and his understanding of the past would certainly appear to have been enlarged by his researches. He talks of himself as 'split', and as implicated in splits of a wider incid-ence. A split appears to be spoken of in the conversation from which I have just quoted: formed by the past, he is also de-formed by it. But this is only one aspect of the bifurcation he describes.

Fraser's fork took several forms, as I say: or one might prefer to say that there was more than one fork to reckon with. Born in Hamburg, he was transferred to the Manor House at Amnersfield, the son of a remote German-American mother and of a sour, withdrawn, irritable Anglo-Scottish father, who would retreat behind the *Times* and spend the evening in lonely state, smoking his pipe in his kilt. He was never to say hello to you, and he once said that he would not be interested in his child 'until he can go out shooting with me'. (Elsewhere, another angry gentleman of the period, Evelyn Waugh, had waited for his children to be of an age to converse with him, before taking an interest.) The household shot, and it rode, to hounds and in all directions, but Ronald Fraser had no love for horses. The poor little rich boy was looked after by a second mother in the person of strict Ilse, from Germany: this did a great deal, but not enough, to relieve the isolation he felt— which, as his researches disclosed, was to be a factor in the isolation and rejection suffered in turn by his younger brother, who also left for the Mediterranean. When friendships finally became possible for him they were with children of the lower orders. His parents did not get on and parted during the war, which put an end to the old hierarchic world of Amnersfield, where you were not to look at your masters when they came up the drive, but to hoe on regardless. Mrs Fraser was suspected in the neighbourhood of being an enemy spy; presently she remarried—her new husband a jolly, but for the son disturbing, wing-commander. The testimonies in the book were obtained mostly from the underlings of the house, led by sly, supportive Bert, a man who was able to take and to give pleasure—a fine portrait, which is also a self-portrait, of a second father.

Bert's testimony, and Ilse's, are probably paramount. 'The image you give', Fraser tells Ilse, meaning the image she gives of himself as a boy, 'is one of dependency, extreme docility. It was my natural character, you think, evident from birth . . .'. Ilse had been trained in an orphanage, and he then tells her, with a smile: 'I wouldn't claim any privilege that an orphan wasn't entitled to.' He reverts to the point with the analyst: 'Supposing I didn't have what a child objectively should be entitled to . . .'. In coping with the unsaid and unsayable, oral history is impelled towards aposiopesis. The analyst's reponse is apt to consist of an '. . .' But if the work is oral history, it is literature too—a disclosure of predicament and bereavement. The enigmatic three dots to which it is impelled are those of a romantic orphan, as well as those of his reticent doctor. A romantic orphan, though, who was able to accept that he had caused his brother to suffer.

In all this there was plenty of scope for an awareness and endurance of contradiction. Contradictions, splits, can readily be perceived, by those minded to perceive them; pursuits that can be married, like oral history and psychoanalysis, can be found to separate. What matters is what happens when the individual, who incorporates his past, incorporates and transforms the divisions which are part of that past. Fraser reflects: 'Two mothers and I'm torn between them . . .'. Torn between 'the distant star and the cold, close moon'. And neither of the women was to prove 'sufficient'. 'You split them', prompts the analyst, 'into the good and the bad mother.' The analyst proceeds: 'All mothers have to be frustrating as well as loving. But being consoled by another mother who seems unfrustrating makes it harder to reconcile the two . . .'. This appears to be a key point, but it is one that is left controversial. It is possible to imagine that for some people such consolation might make it easier to reconcile the two, and to wonder what it was that made the difference in Fraser's case. There were other things that had to be reconciled, and we hear presently of 'a role of inherent superiority which came to me from outside, from the servants among others. Inside, however, I felt inherently inferior, inadequate to fill the role. That was the split . . .' (Fraser's dots). He asks the daughter of the refugee cook, remembering the days when he made love with this daughter, if she had known two different boys.

Later in the book Mr Fraser recognises that he has talked both of rubbing out the past and of preserving it: 'The aims seem contradictory, don't they? But they're the same. I kept the past alive out of a desire for revenge. One day I would write it—and *them*—off the face of the earth . . .'. He is referring to his parents, I think. Later still, the analyst suggests that Fraser may want to offer reparation, by writing this book, for the guilt he had felt in relation to his father, and Fraser asks: 'For wanting to destroy him so I could have my mother to myself?' 'Uh-huh . . .'. 'And for wanting', Fraser adds, 'to destroy her . . .'. Is the book, then, a 'monument to destruction'? The servants, who did much of the living which is commemorated here, and his parents, who did so little of it, are placed well within reach of an impartial sympathy in a work which nowhere *feels* vindictive, and which declines to settle for any final understanding of what went on. Despite its title, and for all Fraser's grave and civil investigative demeanour, the book does not exhibit this past as something to be searched for, uncovered, so much as something which is unfindable, interminable. Understanding is deferred, rather as it is in certain recent theoretical accounts of the way literature works. But this does not diminish the importance of the provisional discoveries which it contains, which the writer has moved to incorporate.

From the point of view of the people of the Gorbals in the Thirties, fox-hunting and psychoanalysis would have been practically indistinguishable concerns of the rich in the Sassenach South, of the 'high heid yins' of the world—an expression of the poor in Scotland then, which Ralph Glasser uses. And there is a point of view from which Ronald Fraser might be seen as a man of Marxist leanings who paid a professional adviser what may have been a fair whack of a working man's wages to enquire with him into the deficiencies of his affective life. This is a split that can rarely have been witnessed in Glasgow—which does not indicate that he was at fault in consulting his analyst, but does indicate that these autobiographies are sited in very different places. *Nail on the Banister* by R. Stornaway, alias R. Scott, is an eloquent Scots joke of the Thirties, and it allows one to say that Glasser's banister was a bed of nails, but that his slides may have been less painful than Fraser's. He could well have been called a victim, and his book consigns itself, as Fraser's does, to that large literature in which the sufferings of victims are recounted: but he does not see himself as a romantic orphan.

He belonged to a family of immigrant Jews which had fled to a Glasgow tenement and a community of Yiddish-speakers within the city. Round the corner was Dixon's Blazes, a blast furnace, and the Workers' Circle, where dreams of socialist emancipation were debated—dreams which were soon to fade for Glasser. Nor was he able to believe in the religion of his community. Anti-Semitism was not, it appears, a major threat in an environment where many kinds of threat and affliction— such as its gangster debt-collectors, the 'menodge men'—competed for consciousness. His mother died early, worn out by making ends meet and by her husband's gambling. Glasser still stands in awe of this formidable, feckless man. His sisters were to flee the family, precipitating an ordeal of severance which compounded others and marked him to the quick. He wants to go to university, turns up to listen to Einstein, studies hard; but his father won't have it, and at the age of 14 he becomes a soap boy in a barber's and then a presser in a garment shop.

The Gorbals comes across, in careful descriptions, as a ferocious place. It should be seen for what it was, and especially by those who feel like regretting its erasure, and alleging that its replacement has made an environment which may be even worse—of tower blocks filled with heroin and despair. The trouble is that the allegation has begun to seem convincing. 'The hovels and the vennels' of the nineteenth-century Scottish city have been projected into the sky; the lower depths of the Thirties have not gone from urban Britain. And we have a government which has been slow to worry whether the people there die of Aids.

At one stage Glasser is invited to look at a tenement close— by Bernard, a Communist who was to fight in Spain and return with an altered mind. In Spain Bernard questioned the principle that the end justifies the means—'the human price was too high'—and it had almost 'cost him his life'. (But can this be said to have been what happened? The book has explained that, having been a murderer of unreliables for the Republicans, he was shot at by a rival and went straight back to Glasgow.) At this earlier stage[2] Ralph goes into the close and takes a look at the human price of capitalism.

Nearly all the stone steps in the first flight up to the half-landing were broken, with jagged edges where bits of tread had fallen away. Some had almost no tread left. Plaster had come away from the walls from ceiling to floor, and along the lower part the bared cement, originally grey, was stained yellow and smelt of urine. On a patch where the rough surface of brickwork was exposed, someone had vomited, probably a passing drunk whose sense of propriety, demanding privacy, had deterred him from being sick in the street; or a returning resident who could not wait to climb the few steps to the communal toilet on the first half-landing. The detritus had stuck to the pitted surface in a wide streaky band as it slid lumpily from chest height to the floor. Judging by the strength of its smell, a mixture of beer and fish and chips, the vomit was recent. Another powerful smell, of decaying rubbish, came mainly from the ash-pits at the far end of the corridor, but also from a deposit scattered over the floor. Despite the cold wet wind blowing in hard from the street, the cloud of mephitic vapours lingered stupefyingly about our heads.

'Mephitic' might be compared with Fraser's 'ulcerous' in 'Resentment wells up like an ulcerous vapour'. Glasser's vapours are different from Fraser's. They stink, while Fraser's are mental. Both men lived through the Depression, but Fraser's depressions were only indirectly linked with the hardships of people he knew. At the same time, these hardships are a focus of his attention.

The two words carry a note of declamation—a note otherwise absent from Fraser's account. Glasser's prose is sometimes declamatory and sententious in an old-fashioned sort of way, and sometimes awkward ('Hidden in the near future, he was to be proved right'). But it rises to many of its ferocious and grievous occasions. We are in the Scotland of TB, pneumonia and drink, in which sex is spoken of as a matter of men attacking women. At the end of the corridor which he describes, before you get to the rubbish, is the place where the young make love. Their elders make it upstairs in the flats, attended by small children—brothers and sisters who grow up in the Gorbals, Glasser says, to try it with each other. About these matters it seems to me that he writes really well, in a manner that might suggest the intent translation of a Latin author anxious to tell the truth.

Afterwards she parted the curtains and came out naked to lift the unsleeping, finely aware child back into bed, to lie between her and the man lying open-mouthed in post-coital sleep. And then mother and child might lie awake for a while, locked in unique perplexities. She, her body prompting her still, with no finality in her, turned her world over and over again in her mind's restless fingers. The child, possessed by wonder and nameless hauntings, tried to join together the heavings and creakings and groans and gasps and little cries he had heard as he lay on the floor, his mother's disturbed concentration now, his father's stillness as if felled, and the sticky warmth in which he lay between them, something more than the sweat that was there before, a substance he divined as elemental, mysterious, newly decanted, that touched his flesh and his senses with profound, unattainable meaning.[3]

At the beginning of the book a dear friend, Charlie, another immigrant boy, leaves for Russia with his family—for the land, they hope, of the free. Ralph strives to address 'the high heid yins of Russia' to solicit news of the family, and receives his letter back from the Embassy in London, stamped: 'Communication not permitted.' And the family was never heard of again. Glasser orders his events thematically, while also wanting to tell a story and to spring surprises. Charlie's departure is the first of several, and this event is succeeded by the announcement of a further theme when the rabbi's thunderings pass over the heads of his congregation and the writer notes: 'in later years I would wonder how different my life might have been if a few people, those closest to me, *had* been frightened—just a

little.' Among those closest who should have been frightened
was Annie, his girl for a while. Annie left him, and then,
pregnant, offered herself in order to saddle him with someone
else's child—and this when he had just received a telegram
awarding him a scholarship to Oxford. Just when his ship was
coming in she might have set fire to it. He condemns her for
trying this trick, which is followed by a terrible fall downstairs
in the course of an attempt to end her pregnancy. She had
known that his love for her would remain, and 'for her to have
acted on that knowledge' in resorting to the deception 'made
her deed unforgivable'.

Those closest to him who should have been too frightened
to behave as they did include his father, but they also include
his sisters, who struck out for themselves in a fashion which
has him siding with his father. Lilian, the older sister, errs by
studying hard to become a money-minded businesswoman with
a grudge and a smart flat, and by blackmailing her employer,
also her lover, by means of an abortion. Glasser talks of her as
if, in walking out, she had gone on to walk the streets. She is
seen to suffer for what she did, and Mary, the other sister, likewise 'paid heavily': let down by an Indian student with whom
she had been having a long affair. 'She set higher store by
emotional security' than her sister, 'and thought she would
find it with a man soft-hearted and caring and pliant, far
removed, as she thought, from father's toughness and un-
controllability.' Glasser thunders on: 'Both Lilian and Mary
invested too much emotional capital in their opposition to
father, whose influence naturally remained dominant, try as
they might to escape; and this imbalance distorted their view
of relationships and of the world.' This is a male view of the
matter, in which women are attacked, and which had me
admiring these ugly sisters.

It is made clear that the boy was exposed to serious danger by his father's irresponsibility and by his sisters' departure: but his sisters had been exposed to this father too, and
had had to defend themselves. A father's influence which has
been revealed as destructive and all but disastrous is thought
to have remained dominant—as was only natural—until the
women broke away for good. An author is taking his revenge in
setting down these judgements, begrudging the grudges of

others—while uttering, this once, the cry of the deserted child.

Neither of these books, however, could be said to be intent on revenge. Glasser presents a full picture of the behaviour, good and bad, which he encountered in an area of maximum difficulty, and it is not often that such a picture has been presented. The familiar and approved accounts of Scottish life have long favoured a country of hills and fields and firesides, where braw lads and bonny lasses dance reels and go on, after early struggles, to better things; where the best thing of all is the kind landed family that comes up from London to visit them, famous for its stables, castles and ceremonies.

Another fallacious account comes to mind. The literary naturalism of the last century went to the poor and itemised their way of life, producing for adversity truthful, distressing inventories and interiors—as in George Moore's novel of the Nineties, *Esther Waters*, which starts with a manor-house, servants and horses, and travels to Soho for compulsive gambling and a fatal cough. In Glasser's book, and in Fraser's, the activities of the poor can be seen as activities which had been performed, and written about, in the past: but these are books which intimate that the lists and specifications of a caring naturalism—features by which they have indeed been influenced—were never exhaustive: that the truth-tellers did not tell it, and that the omissions were systematic. The sexuality of the past, and the extent of the intimidatory violence, were only very faintly registered. Esther had quite as hard a time of it as Annie, one might feel, but even so, Moore's spirited novel can be thought to settle for an anodyne poverty. To say this is not the same as complaining of his acknowledgement that poor people can have a good time. No lie in that.

There were pleasures for both boys in the course of their growing-up. For Glasser, there was Annie, study, socialist hikes and camp-fires in the hills outside the city; for Fraser, there were model aeroplanes, and a mute attraction shared with a boy of lower status, and there was Bert and Ilse. But what is most striking about both books is the sense they give of how desolate and enclosed an adolescence could be, at opposite ends of the society.

The better things presumed to be in store for Glasser when he went off as a scholarship boy to a glamorous university in the South of England are, in a sense, the subject of *Gorbals Boy at Oxford*, his second volume of autobiography.[4] The refugee from Glasgow saw through, and stood up to, some famous middle-class progressives, was asked to spy on student Communists, was asked, by a girl at a party, to 'do something! Julian's got a knife.' At another party, in the South of France, a reefer is placed between his lips by a girl whose trousers fall down. 'I had scaled magic heights and found obscurantism, absence of hope, a world infinitely darker than I had ever imagined possible from where I had stood in the Gorbals.' I can only hope that the bursar now inhabits a wholly healthy Oxford.

VI · Long live pastiche

PETER Ackroyd's novels *Hawksmoor* and *Chatterton* do much to explain one another. Both books mingle old times and new times, and both give expression to fantasies of replication, with *Hawksmoor* a hard act to follow.

Its old times are brilliantly rendered, and its appeal is in part generic. The biographer of T. S. Eliot, who was himself to speak of the 'dark' experience, of the 'rude unknown psychic material', incorporated in his poem *The Waste Land*, can be seen in *Hawksmoor* to contribute to the tradition of romantic fabulation which began with the Gothic novel—a tradition in which darkness is privileged, in which a paranoid distrust is evident, in which can be read the evergreen message that the deprived may turn out to be depraved, and in which there can be two of someone.

Hawksmoor speaks the words of romantic duality, and is in a number of ways a double book. It consists of two alternating narratives, one of which is set in the eighteenth century and the other in the present, with the earlier delivered in the first person. Each of the two principal actors glimpses his double in passing, as a reflection in a glass, and each stands to the other in the same relation—a relation which presupposes, as in many other Gothic texts, some sort of metempsychosis or rebirth. Both of these men are disturbed or mad. Nicholas Dyer is imagined as the builder of Nicholas Hawksmoor's churches in the East End of London; the enlightened edifices of a rational Christianity are thereby ascribed to a devil-worshipper, while the name 'Hawksmoor' is assigned to the Detective Chief Superintendent who, in the later narrative, frets himself into a delirium over a series of stranglings which takes place in the vicinity of the churches. The later crimes duplicate those committed by Dyer, who has wished to baptise his churches with the blood of young victims.

Dyer thinks of himself as 'a stranger to mankind'; his life is led apart, 'in a Corner'. He has grown up as one of 'the orphans of the plague' who roam the streets of the city in the aftermath of the plague and of the fire that followed it. The romantic equation of orphan and monster makes a Satanist of this forlorn Dyer: 'nor can we but by doing Evil avoid the rage of evil Spirits.' His is a theology in which Adam is unredeemed, and life itself a plague. London is a necropolis, its every corner the site of a murder, its soil a pudding of blood and tears. Out of this soil soar elegant churches, each of which encodes the symbols of an alien religion. The St So-and-So's which Dyer has been commissioned to build are so many secret temples of Moloch. The experiments, proofs and improvements espoused by such scientists as Christopher Wren, Dyer's patron in the building trade, Dyer pisses on. The homicides and post-mortems in the book permit the new religion of science to exercise its power: but they also occasion the necrophile brood-ings which exude from Dyer. Much of this material—this archaic London, the Hawksmoor churches, their magical meaning, and the tramps who haunt them—comes from the striking poem *Lud Heat* by Iain Sinclair,[1] where the churches are taken to be geometrically interrelated in the form of a pentacle, the sorcerer's five-pointed star. The poem is dark, dense and learned—Yeatsian, and maybe also Yatesian, in inspiration, amid much else. It is hard to be sure how much of this dark stuff Sinclair believes—as it is hard to be sure how much Eliot believed of the lore which accompanies the dark stuff of *The Waste Land*, another London poem. The two poems could be thought to occupy a common ground which goes some way beyond topography, and includes a stretch of the common ground occupied by imitation. Sinclair's, at all events, is the work of a Modernist, and is unlikely to be that of an occultist. This makes it, in a sense, compatible with *Hawksmoor*. But *Hawksmoor* is a different beast. The novel suggests itself as the work of a novelist intent on a gruesome entertainment. Both works, however, may be thought to share a secret, and a set of clues, which bear witness to the recrudescence of a hippy magic.

Peter Ackroyd is all of the formidable pasticheur that he is praised for being, and Dyer's tale, which affects to be that of someone who lived in the eighteenth century, and in which the element of imitation, present in writing of every kind, is more obtrusive than it is in the other tale, is the livelier of the two.

Pastiche is a dualistic activity, and it is an activity which can lend itself to the expression of paranoid feelings and unacted desires. A writer is copied by 'someone other' than himself, and that 'someone other' can in a manner of speaking become the writer he copies: the biter bit. The expression I am quoting is uttered by Dyer, and it is an expression which Ackroyd is given to using in his books. In pretending here to be someone other than himself who keeps murdering people, he does a tremendous job: this is a more than serviceable argot for the age in question and for the wizard in question. The suffering and self-conscious first-person singular manifested in Dyer could be considered a creation of the Gothic novel that came after him, and Dyer can also bring to mind the magus of a time before. But there is no nagging sense of anachronism. How could there be? the novel seems to be saying. There is no such thing as anachronism. All ages are one.

The later stranglings look like a copy of what happened, at the hands of a sorcerer, in the loamy past, and Peter Ackroyd is very interested in copies. As is usual in such cases, the copy is not exact. Dyer's doings are the same as but also different from those investigated by the fretful man he resembles, just as Hawksmoor's investigative Scotland Yard is the same as but also different from the architects' department of that name attended by Dyer. Ackroyd has given some readers the impression that the modern narrative, the paler of the two, is paler on purpose—in obedience, presumably, to the doctrine of time, of its runnings-down and recurrences, which figures in the novel.

The pale Hawksmoor is an inhabitant of the present day who reminds one not only of Dyer but of P. D. James's character Inspector Dalgliesh—one of her novels, *A Taste for Death*, published a few months after *Hawksmoor*, has a church murder in London, draped in the poses of this sensitive, cultivated policeman, and it also has, like *Hawksmoor*, a suspected tramp. Both inspectors are presented as more interesting than the colleagues and suspects they move among. With the James, we are told who did it; in the Ackroyd, the matted fellow who is the chief suspect is never very securely identified as the author of the crimes—it is almost as if the inspector could have done it: so that Ackroyd's is an authorially uncertain work in which the authorship of its crimes is uncertain too. Meanwhile the interesting Hawksmoor is less interesting than Dyer, and may be meant to be. 'Time will tell, sir', a colleague remarks, and Hawksmoor replies: ' "Time will not tell. Time never tells." Once more he raised his arm involuntarily, as if in greeting.' It is hard to think that the novelist *intended* the reader to find this even more gnomic and exasperating than the colleague seems to find it. But there may indeed be some such aim.

Can the author be detected in this novel—come upon in his dark corner? The attitude to time might tell us what he thinks, but it is the most inscrutable aspect of the novel. *Hora e sempre*— this motto is inscribed on the front of Hawksmoor's, the real Hawksmoor's, Classical house at Easton Neston in Northamptonshire: Easton Neston has been reputed or imagined to be the original of Mansfield Park, which may be described as a house imagined by an opponent of the Gothic novel. The motto refers to a dynastic permanence; but it could be stolen for this novel, where a 'now and always' is on show. We may be meant to think that time is simultaneous, in a way that may owe something to the simultaneity propounded, 'perhaps', in Eliot's *Four Quartets*, where 'History is now and England'; or that it is cyclical, a turning wheel, with human depravity paling into insignificance as the wheel turns into modern times.

Interpretation is allowed to copy what it finds, and to distort it, and it may be that the novel can be interpreted as an entertainment which conveys that doctrines of science and improvement can't encompass what happens in a frightening world, where motive is dark and ill-will ubiquitous. The Gothic novel was shaped to take account of such a world, and to do so, very often, in the guise of entertainment. Since its arrival in the eighteenth century, this is a literary mode which has recurrently been pronounced dead but which has been capable of renewal, and now Ackroyd has given a further turn to the wheel. Once again, a sufferer is seen to be mad, and his fearful sense of what he is up to can be seen to dominate the book in which it is in the end defeated or controverted. Such a book has to be divided—between hope and fear, improvement and depravity. It will be the work both of one hand and of the other. And one of these hands may wield the instrument of pastiche.

Hawksmoor, which came out in 1985, was preceded by the Eliot biography of 1984, which was preceded by *The Last Testa-*

ment of Oscar Wilde of the year before, and in 1987 these annual events were pressed upon by *Chatterton*. All four books reveal a steady concern with imitation and interpretation, and to read them together is to be clearer about what it is that the writer intends us to think that he thinks about things. He would appear to believe in an invented truth, an invented reality—a Rortyan reality, one might be inclined to call it at times. He believes that a writer will often find himself through exposure to some other writer. And it is apparent that Ackroyd has found himself in this manner—through exposure to Wilde, Eliot, and now Chatterton. This brings with it the corollary that it is not always apparent whether the beliefs he expresses are Ackroyd's or those of the writer to whom he is exposed, or both. Interpreters must therefore beware, a little, in doing what they are generally allowed to do.

All four books speak of a 'someone other'. In *Hawksmoor* Ned the tramp encounters a 'someone other' in his double, and in *Chatterton* Charles Wychwood's double is another 'someone other'. Eliot was able to 'recognise himself through someone other'—a changeable other, but at one point it was the Frenchman Laforgue. 'The first law of the imagination', states Ackroyd's Wilde, is that 'in his work the artist is someone other than himself.' Greek love is virtuous, Wilde is also represented as saying, because 'men can live in perfect equality, each finding in the other the image of his own soul'.

It is plain that there are many ways of being and of imagining a someone other. Art may imagine one, and Greek love may. Paranoia imagines one, and so does pastiche. And Ackroyd comes to vivid life as a pasticheur. 'The truest Plagiarism is the truest Poetry', claims Thomas Chatterton, warming to Ackroyd's theme, and perhaps overdoing it, along with Ackroyd's Wilde, who had been able to believe that 'almost all the methods and conventions of art and life found their highest expression in parody'. Still, such claims do seem to have force when fitted to the case of the writer who is making or mediating them. Ackroyd's truest prose occurs when he applies himself to the imitation of ancient and recent writers—a repertoire of others. This, of course, is what Chatterton, Wordsworth's 'marvellous boy', did in the plagiaristic eighteenth century. Like Chatterton, Peter Ackroyd is, in the words of his novel about Chatterton, a 'great Parodist', a 'great Plagiarist'.

It is deemed to follow from such claims that human history is 'a succession of interpretations', a piling-up of imitations, an accumulation of metaphor which will be perceived as reality. And literature will amount to the same thing: all writers are copycats. Those who prefer to believe in an indivisible single self capable of originality will be sceptical of the Ackroyd scepticism. They will make less than he does of that part of Eliot which was a 'good ventriloquist'. And they will undoubtedly object to the more unbridled formulations that enter the three fictions; the biography of Eliot has plenty to say on the subject, too, while maintaining a comparative, and suitable, reserve. They won't accept with Charles Wychwood that 'everything is copied', and won't accept his opinion of Chatterton: 'Thomas Chatterton believed that he could explain the entire material and spiritual world in terms of imitation and forgery, and so sure was he of his own genius that he allowed it to flourish under other names.' The second half of this can be seen to coincide with the opinion of Chatterton which is expressed by Ackroyd's Wilde: 'a strange, slight boy who was so prodigal of his genius that he attached the names of others to it.' Peter Ackroyd has here performed the not impossible feat of plagiarising himself—while leaving the reader in doubt as to whether the writer shares this implausible estimate of Chatterton's marvellous buoyancy.[2]

As Ackroyd's ventriloquised Wilde makes clear, Wilde was a great exaggerator and, like his friend Whitman, a great contradictor of himself; and he is certainly a great source of dualistic formulations, in all their slippery bliss. He is the artist's friend, and a friend of the mimic and poseur, in a world of masks, multiplicities, contraries and successive interpretations. The Wilde apocrypha contains a joke which says it all—or a fair part of it. Some good thing had been voiced, and Wilde had remarked that he wished that *he* had said it—and was then told: 'You will, Oscar, you will.' The Marquis of Queensberry may be judged, in this context, to have made an involuntary and uncharacteristic joke in accusing Wilde of 'posing as a somdomite': a phrase that smells of the multiple self, and of the uncertainty of interpretation—and indeed spelling (Ackroyd, as it happens, interprets him as something other than a sodomite). Ackroyd's

Wilde complains of the 'sordid' interpretations of his conduct which had influenced the outcome of his trial, while himself, on other occasions, interpreting his conduct as sordid. He also confounds his own dualistic zeal by recalling the wise words (as one may truly think them) of the dualistic mage Paracelsus: 'Be not another, if thou canst be thyself.'

In the literature of duality it is the outcast or victim who has dealings with a double, and in the second of the two novels Charles Wychwood is an outcast whose condition copies that of Thomas Chatterton, who committed suicide in 1770 at the age of 17, having invented a medieval monk, Rowley, and written poems for him. Romantic poets were keen to vindicate Chatterton, and to cherish his untimely death as that of a sacrificial victim: here was a spilling of young blood that might have watered the purlieus of a church. Charles belongs, more-over, to a cast of outcasts, monsters, hustlers and impostors which composes a literary London reminiscent of the early novels of Muriel Spark, and far from brutally inauthentic. The queen of the authors is Harriet Scrope, novelist, plot-stealer, and ferocious egotist, whose war against the world she inhabits extends to her best friend and her cat. As a comic portrait of the artist, Harriet scores high. She is estranged and she is hostile. She is a bit like Dyer.

'Tho' I was young Thomas Chatterton to those I met, I was a very Proteus to those who read my Works': Chatterton's story is mostly told by himself, and with a felicity of cadence and of reference which can be caught in the sentence I have just quoted. His story is interwoven with, and is replicated by, a modern tale, in which Charles Wychwood's comet-like career is featured. He too dies the early death of romance—*en poète*, as the poet Burns put it with reference to his own fate—and his end is enveloped in the consequences of his supposing that he has lit upon some Chatterton manuscripts. Charles is touchingly done—a frail unpublished poet kept going by his wife and son (the wife is called Vivien, presumably by design, though she is no copy of the first Mrs Eliot), their household a breath of fresh air in the conniving, phrase-making milieu to which Charles clings. Then there is a third story. Chatterton is as much as anything the famous painting of his death in a Holborn attic done in the 1850s by Henry Wallis—with the poet lying across the bed in a kind of frozen *entrechat*. It looks like an enlargement of the postcard which, in an age of mechanical reproduction, it was to become, commemorating the tourist attraction which it was also to become. The third narrative tells how George Meredith modelled for the corpse in the painting and how his wife then ran away with the painter (see also the sonnets in Meredith's *Modern Love*). The three tales are deftly assembled and get on very well together.

Chatterton is represented in the novel as an accidental suicide—slain by a cocktail of arsenic and laudanum swallowed for a venereal infection. Poor Charles brings him to life again, however, for some further plagiarisms: a nest of antique-dealers, of antic disposition, in Chatterton's native Bristol, have passed to Charles a cache of papers which, together with the discovery of what seems to be the portrait of an adult Chatterton, persuades him that the poet lived on. The portraits of Chatterton have something of the importance to the novel that the living and ageing likeness has in *The Picture of Dorian Gray*.

Like *Hawksmoor* and *The Last Testament of Oscar Wilde*, this novel is a *tour de force*. And it could be said that not only is it about imitation—it is also, as are other *tours de force*, itself an imitation of something. Like other *tours de force*, it is done in a spirit of play and of emulation. It is a contender: a colleague of Ackroyd's on *The Times* announced that it was a 'sure contender' for the Booker Prize of 1987 (which it didn't receive). It observes one of Wilde's principles of literature in responding to the importance of not being 'serious'. It shows what the writer can do rather than what he thinks.

In order to find out more of what this writer thinks about imitation, we are in a position to consult a work by him where a treatise on the subject is developed at intervals and where he writes *in propria persona*. In Ackroyd's life of Eliot we read about a major poet who was a good ventriloquist; a man of multiple personality who swore by a principle of impersonality in art which he was later to unswear by locating *The Waste Land* in the stresses of a domestic life, and whose art bears the indelible signature of that distinctive protean character of his; a man who was often miserable and tormented. The book says that Eliot's truest poetry was a form of plagiarism, in the benign sense that 'it was only in response to other poetry that Eliot could express his own deepest feelings'. A little earlier, a view of Eliot's has been paraphrased: that 'there is no "truth" to be found' in the world, 'only a number of styles and interpretations—one laid upon the other in an endless and apparently meaningless process'. Ackroyd notices that the Eliot who had once called poetry a 'mug's game' was eventually, in his play *The Elder Statesman*, to use the same expression for forgery. Ackroyd warns us not to jump to a conflation here, but he is intrigued by the coincidence, and it might almost serve as an emblem of his concern throughout the biography with the connection between poetry and feigning, and with the potency of parody.

The biography suggests that Eliot was never to lose the divided sense of his youth that human life is futile and meaningless—that man is 'a finite piece of reasonable misery', in the words of William Drummond of Hawthornden, a good poet who was also a great plagiarist, and a great seeker of shelter in books—but that an eternal order might be felt for, or invented. That order was eventually discovered in the teachings of Christianity. When he turned to God it was to someone other: he was surrendering to 'something outside oneself'.

The book depicts Eliot as a parodist, a plagiarist, a responder to other people's poems, and as a seeker of shelter. And yet in its closing passages we learn that as a poet he had 'no real predecessors'. He was his own man, after all. The book is cursory in its treatment of Eliot's literary background: there is no mention, for instance, of Wallace Stevens, Ivy Compton-Burnett, of Empson or Leavis, and no adequate picture of what Eliot meant to later generations of intellectuals in Britain. In other respects, however, this is a cogent and sensible account (which was constrained by a barbarous embargo on quotation). I don't think that its readers can have had much trouble in finding in the life and work the responsiveness Ackroyd finds in them. But perhaps it is the paradox conveyed by that closing glimpse of a parodic but unprecedented Eliot which carries the sharpest conviction of any feature of the book.

Eliot comes across as the sad man who sees double, as a living embodiment of the proposition that the double has to do with pain and with relief from pain, with the search, in such circumstances, for someone other. From the ordeal of his first marriage to the late happiness of the second, the book locks, at one level, into a recital of misfortunes and a medical record. Influenza after influenza. Constant debilitating 'work', in publishing and public life, and a constant invocation of the claims of such work. Lecture after lecture, accompanied by complaints about the futility of lectures and his reluctance to give them. The book makes one conscious of Eliot in the sarcophagus of his upper-class eminence; of a sad face of clerical cut—once the face of a delightful shy child—bleakly sprouting from a sartorial apparatus that resembles the mourning clothes of a cabinet minister; of a masterly poseur, an honoured invalid and recluse, of someone snobbish and sometimes selfish and inhumane, who sought relief in literature and in imitation, and who also embodied the opposite of these qualities.

It is almost as if we are confronted here by a replication of the poor Tom described in Ackroyd's novel by another poor Tom of later times. And perhaps we might imagine that they are the same but different. Eliot was to tell the poet F. T. Prince: 'Not everything you write is very *interesting*.' This could be said with some emphasis of Chatterton, but not of Eliot himself, who moreover survived, who grew to be famous, who did not kill himself, though he was to wonder how one might set about dying. Chatterton died the romantic and traditional early death of the divided, the invaded man, while Eliot did not.

It isn't that Ackroyd asks us to compare these two poor Toms, in pursuit of a theory alleging the importance of imitation. But they are brought together, in successive books, by the force of this preoccupation, and the reader has to make what he can of the resemblance between two figures quite remote from one another in any coarser understanding of the matter, to do this while adjusting his sight to a vista of copycats, impostors and successive interpretations—a vista which is far from unfamiliar now and can be caught, for instance, in the productions and reproductions of contemporary literary theory.

Imposture is shown in Ackroyd's novel, in this burlesque of the literary life, to be an interesting business, but it is unlikely to cause Chatterton's reputation to inch back towards what it was in the retrospects of the Romantic period. He was worshipped then for his talent and untimely death—perhaps a little as Eliot was to be worshipped, in the 1940s and '50s, for his saintly abstention from the world. Keats placed him among the stars, where Keats himself, for similar reasons, was to be placed by Shelley. Chatterton became a topos, and the numbers lisped: 'O Chatterton, how very sad thy fate', 'Flow gently, sweet Chatterton', 'Good for you, Chatterton'. Readers can be expected to spot which of these quotations are forgeries, and they must also have doubted in their time whether this writer was as good as the early tributes made out.

It seems clear, however, that Chatterton needn't have had prodigious talent for the talent expended in the novel to take effect. It is a novel which communicates the notion that talented and untalented meet in that country of the mind where everyone copies and steals from everyone else, where everything is reproductive or reminiscent of everything else, where one thing leads to another and this person passes into that. It plays with such ideas, to a Shavian pitch of exaggeration: but it is not a novel of ideas, any more than it is a heartless game. It has people in it, with lives to live. It has Charles in it, whose plight is more touching than anything in the nineteenth-century retrospects of Chatterton. It has its predecessors in the romantic tradition—a tradition which includes the self-important single self nevertheless prone to dispersal and division, invasion and impersonation, which includes the victim and his alter ego. At the same time, both here and in *Hawksmoor*, Ackroyd, too, is his own man. For all his standard procedures, I don't think he is actually imitating anybody.

VII · Ariel goes to the police

REVOLUTION, literature and love, and the roads and side-roads which join them together, are concerns which join together the Czech writers Milan Kundera and Ivan Klima, whose name is used by Kundera for the uxorious philanderer of his novel *The Farewell Party*. They are writers who have parted company, but who are in some ways at one. There is a sense in which the hero of Kundera's novel *Life is elsewhere*, published in Britain in 1986, is also the hero of Klima's collection of stories *My First Loves*, published here in the same month of the same year. These are portraits of the artist who grows up in an age of revolutionary socialism and who has to make what he can of it. Revolution, and its betrayal by a regime which both prescribes and proscribes literature, are described in both works. Both men are interested in the subject of remembering and forgetting. In the books they write, music is heard in country places—trumpets, fiddles, the cimbalom—and love shows its face in pleasant country hotels, set down beside a stretch of water.

Klima may perhaps be a common name in Czechoslovakia, and Kundera has become a common name in the conversation of Western readers, who are drawn to these reciprocal concerns of his. In the days before *glasnost*—which his fictions may be thought to have rehearsed and predicted, but which could well mean that his fictions will no longer be for the West what they have been so far, when the thing that they deplore was still there in its entirety to be deplored—Kundera was forced into exile in the 'free world' of the time. So far, the free world has liked him both for having been, and for having ceased to be, a communist of a sort, for the freedoms he seeks in matters of literary form, for the modern inventiveness and manipulation of the literary games he plays, games that none the less commemorate, as he acknowledges, Cervantes, Sterne and Diderot, and for the sexual games which he plays in an age when, as he once put it, sexuality has ceased to be taboo. We have liked him for being into free speech and free love, and for what he has to say about convergences of the two, and about the curbs which revolution and its regimes have placed on them.

The West has been grateful to Kundera, extravagantly so at times, and has shown an impulse to beat itself with his playful fictions. Heads have been turned, and have begun to swim, amid the flow of invention, delivered in works which have been Englished in rapid succession and which are not always easy to tell apart. Which is the one that has *litost*—a form of self-pity—and what does he mean by 'unbearable lightness of being'? Which of these two conceptions, for that matter, we may even sometimes wonder, is which? But it seems safe to say that there are circumstances in which *litost* and *glasnost* can be recognised as enemies, and that this enmity can be recognised in the novel *Life is elsewhere*. His fertility, narrative gift, gift for experiments and impromptus, are such as to bewilder the attempt to form a judgement of any particular work. Not that he can mind that.

What he does seem to mind—and what even the most arbitrary-seeming, the most ludic, of his ironic and erotic diversions and excursions show that he minds—is the regime that came to power in his native country after the revolution of 1948. Many of his most memorable literary effects attest to this. In *The Unbearable Lightness of Being*, the Czech exile Sabina disturbs her French friends by being unable to last out a parade held to protest against the Soviet invasion of Czechoslovakia in 1968: 'She would have liked to tell them that behind Communism, Fascism, behind all occupations and invasions lurks a more basic, pervasive evil and that the image of that evil was a parade of people marching by with raised fists and shouting identical syllables in unison.' The British reader, who is likely to have been spared certain of the varieties of suffering which are spoken of in the writings of Kundera and Klima, where a joke, or no joke, or nothing whatever, can sequester you for years from the people you grew up with, is in a position, for all that, to know what Sabina means here. The British reader has only to listen to the sounds that protest makes in his own streets, to the cruel, brutal voices that bellow over loudhailers about injustice and the disadvantaged.

In thinking about what Stalinism brought to his country, Kundera thinks of the support this despotism has received from the writers of his country, and of other countries. Literature,

with its store of memories, is suspected by the state: and yet
the state is served by certain writers. In books and interviews
he has reminded the world that the French Surrealist poet
Aragon, having praised Kundera's excellent novel *The Joke*
in 1968, and having fulminated against the Soviet invasion of
Czechoslovakia—his legs would 'refuse' to take him to Russia
any more—made it to Moscow four years later; and that another
French poet, Eluard, abandoned his Prague friend, the Surrealist Kalandra, to the executioner.

Nowadays, people all over the world unequivocally reject the idea of
gulags, yet they are still willing to let themselves be hypnotised by
totalitarian poesy and to march to new gulags to the tune of the same
lyrical song piped by Eluard when he soared over Prague like the
great archangel of the lyre, while the smoke of Kalandra's body rose
to the sky from the crematory chimney.[1]

Tyranny is a force which locks writers up and which self-serving
lyrical writers may assist.

Eluard's soaring 'lyricism' helped to perpetuate a tyranny,
and is the kind of thing which led Kundera to employ the title
The Lyric Age for the work which first came to him in the mid-
Fifties, and which his publishers prevailed on him to retitle *Life
is elsewhere* when it was completed in 1969. It was published in
America in 1974, translated by Peter Kussi, who has revised
his translation for the new edition of 1986 which I am discussing
here. The provisional title referred to the life-span of Jaromil,
who dies young, as lyric poets will, but also to the enforced,
mass-produced, writer-proclaimed revolutionary ardours which
ensued in 1948. At the outset, Jaromil's lyricism is a Modern affair in which biological compulsion and biographical
reference—peeps at the maid Magda in her bath, for instance—
are enveloped and disguised in a poetry which his doting and
self-pitying mother finds inscrutable. His first loves—to make
use of Klima's title—prove to be his last, but prove as engrossing to him as the lyrics in which his emotional development is
encoded.

Jaromil is not so much a character as a type, and is not
unlike the Shelleyan poet in Shaw's *Candida*, Eugene March-
banks. Aerial creatures, these, ineffectual angels. Eugene, 'so
uncommon as to be almost unearthly', wants to go 'up into the

sky'. His brow is 'lined with pity'. He speaks with 'lyric rapture'. But he is all right when you get to know him. 'Don't say that Jaromil is a bad poet!' Kundera's 1986 Postscript implores. He is a 'sensitive young man'—a monster too, but the same monster is in you and me. And the same monster was in Shelley, and Rimbaud, and Victor Hugo. Jaromil and his mother are portrayed, we learn from the Postscript, quite without any satirical intention. In that respect, Kundera could have fooled at least one of his readers; but I do see that it belongs to the point of it all that the uncommon Jaromil should be thought humanly representative.

By a painter who befriends him, and who sleeps for a while with his mother, Jaromil, already self-perceived as exceptional, original, is introduced to modern art, which 'had not yet become the shopworn property of the bourgeois masses and retained the fascinating aura of a sect, a magical exclusivity fascinating to childhood—an age always daydreaming about the romanticism of secret societies, fraternities and tribes'. Soon he is writing modern poems. 'This verse described a boy who had been trembling in front of the bathroom door, but at the same time this boy was swallowed up by the verse; it surmounted and survived him. *Alas, my aquatic love*, said another line, and Jaromil knew that the aquatic love was Magda; but he also knew that nobody else could find her in that line . . .'. These lines are short and do not rhyme. They are free. Magda was lost in a poem which was 'as independent and unintelligible as reality itself. Reality does not discuss, it simply *is*. The independence of the poem provided Jaromil with a marvellous world of concealment, the possibility of a *second* existence.' Jaromil has discovered that writing can be what reading has familiarly been for the ordinary person: an escape, a shelter, a door to the alternative self.

Much later we read:

Everything seemed to indicate that Jaromil's enormous yearning for newness (the religion of the New) was only the disguised longing of a virginal youth for the unimaginable experience of the sex act. When he first reached the blissful shore of the redhead's body, a peculiar idea occurred to him: he now knew at last what it meant to be absolutely modern; it meant to lie on the shore of the redhead's body.

By now he has also reached 'the realm of real life'—by which he 'understood a whirling world of parading throngs, physical love and revolutionary slogans'. It turns out that real life rhymes, that the revolution wishes its poetry to do so. There is a magical power in rhyme and rhythm. 'Can a revolution dispense with repeated affirmation of the new order? Can a revolution dispense with rhyme?' By now free verse has been exposed as decadent, and modern art as the shopworn property of the bourgeois masses.[2]

Lyricism, then, is the poetry which sings along with the triumph of the proletariat, and with the repressions which accompany its triumph. What is required is a poetry which does not analyse or criticise, and is suitable for throngs and parades: we are in a situation where the self-portraits of the lyric author can be displayed like placards. Lyricism is inexperience, and it is the desire for glory. Such poems 'need not be stimulated by real-life events' such as the plight of the Marseilles dockworkers, which has effaced the sight—darkly limned in Jaromil's juvenilia—of Magda in her bath; and if the poet who displays his ignorant, indifferent self-portrait is hoping for applause, there is a chance for him to do well in the new world of revolution, which rings with applause, and with blame.

By the end of the novel Jaromil has forsworn his artist friend, who is under the ban of the regime and compelled to paint by candlelight: 'The whole world of his pictures has been dead for years. Real life is elsewhere!' We are told that these last four words are Rimbaud's and the Surrealist André Breton's, and that in 1968 they were a slogan of the protesting Sorbonne students. They are words that can be made to mean different things, and are applicable as such to the story of Jaromil's poetic progress from private to public, which can also be recognised as a simultaneity of the two, based on an enduring self-engrossment. Kundera asks us to join together two things that are often kept apart: lyrical effusions and public poetry. The quoted words point back to the privileged second existence which poetry had once promised Jaromil, and they point ahead: the old meaning has been reversed, with the claim that real life resides in a revolutionary solidarity. Just before this snarl about real life, he has betrayed his redhead to the police, by swallowing a lying excuse of hers concerning a subversive brother.

The poets Czeslaw Milosz and Donald Davie have been bothered by the insufficiency and irresponsibility of the lyric genre, and it could be felt that Kundera goes further than they do in denouncing the lyric, and fares worse. The lyricism that sells out to a state-ordained reality and solidarity is not the only lyricism we know, and it is the opposite of much of what we know by that name. Youthful as some of them are, the lyrics of Heaney do not embody the genius of inexperience, whatever some of Shelley's may do. In other words, Kundera's novel isolates certain tendencies in the behaviour of poets (and others) in order to prosecute an attack on Stalinist Czechoslovakia. It will be clear to most people here that the attack is deserved, and that writers sold out. Jaromil's adventures, moreover, are shrewdly observed. Lyricism can indeed be very like this description of it. Poetry has often been a form of self-pity and a means of self-advancement, and it has often pretended otherwise: Kundera's book rumbles such pretence, as in the comedy he stages of an embassy of poets to a college of policemen and a debate there about the aesthetic of the socialist love-poem. But he does all this at the cost of suspending a due sense of the tendency there has also been for poets to see further than their noses, and to speak out, and to go to the wall for it.

His Postscript evokes the aim of a white-coated Doctor Kundera 'to solve an aesthetic problem: how to write a novel which would be a "critique of poetry" and yet at the same time would itself be poetry'. This aim has a sweepingness and a suspendingness which are apparent, too, in the novel to which it relates. Many poems contain a critique of poetry, just as many contain a critique of the self-portrayed poet, and of his intention to serve a social or doctrinal system, or of his claim to be a special case. The lyric is not generically debarred from standing out against the state, or from taking a generous interest in what goes on in the world. Mandelstam's lyric about the 'Kremlin mountaineer'—Klima's 'great Generalissimo', Stalin—sent him to the camps.

Ivan Klima could be called a lyric author, and the notion of what it is to be such an author is examined in *My First Loves*, whose gentle and deliberate stories read as if they have been grown and stored before being made public. The boy poet

Klima loves literature, and pities himself, in a work which pities those around him. There is a lot to pity them for—the stories touch on ghetto hardships, on murders and deportations. His father, devoutly socialist, is jailed by the socialist regime whose discipline replaces that of the SS. Klima's first loves have a way of not working out; and what may have been his longest affair is the one about which least is said. In the opening story Miriam distributes milk to the tenement building and favours the boy with an extra helping: but he never gets to tell her that he is the lyric author of poems 'about love. About suicide.' The second story is set in and around a country hotel, where the wife of a coarse doctor takes a more than kindly interest in a Klima wide-awake to the sights and sounds of this paradise. The story ends at a funeral, hovered over by a surreal balloon, from which hangs a fancied female acrobat. The boy's hand is squeezed by the weeping wife. He is in two minds. 'I was able to soar up, to fly, I could rock in the air like that balloon, I could fly away with it, choose any of the four points of the compass, but I remained where I was, I stopped above this small, painful, blessed piece of earth.' Then there is the tale of a lying girl, as she may be, with whom he makes love, and who alarms him with word of a threatening German—a former SS man, perhaps. He has her report the matter to the police. This is a lapse on his part, but is hardly comparable with Jaromil's treatment of his mendacious redhead. Klima's girl disappears into the Prague bars, leaving him with an imaginary address. She is rather like a lyric author herself, a bit of a lyre.

The last story has to do with the girlfriend of a friend. Literary, second-sighted, sick, she holds out a hand to him: he clasps it, but then decides he can't go on. Is Klima, as the angry friend alleges on this occasion, a flirt, who goes from girl to girl? The stories do well to return an uncertain answer. Through them, somewhat in the spirit of Chagall, runs the aerial preoccupation of romantic escapism. Balloons float, a high-wire circus act teeters. In the last story Klima comes to see 'the connection between heights and vertigo, ecstasy and ruin, soaring and falling'. The literary girl waxes lyrical.

A person who accepted love was like a passenger. Maybe on a boat, at

night, on some vast lake. Whichever way you looked there was
nothing but calm black water. It was true that the water might rise
and swamp you. But to love someone meant to fly, to rise above the
earth yourself. So high that you could see everything. Even if the
world looked different from that height, even if it looked changed,
even if what on the ground seemed important was transformed into
insignificance. She'd say, moreover, that you could always get out of
a boat and go ashore, but from that height you could only crash.[3]

The blessed piece of earth over which float these balloons,
over which are poised these acrobats, is a corner of painful
Czechoslovakia. Klima's stories breathe a delicate patriotism—
which is not absent, either, from Kundera's accounts of a
country which is harder to inhabit, or remain in, or return to.
For both men, Czechoslovakia is both painful and blissful. It is
not surprising that the Czech novelist Josef Skvorecky should
be keen on *My First Loves*. Skvorecky left his country to teach
in North America—as did the Dubcekite Klima—and has
improved the shining hours of a Canadian exile. But Klima
has gone back. It has been said of him that he would rather live
in his native country, and not be allowed to publish, than go
elsewhere and be free to do so. Reality is in Czechoslovakia? A
challenging attitude on his part, if the story in question is
correct.

It should not persuade us that this writer has yielded or sold
out, any more than it should persuade us that the boy poet
Klima is in every sense the boy poet Jaromil. It is possible to
suggest that the two poets resemble one another. Each is in-
experienced, youthful. Each fancies a second existence, wants
to float free. Each feels sorry for himself. Each is lyrical. But
the lyricism of the character 'Klima' can be considered an
element in the lyricism of Ivan Klima, and be thought to
encounter there its own critique. As for that business of going
to the police, I am sorry I mentioned it. There is nothing in the
stories to suggest that either of these lyrical Klimas has the
makings of the hero of the state imagined by Kundera.

VIII · Kapuscinski

WE live at a time when reporters go to foreign countries where there is trouble and come back to write books in which they say that it was hard to make out what was going on. When they say this, they are apt to be called writers. Writers don't know what is going on. But they can be good at conveying what it was like for them to be there, and to be writing it down. The journalists to whom I am referring can more solemnly be said to be practising a modern art of indirection, of the unintelligible and the interminable. It is as if the war, crisis, living hell or chaotic backwater can never be known and will never end. After a while you fly out.

A leading exponent of these mysteries is the novelist and journalist V. S. Naipaul, whose foreign countries are, as we have already seen, areas of darkness, where coups and crises are glimpsed but may remain enigmatic. Another is Ryszard Kapuscinski, an expert in what he calls 'confusion', who has attended twenty-seven revolutions in the Third World. These revolutions, he believably reports, have been confusions. There he sat in his writer's hotel room, venturing out into a series of tight corners, filing his copy, then leaving for Warsaw to compose his short books—objects physically slight but charged with these confusions. They are marvellously done, and they have caused a stir of approval in this country, while also raising doubts. In the *New Left Review*, Benedict Anderson has made sharp criticisms of the work of the journalist and poet James Fenton which compare it with that of Kapuscinski and Naipaul. These three writers are tagged as representatives of two hardly very different types of crisis-fancying, Third Worldly literary tourist.[1]

Kapuscinski exercises a personal charm which must have helped him to establish friendly relations with the people he met, and to gather material, and which can seem to befriend the Western reader. Born in 1932, he retired as a foreign correspondent for the Polish Press Agency in 1981, by which time his three books had started to come out.[2] They describe three falls: that of the Emperor Haile Selassie, that of the Shah and that of the colonial masters of Angola. No fall from power within the Eastern bloc of nations is mentioned in any of the books.

The Ethiopian book, published in Britain in 1983, showed him to be a writer interested in 'autocrats'—in absolute power and in the transformation of that power into its indistinguishable opposite. He says that it is 'difficult to say when omnipotence becomes powerlessness'. Not that the stories of Haile Selassie and the Shah are any great advertisement for the omnipotence of omnipotence. Both rulers had reason to fear. Both of them, though, were rulers whom Western journalists used to admire: they were jewels in the crown of freedom, and yet endearingly autocratic. Kapuscinski's first two books will serve to deter any cult of the dear dead kings in question. In *The Emperor* he writes:

For the starvelings it had to suffice that His Munificent Highness personally attached the greatest importance to their fate, which was a very special kind of attachment, of an order higher than the highest. It provided the subjects with a soothing and uplifting hope that whenever there appeared in their lives an oppressive mischance, some tormenting difficulty, His Most Unrivalled Highness would hearten them—by attaching the greatest importance to that mischance or difficulty.

The Emperor has something of the technique of comic and fantastic exaggeration that we associate with Dickens, and something of the manner, too, of Dickens's reader, Kafka:

in the courtyard where the Emperor's retinue awaited him, there were tens, no, I say it without exaggeration, hundreds eager to push their faces forward. Face rubbed against face, the taller ones squelching down the shorter ones, the darker ones overshadowing the lighter ones. Face despised face, the older ones moving in front of the younger ones, the weaker ones giving way to the stronger ones. Face hated face, the common ones clashing with the noble ones, the grasping ones against the weaklings. Face crushed face, but even the humiliated ones, the ones pushed away, the third-raters and the defeated ones, even those—from a certain distance imposed by the law of hierarchy, it's true—still moved toward the front, showing here and there from behind the first-rate, titled ones, if only as fragments: an ear, a piece of temple, a cheek or a jaw . . . just to be closer to the Emperor's eye![3]

It is not easy to know how far Kafka's fictions can be thought to answer descriptively to the historical realities of his time, let alone to those which his fictions are often thought to have predicted. And it is not easy to know how far Kapuscinski's book is a book about a bygone Ethiopia. Is it a book about Poland? It purports to be based on the recollections of courtiers and retainers hunted up after the fall: but I have heard it suggested that the author did not take to the Picador edition's cover display of a picture of Haile Selassie, perhaps on the grounds of a misleading particularity. The reader who believes he is learning things about Imperial Ethiopia may be equally inclined to tell himself that this is a country of the mind, constructed on principles not very different from those of the Samuel Johnson who devised, for the Abyssinia of *Rasselas*, just representations of general truths and of a common humanity.

From Abyssinia Kapuscinski passed to Persia. From Rasselas, as it were, to Ozymandias. Present in the second book as the occupant of an Iranian hotel room sifting through his papers, photographs and cassettes, Kapuscinski recites the history of the region, which has thrust the Shah of Shahs into the sand in the posture of the statue of the 'King of Kings' in Shelley's tyrannophobe poem. The Shah had made a show-place of his country with his colossal purchasing of weapons, and look what it had all come to: 'If you drive from Shiraz to Isfahan even today you'll see hundreds of helicopters parked off to the right of the highway. Sand is gradually covering the inert machines.' Shortly after the point at which the recital ends, sand was to cover some more helicopters—those sent by President Carter to liberate the American hostages seized in Teheran, where Kapuscinski catches a glimpse not of them but of their place of confinement.

At this palace, as at the other, servility shows its face and performs its tricks. Foreign statesmen revere an oil-rich omni-potence: 'Now the whole world was at his feet. Before him were bowed heads, inclined necks and outstretched hands.' Kapuscinski speaks of the liberals who lost out when the Shah was expelled, but Bakhtiar is not particularised. Bani Sadr he does mention, with sympathy. He says of the liberals that they were placed in a predicament by the fall: 'A democracy cannot be imposed by force, the majority must favour it, yet the majority wanted what Khomeini wanted—an Islamic republic.'

The suggestion that democracy cannot be imposed by force has the force of a generalisation. Kapuscinski is a seeker of general truths who is sparing with his generalisations, and who likes certain kinds of particularity but not others. The kind he likes he calls 'detail', as opposed to 'long shots'—the equivalent, that is, of the long shots over-used by cameramen of the Iranian Revolution: 'it is through details that everything can be shown'—that truth can be shown. But in *The Emperor* no detail is adduced that might bring out what differences there could have been between the courtiers and petitioners of Ethiopia and their counterparts elsewhere in the world. Kapuscinski's courtiers and petitioners are about as black as Johnson's Prince Rasselas, who is about as black as he is white.

In the second book, a photograph is spoken of which 'shows the pulling down of a monument to one of the Shahs (father or son) in Teheran or some other Iranian city. It is hard to be sure about the year the photograph was taken, since the monuments of both Pahlavis were pulled down several times, whenever the occasion presented itself to the people.' Here the confusions or uncertainties are the point of the passage: it doesn't matter that the particulars of the caption are missing since this sort of thing was always happening. It matters less and less as we move into an enjoyable account derived from a vocational puller-down of statues of the Shah and his father. The Shah was equal to these demolitions: 'If we pulled one down, he set up three.' The wrecker explains that, one way or another, 'it's not easy to pull down monuments'. Kapuscinski then generalises. The Shah's regime was a transplant that the system had rejected: 'The rejection of a transplant—once it begins, the process is irreversible. All it takes is for society to accept the conviction that the imposed form of existence does more harm than good.' I am not sure how much work these last words are doing, and if there is tautology here, it is compounded by what follows. Rejecting the Shah was

a great experience, an adventure of the heart. Look at the people who are taking part in a revolt. They are stimulated, excited, ready to make sacrifices. At that moment they are living in a monothematic world limited to one thought: to attain the goal they are fighting for. Everything will be subjugated to that goal . . .[4]

Kapuscinski's way with words entails adding, repeating, piling up, for the space of a slim volume. But the 'and's' and 'or's' and the more and more rarely irritate, and are triumphant in the great set-pieces which mean so much to all three books—like that palimpsest of faces in Addis Ababa.

In 1975, the year after the fall of Haile Selassie, and four years before the fall of the Shah, the witness of revolutions turned up in Angola for the abandonment of their colony by the Portuguese: the subject of the third of these books of his. Agostinho Neto, politician and poet, the leader of the MPLA, is about to preside over the new state, but two enemy armies are converging on the capital, Luanda: the FNLA under Holden Roberto and Unita under Jonas Savimbi. All three have international sponsors, and Kapuscinski is to find out that the South Africans have invaded in the south of the country, having fallen in love with Savimbi. As in the earlier books, the bravura set-piece dominates, and the most memorable concerns the crates in which the Portuguese have packed up their belongings, and which were eventually shipped out of Africa— Kapuscinski was to stumble on a few of them in Portugal, sunk, as it were, in the sand. He writes of them as they stay for waftage:

Some crates were as big as vacation cottages, because a hierarchy of crate status had suddenly come into being. The richer the people, the bigger the crates they erected. Crates belonging to millionaires were impressive: beamed and lined with sailcloth, they had solid, elegant walls made of the most expensive grades of tropical wood, with the rings and knots cut and polished like antiques.

The passage takes off thereafter in ecstatic inventory.[5] At the start of the book there are false notes, those of a Hemingway war correspondent: 'Every knock at the door could mean the end for me. I tried not to think about it, which is the only thing to do in such a situation.' But matters are mended with the arrival of the crates—antiques that epitomised an antique land, brief monuments to the old Angola.

Benguela, in the south, is one of Kapuscinski's ghost towns. A deserted European quarter is twinned with an African settlement out in a desert 'white and glimmering like a salt spill, without a blade of grass'. These Africans have not moved into the houses of the Portuguese. They are passive, we are told; moral scruples don't come into it. Kapuscinski generalises: 'the degree of consciousness that drives one to demand justice or do something about obtaining it hasn't yet been reached.' From Benguela, Kapuscinski and a film crew travel to a scene of carnage, guided by Carlotta, a heroine of the MPLA. When the Europeans decide to return, their guide decides to stay, and is immediately killed. 'We are all culpable in Carlotta's death, since we agreed to let her stay behind; we could have ordered her to return.' A colonial 'could'.

Kapuscinski is soon in a still hairier place, further south, where he is told of the South African intervention. This is a scoop, and he fights his way back through wildernesses, road-blocks, threats of ambush, to inform Warsaw. The last Portuguese leave Luanda. Independence is declared, and Neto's position as head of the hard-pressed MPLA improves. By now Kapuscinski is on his 'last legs', and he telexes Warsaw to say that he wants to leave and that it is 'more or less clear' that 'the Angolans will win'. Neto's, and Castro's, Angolans, presumably. On the following page we read that 'things were going badly' for Neto. Since then, for the thirteen years since Kapuscinski's departure, things have gone badly for the Angolans, and they are still suffering terribly. But at last, in the summer of 1988, negotiations are in hand which may end the war. It is a war which has begun to embarrass the interveners.

According to the *Guardian*, the New Year's Honours list of 1988 in Britain contained a knighthood for 'Professor Albert Maillard, the Oxford historian'. Two of the several names owned by another recipient had strayed into someone's word-processor to create a further deserving don, the knowing reference to whom must have ruined the new year for more than one senior scholar. I feel that Albert Maillard, if he existed, would have no time for Kapuscinski's impressionism, for his absence of dates, figures and state papers, and that Albert Maillard would be wrong. There is history in the accounts Kapuscinski gives of the confusions and uncertainties which he has experienced and which he has tried to interpret. All is not dark in these accounts, and indeed they can be said to gleam with a quality of reflected light. I think of him as an artist who writes history, and I take it that the history he writes includes the history he has principally suffered—that of Poland.

An autocrat falls in the first two books; but the only one in the third is the author-autocrat of the hotel room who sallies into the bush, as if on impulse, to visit the mysterious, moveable 'front'. At the same time, he is a shrewd observer who writes compellingly about the people and the landscapes he encounters. A benevolent despot. The same description would not, in my view, be grossly inapplicable to the present ruler of Poland—which has, as it happens, a smaller population than the Ethiopia of chronic famine. General Jaruzelski bears no obvious resemblance to the Third World autocrats discussed in the first two books. But it can scarcely be in doubt that these books have in them home truths, and an ironic obliquity or duplicity, which richly relate to the world of Jaruzelski's predecessors, and indeed to the experience of other countries where literature and opinion have been repressed. Their writing coincided with the rise of Solidarity. They are books which bring together all three of the worlds we inhabit, and they are books which appear to thrive on being seen through—on the transparency of their suggestion that tyrannies, that sycophancy, conspiracy and repression, courts and courtiers, are all on the royal right, and in the bush, and running into the sand.

IX · Heroine of Our Time

SUICIDE was thought damnable in the Middle Ages, and I expect there are those who have been brought to feel by a book called *The Monument* that the Middle Ages had a point. T. Behrens's book[1] commemorates a young couple who lived together for seventeen years in a *solitude à deux* and who then took their own lives—incompetently and lingeringly. Representatives of the few people they had come to know in the course of their wanderings round the world were left to clear up. Suicide tends now to command sympathy, even when the reasons for it are hard to understand. Not everyone who reads the book will be able to sympathise with Justin and Ursula, or to believe that they understand them. But there will also be those who will stay with it for its relish of damnation.

This is one of the many books which address the snobbery of the English, which flash at their readers the lawns of country houses, the baize of gambling-tables, which tell tales of those virtuosos of ostentation and disregard who have in common a contempt for commonness, for the middle class; and it could be said of such books that their chief resource is the eccentricity which has long amounted to a convention of upper-class life. Literary careers can be founded on the impersonation and adulation of privileged behaviour; but the literary works which have been written and inspired by English snobs and sports are by no means all boastful or complicit. The supreme text of recent years is James Fox's account of Lord Lucan and his set, with their *boffes de politesse*.

Patrician insolence has quite often appeared to express a perception of the activities of the levelling Labour governments which have come and gone since 1945. Behrens's book, however, pays no attention to politics or to public matters. His story begins at a time when, as at other times in this century, the patriciate, and the merely rich, had slipped down into marked collusion with the smart, with upstarts and bohemians. The well-born and the well-off have been apt at such times to turn, for diversion and instruction, to foreigners and to members of the working class. These strangers have been sexual, artistic. Theirs was the charm of not being bourgeois, and the foreigners among them could be, or could come across as, princes, pretenders to a throne, descendants of a khan. What survived, in the late Fifties, of the Chelsea set welcomed a refugee from Hungary, after the Soviet invasion of that country. This was Ursula of the long blonde hair and double-barrelled baronial-barbaric surname (withheld by Behrens), who had fled what survived of ancestral estates—on one view of the matter—and had made her courageous way across Europe, shot at and winged by border guards, to Vienna, and on to London, where she fell among art historians and was counselled by Anthony Blunt.

As did the author of the book, who is a painter and who was then at the Slade, she discovered, he tells us, that 'the people with the beautiful faces were also, mysteriously, the ones it was most fun to be with'. The self-proclaimed 'honesty' of the wild, well-born stranger was doubted, but her fascination prevailed. She married an art dealer, Kenelm, understood to be seriously ill, and conducted daring affairs, one of them on the Metro with her friend Monique's friend Gianni:

Gianni and Ursula leapt on just as the doors were closing, but Monique, who was now a few yards behind them and whose move-ments were hampered anyway by her arthritis, was left standing there as the train moved out. Ursula and Gianni got off at the next station but one, having brought their growing mutual admiration to a startling climax wedged solid among the rocking mass of sober commuters. After a quick tidy-up they took the next train back to the Gare de Lyon where Monique had only twenty minutes to wait.

Were the other passengers *all* sober? Startling the commuter is a game in which it is best to think so.

Chapter Five opens with the information: 'Ursula and Kenelm had known my parents for some time, having been introduced originally by a mutual friend. Kenelm had then sold my father a pair of eighteenth-century cupboards.' And so it was that Ursula met Justin, the writer's moody adolescent brother, and ran away with him.

Away! They were off on their seventeen years of Tristan and Isolde. Justin, who would appear to have lost some of his old

charisma, became the straight man of the act—always mending
things. They lived frugally but in style. They rented a flat in
Rome and built a house in Greece. Here they are, unisex and
colour-supplement-magnetic in an Italian 'working-class'
restaurant: 'Justin and Ursula, with their measured dignity
and impeccable, interchangeable clothes—perhaps soft leather
waistcoats over silk shirts and linen trousers in colours that
rarely overstepped the narrow arc of the spectrum between
cream and ochre—were immediately noticeable.' They turned
nomadic and mingled with the nomads of the Sudan, where
they were to consider building a further house and perhaps
settling down. They swam, they talked, they wrote their diaries
and stories, and were at ease in a succession of remote and
sticky places. Ursula's bad back was religiously exposed to
unmanageable African horses and jolting lorry rides. England's
wealthy and wonderful—their scams and scrapes, their port-
folios, clubs, night-clubs, champagne and cocaine, the Cockney
accents of their young ones, their gossip-columnists and their
art historians, their Lucan-like zombies and their zoos and
safaris—were avoided.

     T. Behrens kept up with the fleeing lovers, at intervals. He
visited them in Egypt, accompanied by a girl he'd met in a bar,
who proved to be a lesbian. His own vicissitudes in love are a
feature of the story he tells, as is his attempt to understand
his disconcerting brother and to produce reflections on the
meaning of it all. Ursula's diary is reflective too, but is at its
best in its evocations of place—of the nothingness of the desert,
especially. She can, against the odds, be funny: 'Dinkas in
the market have long, brass-bound pipes. One of these smokers
wears a T-shirt with the words "ever ready". He looks less
ready than anyone I've ever seen.' One of her sententious
entries reads: 'Tactlessness is often taken for sincerity, and
sincerity is in turn often taken for a compliment. Let no one
ever be sincere with me—it is a failure of respect, and respect is
a thing one can never get enough of. And the only kind of
respect worth having is the insincere kind.' Another reads:
'Where would we be without that much-maligned virtue,
vanity?'

     These upper-class *pensées* lighten the load of an odyssey whose
ports of call, for all her evocations, are barely distinguishable

from one another. Struggling with his maps, the writer is forced into sheer itinerary:

They drove directly south-west into Algeria through Guelma, Bou Saada, Ain Sefra, Colomb Béchar near the Moroccan frontier, Tindouf, into Mauritania through Chinguetta, and reached the Atlantic coast at Nouakshott. Then down the coast to St Louis in Senegal. At Dakar they cut sharply back into Mauritania through Kiffa, then south again to Kayes in Mali. On to Bamako, then eastward into Upper Volta through Bobo Djoulasso and Ouagadougou.

But this, too, is upper-class, this recital of exotic place-names— so often the spoor of the doughty, ascetic, astringent English traveller who has left his privileges behind.

As the years go by, Ursula's body becomes a bore, and she experiences a fear of ageing: 'I shall have to die fairly young, because I won't be able to live with the infirmities of old age.' She is indeed ready to die, and it is a difficulty that Justin may feel that he has to do the same. In the Sudan she declares: 'My time is up.' She is infatuated with a handsome police chief, goes rather grimly to bed with him in the time he can spare from gambling sessions, and then kills herself. Justin goes back to England for a while, and then, having broken some hearts, arrives in the Sudan to perform his own suicide. They now lie together in a single lot in a local cemetery. The headstone is inscribed with the words: 'Ursula and Justin—One'.

'One' was a word of the Chelsea set for the first person singular, and one might perhaps venture the thought of a pun in the words of the inscription. These two people had enacted what we have long been accustomed to think of as a romantic programme, whereby love and death converge, and dying young is the thing to do, whereby other people, and common life, are a thing to be escaped from, and a tension develops between the duty to a partner and a cultivation of the self, between the dictates of an *amour fou* and an *amour de soi*. 'Most people addicted to romancing are their own heroes': when a second person enters the solitude in question, Louisa Stuart's maxim becomes harder to apply. But I have the impression that Ursula was very much her own heroine.

T. Behrens is considerably baffled by this strange case, by the question of what it was that determined Ursula's adherence to this programme, and of what it was that caused her to bring to an end her loving friendship with Justin. Guesses are hazarded, and are quoted from interviews he conducted. A hint of child abuse may seem to be imparted by his account of a Gothic moment which came about during a walk with her father, at nightfall, in a setting of peasants and forests. Ursula figures as 'some sort of Hungarian countess' whose parents were estranged and who was to be estranged from her ominous father. There she once sat in some sort of castle, or not, reading, for sure, the literature of Romanticism, and growing up to resemble—in the opinion of the writer's aunt, the historian C. B. A. Behrens—a character out of Lermontov.

Lermontov, for his part, was a character out of Byron, and so was Pechorin, the 'hero of our time' in Lermontov's novel of 1839, one of those people 'who are fated to attract all kinds of unusual things'. Pechorin is a cold-hearted, stylish fatalist, experimentalist, existentialist and divided man, a traveller, gambler, heart-breaker and forgetter of old friends, who loves to ride 'a spirited horse through the long grass against a desert wind'. Blond and beautiful in his leg-ribbons, his high-heeled shoes, 'fitted with the greatest possible exactitude', his 'long white tunic' and 'dark-brown Circassian coat'. Byron's is not the only ghost to be detected here: the cold hearts of his precursors Lovelace and Laclos's Valmont are present in Pechorin, who has succeeded in attracting a certain princess.

'I'll tell you the whole truth,' I answered the Princess. 'I won't excuse or explain my conduct. I don't love you.'
The colour faded from her lips.
'Leave me alone,' she said, barely audibly.
I shrugged my shoulders, turned, and walked away.

The shrugger doesn't care whether he lives or dies—and the designer duel arranged for himself by this divided and indifferent man is a form of Russian roulette. The duel in which Lermontov was soon to die is said to have been patterned, so far as its arrangements went, on the one in the novel: the outcome, however, was perceptibly different.[2]

V. G. Kiernan's recent book on the history of duelling—the work of a historian who is able to grasp, as many historians now are not, that the literature of the past is evidence of the past—discusses Lermontov's real and imaginary duels.[3] The book indicates that duelling and gambling have been co-ordinate activities: both, we may feel, are poised on a knife-edge between accident and intention. If there is an element of design on Pechorin's part in the duel he fights, an element which incorporates a knowledge of the loaded dice to be employed by his opponent in the form of an unloaded pistol, the outcome can still be ascribed to chance, in a sense that must be meant to characterise the hero's fine indifference. Kiernan reports suggestions that Lermontov's own death (like Pushkin's in another duel a few months before) may have been murder, a murder planned by court reactionaries.

Outcomes are uncertain, games of chance can be rigged—but this is not what we are conscious of in reading about Ursula. We read that she intended, in Hamlet's words, to 'leave betimes', and that she did what she intended. That there was a pattern for her in Lermontov's novel is conceivable: but it can't be claimed that it fits her with exactitude, or that it provides an explanation of her conduct. It is clear enough, none the less, that the hero of that time is like the hero of some other times, including Hamlet's. Shakespeare's play has an arranged duel which miscarries, and which takes off a divided, gambling man who has wondered whether or not it might be better to end his life. Here, too, the uncertainty of a duel utters the uncertainty of internal division. Those who pursue comparisons of the kind I am referring to are likely to be impressed by the staying-power of a literary preoccupation to which a variety of temperaments and compulsions has been attracted, and could well be inclined to believe that Pechorin's duel and indifference may have been among the precedents that weighed, a century later, with a woman bent on contriving her appointment with destiny.

Not much is made, however, in the book she has become, of the cultural provenance of this Russian-style *belle dame sans merci*. She is present in the book as narcissistic, driven and depressive, with the fascination of such people, as the enigma of an exceptional vitality drawn towards 'laziness' and extinction, as a suicidal survivor, her life a chapter of escapes. But she was also, among other literary things, the wonderful and baleful orphan or isolate who is seen to advantage in the books

she read: and it may be that cultural history is especially worth
attending to in cases such as hers, where the subject is a dedicated reader, and the basis for a directly psychological account is
even more than usually insecure. Not that T. Behrens sets up
as a psychologist. To read about her here is like being shown
someone's snaps or scrapbook—perhaps an underrated pleasure.
It is like an evening spent in a restaurant—let's say Olwen's
French Club, mentioned on page one, a latter-day refuge of the
Chelsea set—listening to a story of mutual friends. And it is a
trip in its own right, on the teller's part. T. Behrens gives the
impression that he has more to say about himself than the
progress of this mad love—to which he did not stand all that
close at the time, brother as he was—has allowed him to come
up with. It is also possible to feel, and to be told in London, that
there was more to be said about the mad love than he allowed
himself, or was in a position, to come up with. And it may be
that Justin, too, has more to say, from beyond the grave.
Waiting in the wings is a book by him about Ursula, entitled
Style, which, according to Graham Greene, who was sent the
manuscript, could be edited for publication. There may be a
cult in the making—and one could imagine a film by Antonioni,
whose script-writer, Mark Peploe, was intrigued by J. Behrens
in his last days.

X · Kingsley and the Women

A RECENT photograph of Kingsley Amis shows him with a cat, which is standing beside his typewriter. The author's face wears a witch's smile of appreciation. He is clearly familiar with and fond of that cat. The smile may have come as a surprise to connoisseurs of the pictures of him which have been issued to the world. These pictures, rarely cordial, have become more and more baleful: it is as if he is holding himself back from physical assault on a reader supposed to be a trendy and a lefty, which is, indeed, what many of his readers have always been. The smile contrasts, moreover, with the expression to be imagined on the face of the male lead, Patrick Standish, in Amis's novel of 1988, *Difficulties with girls*, when the cat in Patrick's life pays him a visit. You feel at first that on a bad day (there are quite a few) Patrick might give it one of the kicks that the novelist seems about to direct at his readers. Then it turns out that Patrick rather likes it after all. But then it turns out that the female lead, his wife Jenny Standish (née Bunn), unreservedly cherishes their cat. All this could suggest that Kingsley Amis isn't altogether sold on Patrick Standish.

Readers of Amis can be expected to remember Patrick and Jenny from the past. They appeared in his novel of 1960, *Take a girl like you*, in which Patrick gives freezing looks, and a group of children wears the 'expression of being proud of being serious, like some famous author photographed in the *Radio Times*'. The new novel has married the pair and moved them on into the mid-Sixties and from the provinces to London, where Patrick works misgivingly in a fashionable publishing-house. And there are other reappearances from the earlier novel. Each of the novels has an alluring Wendy. Graham McClintoch of 'the indefensible ginger-coloured suit' has returned, and there are commemorative mentions of a ginger this and a ginger that. Patrick is still having difficulties with girls: the married man keeps going to bed with them, not liking it very much and not liking the distress it brings to a wife whom he *does* like and who is carefully crafted to be likeable.

I reviewed *Take a girl like you* when it came out, and took pains to convey how much I enjoyed and admired its incendiariness. The review seemed to think that the swinging Sixties contained a readership that would be troubled or shocked by the novel's candour and scabrousness about sex—'no doubt he has touched himself on the raw. He will touch everyone on the raw'—while the young would receive it as an account of what they were up to. But it was clear, and is clearer still in retrospect, that on a number of occasions an old decorum had been deferred to, or embraced. Jenny's Jack the Lad is addressed by her as 'my lad', and she firmly refuses to rush into bed with him. The narrator may not wholly be in jest when he refers to sexual intercourse with a certain girl, 17 or thereabouts, as 'the ultimate indecorum', and rereaders of the novel are likely to be mindful of the survival here of an old England lived in by people like the middle-aged T. S. Eliot, exponents of a disgusted chastity. It seems appropriate that the language of *Four Quartets* should enter the novel at one point—appropriate, too, of course, that it should be mocked.

So the piece was solicitous in trying to alleviate the shocks by explaining that the novelist himself was shocked. And I think it was right to argue that the book has its 'strict disclaimers' and that goodness of heart, chiefly Jenny's, is defensively displayed amid a welter of misconduct. There is a bleakness which centres on Patrick's infidelities: but it may also be true that the rudeness and aggression with which Jenny, their sex object, is treated by various chuntering males has grown grimmer with the years than it was reckoned to be, by the author, by me and by many of his readers, at the time. The review predicted that 'any eventual mating' between Patrick and Jenny 'will have something permanently bitter and irresolute about it'. A linguistic point was made in the course of the review—that Julian Ormerod's lounge-bar slang is 'continuous, in a way, with Patrick's cool utterance'—and the review also made out that Ormerod's overdone good heart is continuous, in a way, with Jenny's.

'No wonder we like them', said a poem of Amis's once. The poem says that women are 'much nicer than men'. But the novels were soon to exhibit an interest in misogyny, and to see a connection between 'the old hoo-ha' and 'the old last end'—

expressions used by Ormerod and Standish respectively, in *Take a girl like you*, for sexual intercourse and death. Thinking about women is a way of avoiding the thought of death—and yet women may be the end of you. No wonder we fear them. A paranoid reproach is aimed at all females by an Amis-like figure, who then reproaches himself, or is reproached by some other Amis agent detectable in the novel. At times a golden girl is present in the vicinity of the discussions of the subject that keep happening, and is felt to restore a balance. Fairly early in *Take a girl like you*, Patrick delivers himself of an unqualified condemnation of women, which is followed by a sentence from the narrator concerning and presumably condemning Patrick's attitude to Jenny at that stage, as a girl to be taken and left: 'He wanted more than his share of her before anybody else had any.'

These 'Jenny-dealings' have now, after nearly thirty years, incurred a sequel, in which the discussion, and the former comedy and bleakness, are resumed, and in which the question of continuity of utterance within the novel once again arises. The beauty of the earlier prose is, in part, a beauty of grace notes, the pointing of sentences, charged elegance and buoyant, intelligent wit. In *Take a girl like you* a great sentence falls like the dew from heaven during one of the scenes in Amis when a terminally drunk man endures a sexual turmoil and fiasco, is stunned by a stunning but not very nice girl. This particular girl, a model, is putting Patrick in his place by going on about cars: '"Most of my friends have them on the firm", she said, with the sort of lift of the old proud head that he could hardly believe had not accompanied a limiting judgment on Villiers de l'Isle Adam.' In *Difficulties with girls* there are passages which recall that lift of the old proud head. 'In silence, the two almost bowed almost stiffly to each other, behaving rather like two— well, two somethings-or-other, thought Patrick. Two climato- logical dendrologists or career torturers, pre-eminent in their respective domains but divided on some technical points.' The new prose, however, is in general less embellished, more ellipt- ical, even quite taxingly so on occasion, and yet more colloquial too. There is less style, of the kind known to Villiers de l'Isle Adam. Fewer jewels. Excellent use is made of the text of *Tom Jones*, but it is now less detectable that this is a writer who has done his stint of teaching English literature at university level.

The voice of the novelist is heard continually in the speech of his characters. Patrick is a lord of language, as he was in the previous novel. But this novel has not just one but two barmen who could also at a pinch be hailed as lords of language. Even schoolteaching Graham, who is meant to be amusingly boring, is good with words, in one of the ways that teachers sometimes are. And even Jenny, who is meant to be a mistress of plain speech, is allowed, in this comparatively austere book, a quiet felicity of phrase based on the justice of her perceptions. The lordship in question is the novelist's, not only in the usual sense, often forgotten, that every word of the novel is his, but also because the speech of its characters can be like that of the narrator, and indeed like that of the writer of Kingsley Amis's discursive prose.

This is not the first time that such considerations have arisen for readers of his fiction. Readers of *The Old Devils* have asked: are its Welsh Welsh? Its characters have been said to sound English. (Northern Jenny Bunn, incidentally, sounds, to me, Welsh.) There may be a matter of principle here for some of those who wish their authors to be concealed: such authors should not sound like the characters they invent, any more than they should express opinions. But the raconteurs of the extra-literary world are permitted to shape and turn the speech of the characters in their stories, and to play the pervasive evident author. And anyone who doubts whether the method can safely be transferred to literature should consult one of Amis's best novels, *Ending up*. Raconteur and *raisonneur*, in his art as in his personal life, he is a concealed author who is evident enough in his hotly opinionated fiction: he is not given to expounding his own passionate opinions there, but can be recognised without difficulty in almost every aspect of every one of his novels, including the speech assigned to his often disputatious characters. There is a sense in which each novel of his is an opinion of his, coextensive with the work itself and rather hard, as a rule, to read off in summary.

These considerations affect the difficulties which attend *Difficulties with girls*, and which come to the fore with the most Amis-sounding of its characters, the male lead. Amis's novels have always been full of opinions, and have, I think, become prone to a marked ambiguity of effect, especially with regard to questions of gender and race. Patrick has plenty to say on such subjects, and he says it in the lordly way which does much to furnish the book with its presiding idiom. But are we meant to sympathise with what he says? Here and elsewhere, the method, for all that Amis would hate to hear it, is dialectical.

In the novels I am thinking of he attributes certain ideas to certain characters and utters them in the prevailing manner of the novel, while also submitting them to question within it. He can appear in so doing to have his opinions and to eat them too. And he can also appear to place the novel in a state of suspension. If the state was not present in his novels from the first, it is there in *One Fat Englishman*, and in *Jake's Thing*. It is there in *Stanley and the Women*, which persuaded Marilyn Butler—somewhat against the odds, but none the less intelligibly—to interpret it in the *London Review* as a critique of male supremacy, but which has left a very different impression on others.[1] It is compatible with the canon of artistic detachment, but it can cause controversy. Heirs to the freedoms which, on the threshold of the Sixties, *Take a girl like you* may be thought to have assisted in inaugurating, but which it also contrived to criticise, young people now seem to feel that the old Patrick belonged to a sexist work, and they may well feel that the old Adam has surfaced again in the new Patrick. But a solicitous critic (Amis has had his share, for all the faces he makes) could perhaps be counted on to demonstrate that the novelist is sorry that Patrick is sexist.

Take, for example, the Jewish question as it arises in the novel. Patrick has been hired by an obnoxiously trendy mismated publisher. He labours scornfully for this Simon Giles, faintly comforted by a corner in Classical studies which has been granted him for reasons to do with the firm's image. Between Patrick and Mrs Giles there flows, or gutters, a current of dreary sexual electricity. He fancies that Simon is Jewish, and that he gives off 'a slight hot smell'. We are later tolerantly informed—in the presiding idiom of the book, by a narrator keen, as ever, to monitor Patrick's impressions—that the smell was not atrocious: 'not strong but easily perceptible, like a large zoo passed at a distance.' By then, however, Patrick has been informed, by an office placeman and fuddy-duddy who believes that trendiness has ruined everything, that smelly Simon, though he may be obnoxious, is not Jewish. This is a bad day for Patrick, who had volunteered that Simon was 'one of a certain . . . persuasion'. According to the narrator, Patrick is 'so far from being anti-semitic that a couple of his best friends really were Jews' (but who can these two best friends be—can Ormerod, unmentioned in the later novel, be one?). And now he has been put down, made to seem anti-Semitic, by a probable anti-Semite. The encounter could be read as establishing that he has been silly, while clearing him of a certain . . . imputation. But it could also be read very differently. For some, it may serve as a reminder of the Kingsley Amis who once unambiguously remarked, in the course of a berating of Philip Roth, that 'Jewish jokes are not funny'.[2]

Then there is the woman question, which arises in the novel in a fashion which sets us wondering, as in the past and as in the case of the above encounter, which parts of the bad behaviour on display Amis quite or largely likes. The woman question is treated together with the homosexual question. This is the mid-Sixties, and homosexuals are being released from the closet by a law enacted by Parliament late in the novel. Patrick is far from anti-homosexual, though not entirely patient with the relevant practices and pretensions. This standpoint is gathered up with others in a book which is free with descriptions of creditable and discreditable dealings on the part of those of that persuasion. Two, or three, of them are in, or moving into, the far from populous row of flats, just over the river in South London, which is inhabited by Patrick and Jenny, and by a stunning, boring wife who affords Patrick one of the novelist's turmoils in a vulgarly-appointed borrowed flat some miles to the north. Among the few Standish neighbours on the row is Eric, long gone from the closet and married to Stevie, a he-man former semi-film-star, whom he eventually stabs. Eric is represented as sympathetic, and the counsel he imparts to Patrick on the subject of gender might almost have been imparted by Patrick:

'You and I are by nature, by our respective natures, males who are irresistibly attracted by a non-male principle. In your case, straightforward, women; in my case not straightforward, not women—*but*, non-male, except anatomically. And it's the clash between male and non-male that causes all the trouble. They're different from us. More like children. Crying when things go wrong. Making difficulties just so as to be a person.'

But when Patrick says that sort of thing to Jenny, he adds that *she* is an exception to this law of nature. She is not, as he puts it, 'that sort' of woman.[3]

Meanwhile the also sympathetic but Grahamly maddening Tim is struggling to move into a flat on the row, while supposing himself to be struggling to come out of the closet. A third homosexual on the row? What he has to come out with is not initially clear, but it becomes clearer when a taste of gay night-life turns him off, and he trails back to his dull wife. This could be termed an uncomely version of what happens to Patrick, whose wife discovers that, at long last, she is pregnant. She is sure that this will settle them for the foreseeable future. Their relationship is still unresolved, as wise heads had foreseen in 1960: but their marriage has gained a lease of life. The woe that is in marriage is not all that bad really. Jenny has urgently advised Tim to return to his dull wife, telling him that her dullness is the 'whole point'. Those who think that Jenny herself is a little dull at times might conclude that Patrick has impaled himself on that point, like one of those Romans whose language he used to teach. He is to do a lot less swinging. 'She was going to have him all to herself for at least three years, probably more like five, and a part of him for ever . . .'. The novel is no persuasive advertisement for marriage, or for Jews and gays. But it isn't plain sailing either to claim it as racist and sexist.

There is a difficulty with Jenny, of a kind that came with the innocent of the previous novel. She now knows more, but the iron has not entered her soul. Amid the general ventriloquism she does often manage to speak for herself. The novelist is less inward, less collusive, with her than he is with her husband—a relation fully consonant with Eric's law of nature—but he wants her view to be respected, and works it too hard as a purchase on wrong thinking. Amis is still soft on her, a sentiment which is likely to strike most of his readers as natural too. She is entrusted, on one occasion, with what might seem a rudimentary version of one of his own opinions. On this occasion[4] she is at a posh party, where she has taken a glass of champagne, but only 'to be sociable'—a motive which in anyone else would have driven Patrick to contemplate another of the umpteen blows he feels like unleashing—when the novelist unleashes one of his phonological jokes, which play on vagaries of pronunciation. A man, back from Spain, addresses her in tones that approximate to what the *Independent* thought was the 'well-educated voice', and to what the *Guardian* thought was the 'assured accent', transmitted by the Intelligence chief responsible for the shooting of the IRA bombers in Gibraltar which preceded the arrival of the novel. Jenny understands him to say that he has had trouble on his travels 'with the Reds'.

'Oh, I thought they'd taken care of them,' said Jenny. 'Since that war they had there.'

'They haven't, believe me. Well, not up anything you could call a mountain.'

'No, I suppose that's where they would tend to hole up.'

Where can Jenny have been, in the course of her adolescence, to be willing, if only out of nervousness, to accept that the Reds in Spain have been swept out from under the bed and up into mountain caves? It's a very funny joke, but it works at the expense of treating her like a child, which is not at all what the novel usually intends.

Amis writes here, as he has written in other books, about the distance between men and women; here, too, is the trouble that awaits the rational hedonist who deceives the woman he lives with and loves. It isn't every comic genius who would undertake to send his talent into such painful places. Both this novel and the one which it resumes are 'hung' books, in the sense that Parliaments are said to be hung. Adultery has been a hanging matter—both in this and in the usual sense of the phrase—for the literature of the past, and perhaps it could be suggested that both senses may at times be presented to the mind by what Amis does with the subject, and that there is no striking difference in this respect between what he did in the Sixties and what he has done in the Eighties. I don't think this means that there is no saying what he is getting at in these works; opinions can and will be formed, and for the extent of the present discussion I have been attempting to express one. Any such attempt has to look closely at their chastened but ultimately unchastenable hero, at his hostility, at his stylistic authority and command of the books he belongs to.

Maybe there will one day be a novel from Amis which portrays the Patrick Standish of the Eighties—more baleful, no doubt, on certain subjects, nicer to his cat, surrounded by the monuments of the New Right and by the debris of the swinging past to which he had once been a contributor. The two Patrick books are stations in a progress—what Amis has encouraged us to call Lucky Jim's turn to the right. This is a progress which has found its haven in the achievements of Mrs Thatcher, and the Patrick of the Eighties will have to deal with that. It will be difficult for him to be baleful about the Millennium.

I would like to say a last word about Amis's voices, and about the long words which have been or might be laid on his confident art—a terminology for which he is unlikely to be grateful. There is a poem by his friend Philip Larkin, entitled 'Letter to a Friend about Girls', which was never published during Larkin's lifetime but was retrieved for the *Collected Poems* of 1988. It is dated December 1959, and may therefore have been written at the time that *Take a girl like you* was being completed. And it might almost be the work of Graham McClintoch. To imagine this is to be aware that the aggressive term which I have applied to Amis's novelistic method, 'ventriloquism', has the drawback of suggesting that when an author throws his voice, the character who receives it will necessarily be found to be inanimate, a dummy. This is not, of course, the case. Dummies can come to life in books, as it seems they can do for their masters on the stage: and this miracle depends, not only on the author, but also on the people he knows, who may indeed be thought to participate in what he is, and who are likely to participate in his ventriloquism. It may be that Larkin's poem and the person we meet there participate in the ventriloquism of Amis's novel.

At a mid-point in the novel there occurs McClintoch's complaint that people are divided into the 'attractive' and the 'unattractive', rather as, according to Disraeli, as Graham

duly notes, Victorian England was divided into the two nations
of rich and poor. There is a 'barrier' between the attractive
and the unattractive—between, as Graham puts it on a later
occasion, the 'beggars' and 'choosers' of the sexual life. Convinced of his own plainness, Graham is here engaged in
taking Jenny out and making a mess of kissing her. Jenny is
nice about the mess, but disturbed by what he tells her—in
words that call to mind the language, and the drift, of this
poem and others by Larkin, and of passages in Larkin's fiction
where Jack is denied his Jill.

'You can't imagine what it's like not to know what it is to meet an
attractive person who's also attracted to you, can you? Because
unattractive men don't want unattractive girls, you see. They want
attractive girls. They merely *get* unattractive girls. I think a lot of
people feel vaguely when they see two duffers marrying that the
duffers must prefer it that way. Which is rather like saying that slum-
dwellers would rather live in the slums than anywhere else—there
they are *in* the slums, aren't they?'[5]

Larkin's poem complains in concert; it takes up the question
of what it is to be sexually debarred. The letter it sends is to an
attractive friend who goes about 'bagging birds', and who
belongs to a world in which the beautiful say yes to the
beautiful and wildly misbehave, a world which is said to be
'described on Sundays only', in papers like the *News of the
World*—but which is also described in *Take a girl like you*. The
poem begins:

> After comparing lives with you for years
> I see how I've been losing: all the while
> I've met a different gauge of girl from yours.
> Grant that, and all the rest makes sense as well . . .

As for the different 'sort' of girl known to the loser:

> They have their world, not much compared with yours,
> But where they work, and age, and put off men
> By being unattractive, or too shy,
> Or having morals—anyhow none give in . . .

By now, the reader may be on his way to deciding that this is
the better world of the two, and to wondering if the poet is
trying to get his own back.

The poem might be thought self-pitying if it were more believable. Can *this* ever have been the trouble with Larkin? But then I'll be told that it's not about *him* at all, in that silly sense. Whether it is or not, the poem can be called distinctive— distinctive both of Larkin and of Amis. The mutualities of their friendship have been incorporated in the two worlds in question as they figure in Amis's novel, where unattractiveness is a category as definite as mumps and the unattractive are abso- lutely and permanently unattractive to one another. These two worlds, moreover, are like the two worlds of men and women in Amis. Between men and women, too, there is said to be a barrier. And there are, in fact, several barriers in his writings: that between Jenny and the Reds could be considered another. In all this sharp distinguishing, in all this enemy thing that Amis has, there are elements of anxiety, and of misrepresenta- tion. Many of the actions performed by many women, accord- ing to the misogynists he likes to write about, are performed by many men, and many ugly people would appear to be just as happy, and just as emotionally fulfilled, as many lovely ones. Amis also likes to write, as Larkin liked to write, about the fear of death, and it may be that this fear can be detected in the failure to notice here that both sorts of people are subject to it, as to other unavoidable misfortunes, and that both sorts die.

Amis and Larkin are the same but different. The poem and novel I have attributed to them respectively can also, for certain purposes, be attributed to them both. They are pieces of writing which are distinct in law; the author of the one could not be sued for the other, or for collaborating in it. Nevertheless a togetherness is apparent, of a kind that characterises colluders —or friends—rather than collaborators. It can be said of these strong-minded and independently gifted accomplices that their work shows a dimension of reciprocity and replication, of the production unit, which stands at an appreciable remove from parody and plagiarism, and from the mimicry of other people's voices which is comprehended in the term 'ventriloquism', which Amis goes in for in private, among friends, and which is also a pleasure of the novels he writes. Their work bears witness both to the power of partnership and to the powers of expression which we feel able to attribute to groups, to some circle of friends or literary 'school'—in this case, the group which was at one time drunkenly designated the scholarship boys, angry young men or hypergamists of the Fifties.

I have applied the term 'ventriloquism', in this book, to the fictions of Peter Ackroyd and Kingsley Amis. Elsewhere,[6] Frank Kermode has applied it to the fictions of Evelyn Waugh and Muriel Spark ('no matter what the characters say they all speak in some version of her voice'), while linking it with Bakhtin's distinction, well-known now both in Russia and in the West, between the 'monologic' and the 'dialogic' imagination. The former is ventriloquial; the latter gives 'a carnival sense of the world', and is the more hopeful. True art, or the best art, has a dialogic structure, many voices, and so has the good society. This is an author who has contributed to the Russia which has come after him—to the emergence there, at the present time, of the demand for a lawful Opposition, for the duality of democracy.

The difference yields a political meaning, in other words, and it would also appear to relate to the old theory of the difference between an author who tells and an author who shows, and who employs a medley of voices in order to do so. It is a distinction which may in the end prove more suggestive than serviceable: the author who tells, and who can be accounted something of a ventriloquist, may well, for instance, be more than capable of carnival, and may even be every bit as plural in his works as his dialogic counterpart. But it is possible to believe that the idea of ventriloquism which lies at the heart of it may be successfully applied both to some sorts of contemporary author and to some of what went before. The status of comedy is crucial to the debate, and we can at least be sure that Kingsley Amis would not object to having his practice compared with Waugh's, or to being placed with him among the monologists of the Right.

Against this monologic Amis can be set, by way of alter ego, the modernistic Amis of Barbara Everett's discussion of *Difficulties with girls*, which occurred in the course of an essay on Hugh Kenner's fantasy of a British betrayal of Modernism, and which springs the surprise of conveying that Amis, so often supposed an enemy of Modernism, is really a Modernist.[7] She begins by recalling a remark made to her a long time ago by Larkin, about difficulties encountered in his private life—a remark which consisted of a joke to do with 'the impossibility of relations between men and women', followed by the notion that 'women ought really to marry each other', followed by 'but that would be wrong, wouldn't it?' And she notes that the same remark, or the same sentences, can be found in Amis's novel. What interests her, apparently, is not the remark itself, but 'the degree to which the piece of recall'—her piece of recall, presumably—'failed to affect the novel in any way'. The novel was left 'curiously unaffected' by this discovery. It is as if the discovery could have no meaning for anyone experiencing the novel—which would certainly be curious.

Barbara Everett's subtle and disconcerting essay proceeds to say that '*Difficulties with girls* is much more like *The Waste Land* than Kenner leaves room for guessing it is', in the book by him which she is examining. 'This theoretically realistic and humorous novel is not unlike *The Waste Land*, the showpiece of Modernism and Impersonality'—which gives the impression that the realistic and humorous can only be deemed compatible with impersonality if they can also be deemed theoretical, and that the novel may not be very funny. Soon afterwards, though, she writes: 'I don't want to suggest that *Difficulties with girls* and *The Waste Land* really have much to do with each other.' So the two works are said to be both like one another and unlike. What they have in common is that each escapes 'the limitations of the personal'.

Everett explains:

All knowledge of life and lives, and indeed of history, is a good in itself, and seems likely to inform literary intelligence; and in addition Amis's novels would rather confuse if thought to be the work of an early Tudor writer. Beyond this, the use of biography, its actual ability to throw light (rather than just to be entertaining and nice to have around), seems to be a fantasy.

Kenner's fantasy is being discussed in terms of the view—with which Kenner can be expected to be very familiar—that the goals of a biographically-minded criticism are in some measure fantastic. 'Beyond this', however, leaves indefinite the point at which, or frequency with which, the use of biography deserves to be called by that name. She is saying that this good thing, this knowledge, can be used—to tell us, for example, that Amis is not a Tudor writer: but she is rather more moved to say at the same time that it can't or can hardly be used, devoted as she is to the thought of a separation between, in this case, Amis's friendships and politics, his life—and his art.

His novel is art all right. It has the *sui generis* of art. It has art's power to translate, to abstract from the circumstances in which it originates. There is no biographical key with which it can be unlocked—and I have not been trying to turn one in this essay of mine, which does not believe it, for that matter, to be locked. Nevertheless it is an utterance of the Amis who has made himself known on other occasions, and it can be none the worse for being read by those who are able and disposed to pay intelligent attention to this range of information—which is not to imply that the information may not be disastrously mis-understood. The choice here may in a sense be one between knowing more and knowing less. Should Amis's friendship with Larkin—which goes unstated in Amis's fiction, but which is not absent from it—matter to the reader of that fiction? Why should it not, if there are grounds for thinking that it matters to the fiction? The report that Eliot was eventually to say of *The Waste Land* that 'to me it was only the relief of a personal and wholly insignificant grouse against life' is no more a licence to treat the poem as totally and unreservedly autobiographical than it is a conclusive estimate of its significance. But the report is worth knowing by those who want to know the poem.

Both Amis and Eliot can be considered seasoned disapprovers, and it is probable that Amis shares the other writer's distaste for the biographical critic, whose activities may be responsibly conducted, and are generally acknowledged to have been successful at times, but have often been reckoned to fail. But if this is so, it can be seen to make possible biographical connec-tions of a usable kind. It connects the two writers, and it connects each one of them with their works. The two works of theirs which Barbara Everett compares are neither of them an escape from the spacious confines of the personal. In this respect they are alike, and like all other works of art. But in many respects they are very different, and they come from different times: they are separated from one another by three-quarters of a century. It would take someone who was very much intent on a punishment of biography to think of pointing the way to *Difficulties with girls* by mentioning its proximity to *The Waste Land*.

XI · Polymorphous Roth

AUTHORSHIP can be called, if anything or anyone can, dual, equivocal. The works of authors are replicas, and they are unique. They are and are not autobiographical. An author is and is not his book. In the later years of the Eighties a series of events and episodes has served to direct the attention of British readers to the issue of authorship and its autobiographical character or constituent. I am thinking of the death of Primo Levi, an autobiographer, and by certain standards an amateur; of the threatened death of the novelist Salman Rushdie; and of the discovery of the fascist sympathies formerly exhibited by the literary theorist Paul de Man. And I am also thinking of the identification of Rahila Khan—a novelist supposedly Asian and female—as an Anglican vicar; and of the attempt to thwart a biography by the Englishman Ian Hamilton of the American J. D. Salinger, whose novels tell the story of his life, but who does not want anyone else to do so, preferring to keep his facts to himself. Soon after Hamilton's battle-scarred book came out, moreover, in the spring of 1988, there appeared in Britain a kind of memoir entitled *The Facts: A Novelist's Autobiography* in which the issue was addressed in some passages of exceptional interest—the gaze and forehead of Olympian Zeus after the outcries and the special and professional pleading which had surrounded all but one of these other events. The novelist was Philip Roth, no stranger to outcries himself, whose fictions reveal a multiple self which corresponds to the multiple self of Philip Roth. They can be said to determine and to indetermine, both to record, and to distort and desert, the facts of his life. He has now told the same story 'straight'—or comparatively straight.

'On the pendulum of self-exposure that oscillates between aggressively exhibitionistic Mailerism and sequestered Salinger-ism, I'd say that I occupy a midway position', explains Roth in *The Facts*—in a prefatory letter to his alter ego of earlier books, the novelist Nathan Zuckerman, who is granted a letter of reply at the end of this one and a perusal of the intervening narrative. Roth also explains that he was 'educated to believe that the independent reality of the fiction is all there is of importance and that writers should remain in the shadows'.

As the world knows, Roth grew up in Newark, New Jersey, a second-generation American Jew, and he was to turn into a citizen of the world, a famous cosmopolitan author. In middle age he has experienced a breakdown, an identity crisis, which followed a long illness and an operation. He felt a need to discover who he was, and to write directly about that, and about his books, to step out of the shadows. His first book, the collection of stories entitled *Goodbye, Columbus*, fixed him in the popular mind, from 1959, as an 'enemy of the Jews'—a condition aggravated by the onanistic bravura and scandalous mad success of the grotesquely imaginative *Portnoy's Complaint* (1969), and not much improved in recent years by *The Counterlife* (1987), in which various escapes from Jewish America, including an escape to Israel, are projected, and in which Zuckerman and his dentist brother Henry are both imagined to have ailing hearts and to undertake gruesome surgery in order to restore the sexual potency suspended by their medication. Defenders of the Jewish American pieties and proprieties, and those in Israel for whom the Diaspora Jew is a rootless cosmopolitan, had marked Roth as a bad man, and in their eyes he has yet to turn into a good one.

In the fine and fairly straight title-story of the first collection, a well-to-do Jewish family expels a poor boy to whom they feel they have been 'nice' and who has repaid them by sleeping with their daughter. The poor boy, who resembles Philip Roth, tells the story in which he takes part, and does so in a manner that can be considered uncontroversial. In the fictions that lay ahead, however, the relationship between the author and his characters is subjected to an intense elaboration. It became, in a sense, the story Roth now had to tell. A dance ensues in which he and his characters exchange identities. The poor boy continued to fight with propriety in these fictions. But now there's the possibility of a truce. *The Facts* shows signs of a wish to be 'reconciled with the tribe', and indeed to be a 'nice fellow'. At the same time, though less abrasive, the book is only intermittently less sophisticated than those that preceded it. The 'distrustful fellow' of the past is present, and not just as a commemorative item. A multiple Roth is again in evidence. He knows how important to the power of his writings have been his fight with the Jews and the outrageous candour of his sexual descriptions, and in the recent writings this knowledge is conveyed by the proximity of an imagined truce to an imagined impotence.

Nathan Zuckerman is a persona's persona: Roth begat Peter Tarnopol—who begat Nathan Zuckerman—in the novel of 1974, *My Life as a Man*. Zuckerman has enabled Roth to deal with the question of the offence he has given to righteous Jews, and to come to terms with the rebellious, psychedelic, philo-Semitic Sixties, when Roth's writing went, with the times, derisive and fantastic. The Zuckerman books are a medley of differences and affinities between what we are able to infer about Roth's life and what he has made of it in art. *In propria persona*, Roth discourses in *The Facts* about his relationship with his younger brother, Sandy. The tone is judicious and kind. This is a nice fellow speaking.

Because Sandy was embarked on a marriage and a career pointing him in a more conventional direction than mine, planning the sort of life that looked to me to have more obviously evolved from the background I'd put behind me, it didn't seem to me that he would have had the wherewithal—'morally', as I would have been quick to say then—to help me through my predicament or, if he did, that it was possible for *me* with *my values*, to solicit his assistance. This was hubris, pure and simple . . .[1]

Zuckerman's relationship with his brother Henry is, in contrast, often sanguinary, as gruesome as their respective operations. *Zuckerman Unbound* (1981) reaches its climax at one of Roth's frequent funerals—in this case, that of Zuckerman's father—after which Henry charges Nathan with killing their parent by writing 'that book', the liberated *Carnovsky*, and with believing like the bastard he is that fiction doesn't have consequences. Nathan is a swinger, who is blamed for whoring after and mistreating gentile women. 'Even your shiksas go down the drain when they don't tickle your fancy anymore.' Meanwhile *The Counterlife* attributes to Henry the verdict that 'exploiting and distorting family secrets was my brother's livelihood'.

Philip Roth's contribution to *The Facts* is (as distinct from Nathan Zuckerman's) significantly milder, in relation to family matters, than what we get in these abrasive comic fictions: but then the fictions can be nice too. The conversation in *Zuckerman Unbound* between the novelist and his mother, in which he tenderly instructs her in how to field the intrusions that arise from the *Carnovsky* outrage, reads authentically, auto-biographically, enough, while showing a good Jewish son. The Zuckerman books help one to imagine how Roth has faced the reproach that he has derided his family and sold their secrets. But perhaps it is not too simple to suggest that we are also conscious of Zuckerman as a deflection of the wrath over Roth which works by making Zuckerman responsible for the outrage. We are conscious of what Zuckerman does for Roth: when he helps a man to gather his spilt heart pills, it is Roth helping himself by assigning a small mercy.

In *The Facts*, the tough guy with his shiksas, the supposedly 'self-hating' Diaspora Jew, can be 'tenderised'—a word Roth likes, for all the awkwardness it imparts to the operations to which it refers—into a sort of uxorious submission where his parents are concerned. This is a state which Zuckerman experiences and which he sends up. In the fictional conversation about adverse publicity a good mother meets a son anxious to reassure her, while alive to the comedy of it. 'As long as you know what you're doing', she ventures, adding: 'And as long as you know that it is right.' 'I do' and 'It is', replies Zuckerman. *The Facts* is the more filial book of the two. The facts show a good son, one who is less quick to see the jokes.

Shiksas were to promise an escape from Jewish America, as the promised land of Israel was eventually to be evoked as doing for Henry Zuckerman. *The Facts* is preoccupied with one shiksa in particular: the deadly Josie, whom Roth marries, who forces his hand in the matter by faking an abortion, who comes near to destroying him, and who may have been, according to the Zuckerman letter at the end of the book, an alcoholic. When Josie dies in a car crash Roth feels relief. Her death delivers him from the ordeal of divorce, as frequent as funerals are in his books. He had left her and gone to live with an upper-class woman, had soared to the opposite end of the scale from Josie, whose attraction for him had been that of a splenetic

victim from the lower depths of the goyim: but Josie had refused
a divorce and the ordeal had dragged on. At one stage no less a
person than Bobby Kennedy, soon to accompany Josie to the
grave, had offered to help Roth gain his freedom. In the liberated world of radical chic, we may be intended to think,
favours could be done for the right person.

The Facts says that the 'crack-up' of 1987 had induced 'fiction
fatigue', a need to 'demythologise myself and play it straight'.
Leaving off with the 'imaginative fury' might make it possible
to 'unlock meanings that fictionalising has obscured, distended,
or even inverted'. At the same time, he accepts the 'obvious'
fact that 'facts are never just coming at you but are incorporated
by an imagination that is formed by your previous experience'.
At the end of the book, though, Zuckerman confronts Roth
with the opinion that the latter has made a mistake in trying to
tame or to shed his imagination in the foregoing text, that
fiction is superior to fact, and that the factuality of The Facts is
specious. Roth would appear to believe both the claim and the
counter-claim as to the value of the text, and to believe, too,
both that the Roth part of the book does not represent an
exercise of the imagination and that it does.

It seems reasonable to think that The Facts is imagined, and
that it could promote a benevolent view of the literal or faithful
—as opposed to the fantastically transgressive—imagination,
which may or may not, in any given case, be directly concerned
with the facts of the author's own life. It is a work which might
well shed a tender light on the novella 'Goodbye, Columbus'.
Later in the present book there is a discussion of Roth's regard
for the literalism of Primo Levi, who is at his most imaginative
when least imaginary, who was not all that successful at imagining things in the style commended in the Zuckerman letter:
and in The Facts a related meaning is apparent.

Portnoy's Complaint is a work of the furious imagination
spoken of, and rendered debatable, in The Facts. It is seen in
The Facts to belong to the times in which the writer lived when
he wrote the novel, when opposition to the Vietnam War, and
to a President Johnson perceived as monstrous, took to the
street-wisdom of a farcical obscenity. The Facts is able to treat
the historical conditioning of Portnoy's Complaint in a way in
which the novel itself was not in a position to do. It has the

benefit of hindsight. But it would also appear to know its own place in history in a way which an exercise of the furious imagination in art can sometimes seem to prevent. Different genres, different imaginations. Roth has left off with his mythologising fury—and his memoir lets us know that the benefits that come to the writer who tries, or even seems, to stick to the facts may amount to something more than those of hindsight. It informs us of the 'forces' which shaped Roth's *tours de force* of the Sixties and early Seventies, and it informs us of how he came to be where he is now. He has travelled from the liberated past, when imagination took power, to the liberation of an interest in fact—a state which may or may not prove to have been, for Roth, partial or provisional, and which *The Facts*, in its totality, manages to enclose in an ironised uncertainty. He can look here at times a little like a man who has taken the first steps in a descent from the high ground of self-consciousness, impersonality, fantastication and ironic indirection—not that this has lately been, or has ever been, literature's only ground. But perhaps it will come to be thought by his readers that these successive attitudes to the autobiographical, and to plain speaking, in art are equally valid, equally reversible. This is a view which would accord with the dualistic tradition to which his novels predominantly belong.

The Facts presents, among its various dualities, the reminder that the one and only Philip Roth is like Saul Bellow. Bellow supported Roth's early work, and Roth's work was to bear a resemblance to Bellow's. They are two of a kind, it seems to me, authors of a paranoid comedy of the dualistic imagination, while also different. Roth got to know Bellow in Chicago, where Roth worked as a university teacher, finding it a lively place. It was lively enough to marry Bellow to a 'stylish Radcliffe graduate' of whom Roth had been 'enamoured'—if we are to assume that *The Facts* has not imagined the connection. It is a connection not unlike some of those made in the fiction of both authors.

The memoir sets us asking if Philip Roth knows who he is. He is angry, suspicious, overbearing; he can be very like the Zuckerman berated in the fiction as 'this unsatisfiable, suspect, quarrelsome novelist'. And yet he is nice. He is tough and he is tender, wrathful and ruthful. This mixed condition he shares with many others, not all of them writers; it is a condition we are entitled to call traditional. And it is a condition which can be recognised in the reception of his work. There are readers whom, as Zuckerman is the first (or second) to acknowledge, he can drive to the complaint that he has sex, and family matters, and Jewish matters, on the brain: 'I want him to take his manuscript and mail it to his mother', as I have heard them cry. There are times when his world can appear to consist of Jews and of those to whom a Jew might wish to escape—such as America's well-heeled Wasps, or the semi-imaginary anti-Semites of Gloucestershire who figure affluently in *The Counterlife*. But he is also a writer of remarkable ability who has managed to capture and to keep the readership he has bewildered and delighted and offended, and whose work is strong in an intelligent and generous-hearted awareness of public matters, some of them quite remote from the Family Roth: *The Counterlife*, for instance, carries a telling serio-comic critique of the hard line in Israel, the Israeli toughness, that refuses to 'give ground'. In *The Facts* he examines his own vexed state with reference to the vexed question of whether it is better to make things up, and to distort them, and by contemplating his earlier re-invention of the time-honoured dualistic account of literature and human nature. His shiksas and replicas, hostilities and escapes, have taken part in a great game of long duration, and he can be said to be reviewing the state of play. Escape, he thinks, is Jewish. He knows that it is also dualistic.

The dualistic ambience in literature has long been influential, but has remained controversial, and it is both influential and controversial in these annals of the House of Roth. Zuckerman's proposal of marriage to Maria in *The Counterlife* is an indication of its importance, and of the importance of escape both for the tradition and for the unsatisfiable Roth. 'Because I've decided to give up the artificial fiction of being myself for the genuine, satisfying falseness of being somebody else. *Marry me.*' Here, it is as if both the single and the plural accounts of human nature were specious. In general, though, he has been faithful, in most of what he has written, to a version of the mobile and multiple, mysterious and fugitive self.

At the end of *The Counterlife* there is a letter from Nathan Zuckerman to Maria on this subject which has the force of a statement of allegiance on the part of Philip Roth.[2] The reader knows that it is Zuckerman's statement too, that it is fiction, and is likely to remind himself that it could well belong to the infinite regress of the dualistic indeterminable, where claim and counter-claim alternate indefinitely. There can be no claim that this is what Roth really thinks: the affidavit that might have been contained in *The Facts* has been withheld. It may be that he really thinks there is nothing that he really thinks. But if Roth dissents from the statement, then imagining how he came to write most of his books becomes a problem. Zuckerman tells his Maria:

Being Zuckerman is one long performance and the very opposite of what is thought of as *being oneself*. In fact, those who most seem to be themselves appear to me people impersonating what they think they might like to be, believe they ought to be, or wish to be taken to be by whoever is setting standards. So in earnest are they that they don't even recognise that being in earnest *is the act*. For certain self-aware people, however, this is not possible: to imagine themselves being themselves, living their own real, authentic, or genuine life, has for them all the aspects of a hallucination.

I realise that what I am describing, people divided in themselves, is said to characterise mental illness, and is the absolute opposite of our idea of emotional integration. The whole Western idea of mental health runs in precisely the opposite direction: what is desirable is congruity between your self-consciousness and your natural being.

Zuckerman is seeking to deny the traditional connection between illness and psychic division which is reaffirmed in the novel as a whole, and which is also reaffirmed in *The Facts*, and at the same time to deny that there is a traditional belief in division or multiplicity, a long-standing sense of selfhood as a chimera. He goes on to say to Maria that

it's *all* impersonation—in the absence of a self, one impersonates selves, and after a while impersonates best the self that best gets one through. If you were to tell me that there are people, like the man upstairs to whom you now threaten to turn yourself in, who actually do have *a strong sense of themselves*, I would have to tell you that they are only impersonating people with a strong sense of themselves—to which you could correctly reply that since there is no way of proving whether I'm right or not, this is a circular argument from which there is no escape.

All I can tell you with certainty is that I, for one, have no self, and that I am unwilling or unable to perpetrate upon myself the joke of a self.

The man upstairs, the first husband whom Maria is to leave, is not 'self-aware'—unlike Zuckerman, who declares, on be-half of the self-aware, that he has no self and that the self is a joke. But Roth must know that it is likely to be no joke to those who are reading his book. Zuckerman says here that perform-ance is all there is, that person and persona are one. But we may feel on reading this that it takes two to perform—that performance requires, in however regressive or circular a fashion, the self that so many people believe they have, and that this epistolary Zuckerman exhibits here, in a display of inadvertence which may or may not implicate Philip Roth. This is a self which there may be 'no way of proving'. It is a self which is proving, for philosophers, hard to prove. But it is a self which readers of the book can only rarely have found it hard to experience. The novelist referred to himself once as 'amorphous Roth'.[3] 'Polymorphous Roth' might be nearer the mark. I think that many of his readers would be prepared to bear witness to the sense that somewhere in there among the changing shapes is the usual nonpareil.

In the ambience and tradition to which I am referring per-sonality is defined in terms of breadth and contrast; the effect is at once stereophonically-internal—a number of speakers has been installed, so to speak—and invasive. There is more than one Roth. And in what Roth writes Roth and Bellow meet. But neither of them is incapable of pursuing the artificial fiction of being himself. No one would lightly believe that either of them has ever found it hard to tell the difference between himself and somebody else. Dualistic explanations are moving, and in-triguing: but they are often thought, even by proponents, to be far-fetched, fictional, theoretical, counter-intuitive. That Bellow, this participant in Roth's inner life, can also be said to be out there in the world as his friend, and perhaps his rival, is a fact which does not help one to decide whether or not to trust the reports of literary duality—what comes in has to have been out—but it is very much in the tradition. The tradition gives many convincing pictures of the inwardness and invasiveness of friends and rivals. Brothers may be rivals, and they may be internalised. Roth's fiction internalises the brother identified in *The Facts*. In *The Counterlife* Henry, the 'distrustful fellow' who distrusts his distrustful brother's 'wallowing heroes', is at one with the creator of those heroes, and with the heroes, and with the creator's creator. Nathan enters Henry and Henry enters Nathan. Maria bursts into italics (and out of character) to say to Nathan: '*You are your brother!*' And Nathan says to Henry: 'We are all each other's authors.' A universal fellowship obtains.

The definition of personality which is harboured in such procedures has moved and influenced several generations of writers. The art that comes of them is one in which imagination takes power, the power to distort and exaggerate, in which difference of person is suspended, in which the experience of time is as it is in dreams. The story that is told is a story which never ends—and which risks losing shape and momentum—because it is a story told of himself by a living author, an author who has yet to end, whose isolate's imaginative fury lives on to tell another tale, some more of his own story. This fury can look like an onanistic or a solipsistic fury. Mail *that* to your mother!

It goes without saying that the definition has been responsible for a major literature. But about many of its manifestations there can be something ominous—something that is acutely understood and eloquently exposed in *The Counterlife*. This is a generic something: I am speaking here of a literary practice long and widely and variously undertaken, in relation to which Roth is both critic and executant. But it should also be said that some elements of this description of mine could be taken to characterise the activity, sometimes ominous enough in its human implications, of all imaginative writers, however remote they may be from the dualistic confederacy. The caveats expressed in *The Counterlife* apply to all occasions when, in whatever genre or style, autobiography imposes itself upon, overwrites, the world.

By Roth, as by his predecessors in the dualistic art, this definition has been correlated with breakdown, madness, though, as we have seen, Zuckerman seeks to exert a counter-claim in his letter to Maria. And it has evolved in contrast with character—that other, earlier product of the literary imagination—and with purpose and achievement. There are times when it might seem that this is a definition which can produce the sense of a self which is both amorphous and autonomous, of a doubtful self which also serves to cast doubt on the human world that lies beyond the subjective individual—a world which some writers are, and some are not, very cunning in, and which is inhabited by people with a working knowledge of who they are and what they are doing. This is a knowledge which has been impugned in literature, and which has deteriorated there. The books I am speaking of are, among others, books which pursue the idea of an escape from personality and from society, and in which personality and society are seen—as in Zuckerman's letter to Maria—to be aspects of a single threat. Roth's turn towards fact—admittedly, an imagined and far from indisputable fact—will appear to some to signal a turn towards the self and towards the outside world. Such a reading could well be found to have attributed too much to a recoil, a respite, a provisional position. He is unlikely to have lost his distrust of the self; and he is likely (and welcome) to resume his furious fictions. But when he does resume them, when the time comes for him to make his next leap, the suggestions made in the course of this affair of his fiction fatigue and literal turn—suggestions which receive both rebuttal and support from within the shape-changing dialectic represented by *The Counterlife*—will not deserve to be forgotten.

XII · Levi's Oyster

THE Italian writer Primo Levi died on 11 April 1987, to the dismay of his readers. There was a time when it must have seemed to many of them that he would never receive a bad review, or even a cross word. His first book, *If this is a man*, about his months in Auschwitz, and its sequel, *The Truce*, were hard to fault, and the successive publications of his middle age have been greeted by an admiration responsive both to his skills as a writer and to his character as a man.[1] In October 1985, however, the chauvinistic American-Jewish magazine *Commentary* did succeed in performing the outlandish act of disparaging Levi and his books. 'Alas', wrote Fernanda Eberstadt, a German-American, the later ones are inferior to the first two, and alas, the personal character imparted by his writings—freely imparted, one might add, and yet not unreservedly—is flawed. 'Reading Primo Levi' is in some respects a strong essay. The later books are in large measure accurately described, and the experience of the assimilated Jew in Italy, where the Jews came to harm under Mussolini but where they were never the strangers they have been in several other countries, is summarised in a well-informed and pertinent fashion. At the same time, the article is tainted by what seems to be a desire to inflict damage on Levi's reputation, of a kind which may be thought to serve the ideological tendency of the magazine in which it appeared.

So what is wrong with Levi and his Levi-like writings? It is made to seem that he was a stranger, a gentleman, a 'watcher from the sidelines'. He was 'cursed with a tin ear for religion'. He could not get on with the believing Jews from Eastern Europe whose religion and traditions he neither shared nor understood. As a result, there are 'no Jews as such' in his Auschwitz book. But many Jews are not believers, and are still, for most people, including themselves, palpably Jewish. He also had, the article conveys, a tin ear for the ordinary man. He is like the poet Ausonius, alas—that Silver Age abstainer from the world and connoisseur of oysters.

Literary criticism is doing here what it often does: it has gone for the faults and, in so doing, inverted the truth. When is a Jew not a Jew? When he does not accept the religion revealed in the Old Testament. The Primo Levi who is read by Fernanda Eberstadt is a man who is unable to write about Jews—though he does in fact write about them with great sympathy, believers and unbelievers alike—and who has no feeling for people whose background and abilities are different from his own, though the joy of Levi's work, for other readers, is very often that he *has* such feelings, that he knows himself to be, while also knowing himself not to be, an ordinary man, a worker, a man who worked as an industrial chemist and who was no less of a worker when he wrote books. The Levi who emerged from a regime of cruelty and humiliation with his judgement intact, his mind not closed, neither vengeful nor forgetful, and who wrote a noble and rational book about what had happened to him, is mentioned only cursorily and as if concessively by Fernanda Eberstadt.

It is not the case that all her objections are mistaken. But their accumulation is very far from the complicated truth. The article leads you to wonder about her religious faith, if she has one, and about where it stands in relation to the outlook of the editor of *Commentary*, author of a book about his ambitions for worldly success: *Making it* must be the least pious book that has ever been written.

The stress on Levi's insensitivity to religion is allowed to suggest that all Jews are religious, and there are readers for whom this might signal the corollary that all Jews are Zionists, and are likely to be supporters of Israeli government policy. By these standards, Levi would appear to be an imperfect Jew, and this could well be an opinion that underlies the talk about his later books being not nearly as good as his earlier ones. Here is an assimilated Jew, a Diaspora Jew, unsound on Zion. Among the principal references to Israel in Levi's writings is one which is, from a Zionist point of view, tin-eared. The reference occurs in *The Drowned and the Saved*, of which a translation was published in 1988, on the anniversary of his death. In this collection of pieces which revert to themes pursued in *If this is a man* Levi writes: 'Desperate, the Jewish survivors, in flight from Europe after the great shipwreck, have created in the bosom of the Arab world an island of Western civilisation, a portentous palingenesis of Judaism, and the pretext for renewed hatred.' There are those for whom it is not Jewish to speak in this way about Israel.

It is odd to speak of the creation of a state as the 'pretext' for anything: the translator may possibly be responsible for the oddity here, as for the orotundity that precedes it. But the passage certainly suggests that there was a distance between Levi's view of Israel and the views that *Commentary* chooses to publish. The second sentence of the issue of May 1988 refers to the first twenty years of the state: 'Threatening to "push the Jews into the sea", the Arab world reformulated the Nazi theory of *Lebensraum* in Mediterranean terms: there was no room in the region for a Jewish homeland.' Arabs who had been expelled from their land and thrust into the condition of Jewish refugees are hereby reformulated as imperialist aggressors and as Nazis. This is reminiscent of the sort of inversion a fault-finding literary criticism can produce—which is not to deny, which is indeed to admit, that the Arab leaders and polemicists of the region have had their faults, including some of those which have been identified over the years by *Commentary*. The magazine's line on such matters would also appear to be remote from, and distinctly harder than, that taken in its dying days by the Reagan Administration. George Shultz travelled to the Middle East in the summer of 1988 to spread the word that 'the continued occupation of the West Bank and Gaza and the frustration of Palestinian rights is a dead-end street. The belief that this can continue is an illusion.' It is a measure of the grim recalcitrance of the region's problems that Shultz's message was reported to have been saluted by a strike called in protest among the Palestinians of the occupied territories.

Meanwhile Fernanda Eberstadt has been practising as an expert on captivity and escape, and on the beliefs established for later generations by the children of Israel. She has written in the same magazine (June 1987) on the Book of Exodus, warning that a reading of the Bible as literature, rather than as sacred text, 'cannot lift heavenward'. In the article on his work which appeared in 1985 Levi is at one point examined with reference to Leviticus. She takes exception to a story of his about a Jewish Communist, an inhabitant of the camps, who fasts there on Yom Kippur. She observes that the prisoner is following a prohibition laid down in the Old Testament, but that a rabbinical ruling had allowed Jews to eat in the camps on Yom Kippur in order to stay alive. It is not clear why this is a reproach to Levi, whose story concerns a man whose piety is idiosyncratic, especially severe.

Two years after this, in February 1987, she praised a Gulag memoir by Gustav Herling. *A World Apart* is a 'truly golden' work, despite the presence in it, apparently, of a foul anti-Semitism. Herling is thought to resemble Dostoevsky, whose prototypical prison book, *The House of the Dead*, has in it a mansion tenanted by obnoxious, caricatured Jews. *A World Apart* is, 'despite' its author's socialism, a 'deeply religious book', in which she has at times the sense of 'a man talking to God'. She displays more sympathy for this anti-Semitic Moses, for this religious man who is against Jews and against the Soviet system, than she does for Jews who are not religious. Whether or not she has talked to God, she has certainly been reviewing for him.

Levi, the expert on metals, would have had no difficulty in telling the difference between gold and tin. I have heard that he was saddened by these writings of Fernanda Eberstadt's, in which his own writings are faulted. Two months after the Herling piece was published Levi committed suicide, throwing himself down the staircase of the house in Turin where he was born and grew up, where he wrote about his life in the camp at a desk which stood where his cradle had stood, a house he shared with his wife and mother. He was 68 years old. I don't suggest that these unfavourable writings pushed him to do what he did, though I don't mind suggesting that the bigotry and vicarious piety they may be reckoned to contain could be classed among the negative experiences of the last months of his life. I have in fact no explanation to offer as to how he came to die, and it may be that no trustworthy explanation will ever be achieved.

Levi was an author who, without detriment to the other people who figure in his books, wrote all the time about himself, both in autobiographical and in fictional form. The modes which he adopted were such as to license elisions and lacunae, to enable him to leave out bits of his life—a procedure which would seem to be connected with his scepticism about what can be known about people by biographers. In *Moments of Reprieve* he remarks: 'What the "true" image of each of us may be in the end is a meaningless question.' In *The Periodic Table* he mentions a woman 'dear to my heart' who was murdered at Auschwitz: but the book on Auschwitz does not discuss his relationship with her. In *The Wrench* he creates the rigger Faussone, the practical man whose cranes girdle the world and who keeps returning, a little heavy-footed, to the house in Turin where two old aunts fuss over his welfare: Faussone was spoken of as 'my alter ego', and the book has to struggle to accommodate him as a second person, available for interview by Levi. These omissions and transpositions indicate that Levi could well have kept to himself any plan he may have formed to end his life. During the meeting with him a few months before his death which was recorded in an article published in the *London Review*,[2] Philip Roth found him as keen as mustard: here was someone who listened, with the intent stillness of a chipmunk. Levi had a high opinion of the grain of mustard, and of salt. Fascism did not like these substances. He associated the grain of mustard with his own activities, with Roth's, with Jews generally, with the awkwardness and tartness and wholesomeness of idiosyncrasy and dissent. It was, or could be called, an impurity. It was the taste of the stranger—who might at the same time be rooted, as he himself was, in some national life.

Back in Italy, after his departure from Auschwitz and his wanderings through Europe, he found that 'the things I had seen and suffered were burning inside of me', and that he wanted to write about them. These words of his, in *The Periodic Table*, refer to some words of the past. 'I felt like Coleridge's Ancient Mariner, who waylays on the street the wedding guests going to the feast, inflicting on them the story of his misfortune.' He began work as a chemist in a paint factory. Then came the meeting with the woman whom he was to marry, a meeting about which he writes in the same book.

In a few hours I felt reborn and replete with new powers, washed clean and cured of a long sickness, finally ready to enter life with joy and vigour; equally cured was suddenly the world around me, and exorcised the name and face of the woman who had gone down into the lower depths with me and had not returned. My very writing became a different adventure, no longer the dolorous itinerary of a convalescent, no longer a begging for compassion and friendly faces, but a lucid building, which now was no longer solitary: the work of a chemist who weighs and divides, measures and judges on the basis of assured proofs, and strives to answer questions.[3]

These remarks concerning *If this is a man* do not describe the kind of book which runs easily to sequels, and which is easy to live up to. Nor do they describe the sort of thing we are supposed to like very much. The first two autobiographies, that is to say, are the kind of book to which a tradition of literary interpretation has been inimical, imagining for itself a literature of impersonality, in which autobiography is subsumed, invisible.

Philip Roth's article refers to this issue in referring to the later book *If not now, when?*—Levi's 'Eastern', an adventure story of Jewish partisans during the closing months of the war, led by the Communist fighter-fiddler Gedaleh. 'With his left hand he snatched the gun from the Pole's hands, and with his right he gave him a violent blow to the ear.' Roth says to Levi in the course of the interview embodied in his article: 'Your other books are perhaps less "imaginary" as to subject-matter but strike me as more imaginative in technique. The motive behind *If not now, when?* seems more narrowly tendentious— and consequently less liberating to the writer—than the impulse that generates the autobiographical works.' Levi explains that he had amused himself by writing a 'Western' and that he had wanted to write a hopeful book.

I wished to assault a commonplace still prevailing in Italy: a Jew is a mild person, a scholar (religious or profane), unwarlike, humiliated, who tolerated centuries of persecution without ever fighting back. It seemed to me a duty to pay homage to those Jews who, in desperate conditions, had found the courage and the skill to resist.

I cherished the ambition to be the first (perhaps the only) Italian writer to describe the Yiddish world. I intended to 'exploit' my popularity in my country in order to impose upon my readers a book centred on the Ashkenazi civilisation, history, language and frame of mind, all of which are virtually unknown in Italy, except by some sophisticated readers of Joseph Roth, Bellow, Singer, Malamud, Potok, and of course yourself.

Levi's explained intention does not mean that there is no autobiography in the book. The wish to evoke a Jewish resistance to Nazism relates to a history which comprehends his own writings and example. And in the portrayal of the mechanic Mendel there is a portrayal of Levi. Philip Roth is right, however, to point to the limitations of the book, and to point to a law of Levi's work in general: the less imaginary it is, the more imaginative—the more literal the better.

Let us praise, more than we do, and as we can here, the literal writer. But there is no doing so unless we accept that the literal writer has an imagination. Levi can sometimes appear incapable of fiction, but it is no less apparent that everything he wrote was fiction. He was well-aware of the sense in which he made up what happened to him, imagined his misfortune. In calling his recent book about his own early life by the name of *The Facts*, Philip Roth is issuing a challenge—expecting his readers to know that there are no bare facts, and obliging them to think hard about what happens in the recounting of the facts of a life. Levi would have understood that challenge, just as I think he would have been happy to agree that it is possible to speak without contradiction of the literal imagination.

Levi's words to Roth about the adventure story *If not now, when?* bring to mind the art of the Russian Jewish writer Isaac Babel, who rode with Budyonny's Red Cavalry after the Revolution, through scenes of hardship and atrocity. Babel's art is imaginative, figurative. It has been said, by Dan Jacobson, that he 'aestheticises' his response to violence. This tendency has no counterpart in Levi, and it may be doubtful whether it could live with the subject-matter of the camps. Babel's bad times could be turned into art—an art which has been seen to release him, as it were, from his subject, and which has also been seen to hesitate. He felt imprisoned by his religious upbringing in Odessa, and was to remember 'the rotted Talmuds of my childhood'. And he was drawn to the grace and violence to be found among his Cossacks. But he was also drawn to the Jews whom he met in their Polish villages, victims of persecution and war, 'old Jews with prophets' beards and passionate rags', to their ruined ghettoes and synagogues. To such scenes his narrator is introduced by the shopkeeper Gedali, believer in a peaceful Revolution. Levi's Gedaleh and Babel's Gedali are opposing faces of the Central European Jew in times of crisis.

Action, power, are thought to be contrasted, in Babel's stories, with learning, devotion, resignation, suffering—those Jewish things. His ambivalence is a bespectacled look at the long legs of the divisional commander, which were 'like girls sheathed to the neck in shining riding-boots'. The image—summoned by a narrator whose exhausted dreams are filled with girls—is like nothing we would ever meet in the literal Levi. But the literal Levi is a writer who has his own way of interesting himself in the contrasts which have been attributed to Babel. Levi was interested in action, purpose, work, and capable of them: and the capacity may have been formed in contention with a desire to withdraw and perhaps to give up. I think myself that this was the case, and that it scarcely makes him very different from many other hard-working people. The desire can be surmised, without recourse to hindsight, in some of what he wrote, but is far from being the point of what he wrote.

Work is the supreme subject in Levi. 'We can and must fight to see that the fruit of labour remains in the hands of those who work, and that work does not turn into punishment.' 'Perhaps the most accessible form of freedom, the most subjectively enjoyed, and the most useful to human society, consists of being good at your job . . .'. These statements are from *The Wrench*, where Faussone is good at his job and Levi is good at getting this across. There can be no doubt that he had an ear for what such people have to say for themselves. Faussone talks about 'the way we bent our elbows'—an expression (for eating or drinking) which I have heard spoken in English, but which I had never before seen written down in a book. Book-writers, Faussone says, produce works 'which may be beautiful and all that, but, on the other hand, even if they were a bit defective, excuse the expression, nobody would die, and the only loser is the customer who bought them'. I have heard that before too, but not from any writer. A builder friend of mine once talked to me about mistakes made by builders. These mistakes mattered —whereas 'in the arts it doesn't matter if you foul up.'

Levi's double life as chemist and writer suggests that if art and work need to be separated, according to a certain sense of what it is to be a Jew, art and work are nevertheless very often the same. I like to think that he would have accepted that art is work, that the work that frees us, and is not just 'punishment', is art, and that anyone who uses his imagination is an artist. The categorical difference of the modern world, between artists and others, does not come well out of his reports.

His chemistry is intriguing from this point of view. Here was a second double life—that of a scientist who was also an artist, a chemist who was also an alchemist, a businessman who was also a magician. He was as keen as mustard, and as Doctor Faustus. *The Periodic Table* reveals that the ancient magic of transmutation and alembics persisted in Levi's laboratory. The book has fumes, stinks, bangs and fiascos. There is more than a hint of the search for the philosopher's stone. It takes its structure from a set of correspondences between elements and persons, and the old definition of temperament as a mixture of qualities is present to the reader's mind—the same definition that permits us to think of Faussone as a part of Levi, or as his alter ego. Levi's paints actually manage to come to life as human beings in *The Wrench*, a less fanciful book which nevertheless claims that 'paints resemble us more than they do bricks. They're born, they grow old, and they die like us; and when they're old, they can turn foolish, and even when they're young, they can deceive you, and they're actually capable of telling lies, pretending to be what they aren't: to be sick when they're healthy, and healthy when they're sick.'

The work that Levi valued is of an order to which Auschwitz —with the lying motto over its gates, *Arbeit macht frei*—was built to be antithetical. In the camps, work was imposed on the prisoners with the aim of exploiting and of destroying them. It bore a hideous resemblance to the blighting, punishing sorts of work which are common in the world at large. And yet there was a work of survival to be attempted in the camps. Intelligence, vigilance, practicality, cunning, luck, friendship—Levi was crucially helped by donations from an Italian workman he barely knew, and by the exercise of his skills as a chemist—kept you going and, in some few cases, made you free. But most of those who stayed alive were 'prominents', or Kapos, prisoners

who were placed in authority, or members of the Special
Squads who assisted with the killings.

One of the late pieces in *The Drowned and the Saved* casts doubt
on this work of survival: 'the worst survived', he writes. In 1946,
a 'religious friend' told him that he, Levi, belonged to an elect:
'I, the non-believer, and even less of a believer after the season
of Auschwitz, was a person touched by Grace, a saved man.'
The friend felt Levi had survived 'so that I could bear witness'.
Levi goes on to insist that the real witnesses are those who died
in the camps, and that those prisoners who did not were mostly
compromised people or privileged people: Solzhenitsyn is cited
as making the same point about the *pridurki*—the 'prominents'
of the Gulag system.

The book is no sequel to *If this is a man*, but its explications
are never without interest. 'In the Lager, colds and influenza
were unknown, but one died, at times suddenly, from illnesses
that the doctors never had an opportunity to study. Gastric
ulcers and mental illnesses were healed (or became asympto-
matic) but everyone suffered from an unceasing discomfort that
polluted sleep and was nameless.' There is a chapter which discusses the letters from Germans—'good Germans' in the main
—which were sent to him in response to his book about the
camps. An eager public woman appealed to him with the story
of her cleaning woman, who had proved herself at fault. The
husband of the cleaning woman had been a soldier, and she
had said that he had had no choice but to obey his orders to
shoot Jews. The correspondent explained: 'I discharged her,
stifling the temptation to congratulate her on her poor husband
fallen in the war.' There is a 'Middle Eastern' recalcitrance
here.

Another chapter, on the Kapos and the Special Squads, exhibits what must surely be judged an analytic understanding of
the concentration-camp system set up by the Nazis—an understanding Eberstadt is inclined to deny him, believing that the
camps are insufficiently construed in the Auschwitz book as an
institutionalised anti-Semitism peculiar to Germany and polit-
ically-determined: she thinks it is soft of him to see them as
belonging to a universal latent hostility to strangers. The chapter exposes a factor of complicity, and regards it, one might
think, as a German invention. The Special Squads were the

Nazis' 'most demonic crime', representing 'an attempt to shift on to others—specifically the victims—the burden of guilt, so that they were deprived even of the solace of innocence'.

He never forgave the Nazis; they were always his enemies. This was not, however, 'personal'. He is among the least ego-bound of book-writers, the least ego-bound of autobiographers, at all times able to look beyond himself and his community. Two occasions in the book about his partisans quietly illustrate what he is for his readers in this respect. In the partisan book Line has been Leonid's woman, and has gone with Mendel. By then a 'desperate man', Leonid is sent as such on a desperate mission, and is killed. Who can be said to have killed him? Mendel tells Line: 'The two of us.' Not long afterwards, his attention fixed on the sufferings of those Poles who had caused their Jews to suffer, Mendel falls silent, thinking: 'Not only us.' For Fernanda Eberstadt, Mendel is 'a worrier afflicted with an ability to see his enemy's side of the question'. Those she doesn't like are 'cursed' or 'afflicted'. There's religion in that.

Levi's statement to Philip Roth about *If not now, when?* did not mention Babel, but it did mention another Isaac—the Yiddish writer, Bashevis Singer. There is a story of Singer's—one of a collection, *The Death of Methuselah*, published in Britain in the autumn of 1988—in which Levi, or a part or perception of Levi, is perhaps faintly distinguishable. 'The Jew from Babylon' is an enthralling tale about a Jewish sorcerer, a believer in the faith, hated by demons and disapproved of by rabbis, who in old age endures a turmoil which ends his life. Singer is a writer of standing in the matter of when, in what he sees as the 'disappointing' modern world, a Jew is not a Jew. Modern Jews, he affirms, are greedy creatures, tormented by their too many opinions. It could well be asked if his is an Orthodox fiction. Is it that of a vicarious believer, if such a person is possible? Is he an aesthete of the subject? Everything he writes is Jewish in the sense that everything he writes is conscious of the Jewish faith, if that can be said without relinquishing the thought that there are such persons as unbelieving Jews. But there is some instability in the accounts he gives of dark professions of faith, in his acerbities and fatalities. In one of the new stories a 'recluse', formerly a womaniser, says: 'One step away from God and one is already in the dominion of Satan and hell. You don't believe me, eh?' Do we believe him? Is this some Jewish joke? Singer can, after all, be very funny.

His religion is as much as anything the regression to a past of obedience, disobedience, sin and doom. Such things are celebrated in his stories with a richness and unction which might appear to make a renegade of Babel and certainly of Levi. Singer's religion is also a feeling for the power of the community to censure and reject. This power is apparent in the story of his sorcerer. It is a story in which the case of Primo Levi, that of a dissident, gifted, magical, mustardly Jew, might at moments be thought to be implicated. But then so might that of the writer of the story, who may be less obedient than the gentile reader immediately recognises. The story celebrates both the sorcerer and his rejection. We mourn his fall. 'In the morning they found him dead, face down on a bare spot, not far from the town. His head was buried in the sand, hands and feet spread out, as if he had fallen from a great height.'

XIII · Glasgow Hamlet

STUDYING the West Coast of Scotland from the yacht *Britannia*, the Queen is said to have remarked, not long ago, that the people there didn't seem to have much of a life. James Kelman's stories make clear what life is like in Glasgow, and what James Kelman's life is like. They are not going to change the royal mind. This is the queen who was greeted, on a visit to a Scottish university, by the sight of a student emptying down his throat, at top speed, the contents of a bottle of alcohol.

One of Kelman's stories, 'Greyhound for Breakfast', the last in the collection of that name which appeared in 1987, is, to my mind, a masterpiece. It's about a fellow called Ronnie, who is on the dole. His son has gone off to London, and he worries that he may lose touch with him. He has dumped down the notes for a greyhound, has given his heart to the beast, and is derided for this by his friends in the pub. He takes it for a walk —such walks have long been a ritual activity of the country's more optimistic male poor, the dog more expensively jacketed than the chap. 'It stopped for a piss. Ronnie could have done with one himself but he would have got arrested.' Its withers will never win any of the races Ronnie had been telling himself about, and he is reluctant to return from this long, defeated, dark-thoughted walk to break the bad news of his adventure to his wife and daughters. The story is wonderfully funny and depressing.

Ronnie, I think, could be held to be a precursor of P for Patrick Doyle in Kelman's novel of 1989, *A Disaffection*. Both works end on a possible return, on what might look like a bleak diminuendo but is really an anxiety state. There are important differences, though. Kelman stands much closer to the new hero, and more is made of what happens in that hero's head. The new book is funny and depressing at considerable length, and there are moments when a wee terror comes of its expanded universe. *A Disaffection* is a problematical book—because of this closeness: we learn very little about how Doyle is seen by companions, very little about the standpoint of those who surround him, those with whom he has his tender and abrasive dealings, with whom he airs his invectives and bitter ironies, with whom he conducts his antagonisms and ingratiations. It's almost all Doyle. If this is a problem, however, it is one the novel shares with many of the novels we now read. We are aware, in the novels we read, both of an authorial identification with the leading character or the first-person narrator, and of material that might constitute an authorial judgement in that respect: but we don't know what the verdict is. *A Disaffection* shares in that uncertainty, and in so doing acknowledges a connection with a certain whether-or-not that we meet with in the plays of Shakespeare.

Doyle—'Patrick' to his author—is of the fantastic-depressive, angry-and-otherwise Scots-Irish clan. He is a schoolteacher, 29 years old—the age of Christ at Calvary, whose name is often in his mouth, averse though he is to 'deities', and perhaps of Hamlet, whose words enter the novel. This Glasgow Hamlet is the latest in a long line of impersonations, and his soliloquies *are* the novel he inhabits, or most of it. Doyle's greyhound is a pair of electricians' pipes, which he lights upon, paints and plays, producing a doleful sound that soothes him—it is like mumbling your mantra or telling your beads. He needs soothing. He has passed into crisis. He is lonely. His aged parents bore him ('Are all parents boring?'). His brother Gavin frets him, and he has a longing for Gavin's wife, together with a more urgent one for a teacher at the school, Alison Houston, who could be felt to lead him on a bit but doesn't want to have a 'relationship' with him. With Doyle it's 'fucking' this and 'fucking' that and the system this and the system that. He is against 'Greatbritain', with its aristocratic capitalists, its MI5 and its MI6. Society is a stench. Shite is everywhere. Crassness is everywhere. He is a schlemiel of the subject.

In such a setting, he believes, his work as a teacher can only be betrayed. His work as a teacher doesn't involve much in the way of teaching. Homework is a thing of the past. His classes are soliloquies and Socratic teases in which his interest in Classical Antiquity, in Pythagoras and Heraclitus, and in Hölderlin, Hegel and Marx, and in James Hogg, is imparted to the young ones. He is the sort of Sixties dominie who used to inveigh in class against the system. His relationship with the kids is one between equals, but they also seem to expect him to be a wise man, and this is what he sometimes expects of himself. The kids are presented as decent and thoughtful, and there's an Arcadian absence of the stress and violence which some might look for in a class where the teacher swears and free-associates, and throws up and bunks off into the bargain. If the Queen's telescope had been able to reach into Patrick's classroom, there would have been a surprise in store for her—but not for Patrick, who at least affects to believe the story that Orwellian minders are peering at the punters from the screens of the punters' television sets.

Kelman makes Doyle charming, and it is impossible to read the book without gaining the sense of a fully-developed authorial fellow-feeling. Not that Doyle isn't taxing and maddening too. His consciousness delivers paranoid images of aggression and hostility. He is against racism and sexism, but is capable of reflecting: 'He was in love with Alison Houston. And he wanted to grab a hold of her.' His crisis is precipitated by word of his transfer to another school; he staggers towards resigning from the school he's at, and maybe from the profession, and then bunks off for a long afternoon's superlager, home-brew and whisky with his brother, who is on the dole, and two of his brother's mates. Eventually, stone-cold-sober-seeming but perhaps too drunk to drive, he treks off through the dubs of a drizzle (Thales said the world was made of water, the 'primary element', and he handni even been to Glasgow) back to his bachelor's tenement flat (Coelebs still in search of a wife). On the way, he is chased, or fancies he is chased, by Police who hate him. Kelman projects Doyle's state of mind virtually without framing or critique. The Queen will certainly need a glossary, but even then she may well be uncertain as to just how much Kelman likes his unlikely lad.

This kind of thing has been said about Hamlet, to whom, as I say, Kelman alludes, and more than alludes. At one point, 'all he sought was death'; and the next paragraph has him aching to be 'out of the road of trouble and strife and all things rotten and putrefied and shitey'. Later he reproves himself for an impulse to be rude to a 'good auld guy' encountered during his terminal search for a bus, and we think of the prating 'good old man' Polonius. And on the facing page he breathes some more of Shakespeare's words: 'To return to Gavin's or not.

Whether it is nobler.' Whether he is sober enough to go back
and fetch his dilapidated car, or should soldier on, is the question here, or at any rate part of it. Hamlet kills his good old
guy, as it happens. He makes mistakes and causes havoc, in
pursuit of the right course. So does Doyle.

A high point in the novel[1] is the altercation and huff with
Gavin and his mates which precedes this: about the long holidays teachers get, or don't get, about the homework they with-
hold, and about the rights of weans—children—and the rights
of parents.

Patrick said: Do you know what I tell parents Arthur? I tell them to
go and fuck themselves. Patrick held both hands up in a gesture of
peace, he smiled for a moment; I'm no trying to get at you personally
but I just fucking feel that you cant expect the teacher to be the everything, the heavyweight boxing champion of the world.
Arthur stared at him.
Know what I mean, I'm just being honest with ye. I dont think ye
should expect the teacher to do everything. If you want your weans to
get homework then give it to them your fucking self.
Gavin said: That actually sounds quite right-wing ye know.
Well it's meant to be the fucking opposite and it is the fucking
opposite.
Gavin nodded.

Then:

Gavin gazed at him, then laughed briefly. He looked at Pat but Pat
looked away. Nor was Pat going to say anything further because he
was fucking off home as soon as he swallowed what he had lying.
There was no point sitting here yapping to a bunch of fucking pre-
judiced right-wing bastards. And Gavin turned on him once more:
What d'you mean ye deny ye get long holidays?
I deny I get long holidays, that's what I mean.
Back it up.
What d'you mean back it up?
Show me what you're talking about?
Naw. You show me what you're talking about.
I think I know what Paddy means, said Davie.
Good, tell me, replied Gavin.
I think I know what you mean Paddy.
Pat nodded.
Ye dont think ye get long holidays because when you're off from

the school you're still doing other things connected with it, making up timetables and all that.

Patrick nodded.

By the end of it you're no all that sure whether teachers get long holidays or no (they do, though most of them have to work hard for it), and whether parents should go and fuck themselves. Soon after this we learn that Doyle thinks he has sold his rights by serving the system as a teacher for 'a large wheen of pennies': 'He was an article that was corrupt . . . corruptio optimi pessima . . .'. This, as he recognises, is a form of self-praise. Throughout, Patrick is both the 'King of the World' that he wants to be—Glasgow belongs to him—and an abject sinner.

The rage of the novel's males can sometimes be made to appear the rage of those who believe themselves permanently beaten and cheated. The women are the vessels of a better spirit; the injury to them is greater, and it is their own men who are responsible for some of that injury. Patrick rages and scorns in proportion to his frustration: Hamlet's 'weakness' has its counterpart here. 'Patrick couldni find a pen. It is most odd indeed how objects disappear in rooms wherein the only moveable entity is oneself.' (He slides into English here for a laugh.) Objects disappear, and for a man of 29 he seems to have grabbed hold of very little of anything except a glass and a book. Drink figures in the novel, in precisely rendered scenes, as a bastion of the culture which is also a slow death. And yet this man is very far from useless. What we are reading is the Book of Patrick Doyle. Whether or not it can be seen as Kelman's self-portrait, it is the portrait of an artist.

The shortest stories in *Greyhound for Breakfast* owe a lot to Kafka's briefer parables, though they are apt to be more difficult to understand; and there can be no doubt that Beckett's solipsistic tramps have left an impression on the earlier writings. These influences, however, would appear to have receded, or to have been digested. The speech of Glasgow people is the big thing in the novel. This is a good Scots which is at once distinctly literary and faithful to the speech of the city. The deferred 'but' as in 'There again but' is a particular pleasure. There are many such verbatim effects, and indeed the oral dimension of the novel is very important. This can be reckoned to contain the succession of anecdotes that occurs and the fine detail of work-ing-class life that is provided. Doyle, for instance, thinks to himself a Scottish thought: 'Would his grandparents ever have had sexual activity in the parlour?' Elsewhere, 'he put a tea-spoonful-and-a-half of coffee granules into his mug and exactly the same into hers.' The measure expresses a mean between saving and lashing-out, and it has remained a feature of my own Scots-Irish domestic economy which I would bet is wide-spread in northern parts.

There is good Scots, too, in *The Book of Sandy Stewart*, which contrasts poignantly with the Book of Patrick Doyle. Stewart is a traveller, one of the people of the road—among them, tinkers, pipers and folk-singers—in whom an oral culture has survived to the present day. Here, too, there is an antiquity to be aware of. The book is a succession of anecdotes carefully transcribed in fidelity to his broad Scots, and largely concerned with the long-since of his early days. A story that would appeal to Kelman concerns some killer donkeys. One of these creatures once slew a butler whose toff gear had proved a red rag—quite a smack, this, at the system.

This gentleman bocht the donkey fae MacGreigor—it wes afore my day though—an it wes two or three days in the field at the front door. This day the butler went oot tae gie it a piece an it tore him doon wae its feets an mooth. They say that it wes the different claes that done it—the way the butler dressed—an it hed looked at the claes an taen a bad wey o the claes. It hed run intae him an tore him at yinst. An they say the butler wes gaithert up intae a white sheet aff the field.[2]

Kelman's work forms part of a flowering of talent which has come about in the urban Scotland of the last few years. These books and plays and films reveal a humanity which surmounts, as has been said, the hardship and brutality they describe—sur-mounts it, as a rule, by laughing at it. The Glasgow they evoke is a very hard and a very lively place. And yet Stewart's small wandering world could well be thought the richer of the two environments. He seldom responds to matters of personality, or individual psychology, is hardly ever in the least 'inward'; much depends on the turn of the tale. They are tales, more-over, which don't do all that much to summon the nostalgic reader. They don't direct us to the late survival of a gypsy paradise. Nevertheless, they contain persuasive evidence to indicate that there was more for his people to do, and talk about, that there was more fun, than there is now in some parts of urban Scotland. Less persuasively, a people which has had to defend itself against an enduring hostility is shown, for the most part, as free from fear, and, in particular, from the fear that exceeds and mistakes its objects. Those under threat in the cities have not always been so lucky. But then the travellers, too, may not have been quite as lucky as Stewart, in his old age, can sometimes suggest.

I remember these nomads myself, from a long while ago in Scotland. I remember dark, solemn and suspicious looks, as a travelling family was given tea in the back-garden of a house in the country. I peered at them round the end of the house. They could not be let into it, but there was a duty to entertain them, and, as I was told, not to stare. They were like spirits, and I loved them.

XIV · Authors

MOSTLY, he hides, keeping himself to himself. He may be a man or a woman, or a man disguised as a woman; it is no longer likely that he will prove to be a woman disguised as a man. His face, when we are shown it, will seem unhappy or hostile. He will seldom tell us what he thinks, or what to do. He does not like us. But we like *him*. He is the author we continue to read.

The portrait is not intended to serve for all authors, or for all seasons of modern literary history. Indeed, the appearances I have described may at times be imperceptible. At such times we may be conscious of an author who is quite as ready as any politician to come forward and talk to us.

One thing we mean by the word 'author' is that no two of them are alike. But we also think that they are a category, a tribe, a profession, an élite. We are persuaded by the language we speak to think of authors as authorities. But we also think that they are like other people, that they are humanly and historically representative. We think that they should be invisible, and that they are instrumental, that their opinions and personal lives should not get into the books they write, and that, when they do get into them, they undergo, together with their intentions, a process of translation or subversion. We think that a book is written by the language it shares with other books, and by the books which have preceded it. Nevertheless, the individual author continues to matter, in ways which suggest that we are also able to think of authors as inherently autobiographical, and, at the same time, as separate from the society which they represent and which wishes to honour them. To their best efforts we assign a public consequence which accommodates itself to the sense we have, and *they* have, of their autobiographical reclusiveness, and to the sense we have, and *they* have, at times, that there is something wrong with them.

Each author is different, and there are different kinds of author. There is an author who has been formed by a society which is no longer predominantly Christian but which is still disposed to worship—an author, for instance, who is immortal, invisible, and yet miserable and marginal. And there are highly professional, trading authors who are more or less at one with other people, and whom it can often seem that only a great willingness would be able to worship. And there are those who scarcely ever write books, and whose books are scarcely ever read, but who nevertheless display themselves, and may nevertheless be experienced, as authors—mostly, of an afflicted kind. But for all the different kinds of author that there are, it is usual to think of them as exercising a single general function, and for this to bear the compacted, contradictory meaning I am writing about here.

The idea of the writer as someone who is both a public figure and a recluse is ancient, and so is the idea of the writer as free agent—free, for instance, to decide for himself what he owes or shows to the people he lives among. Since the early Thirties, in Britain and elsewhere, these ideas have been exposed to an insistence that writers are in various ways formed or forced by the society they inhabit and the medium they employ, and there are writers for whom this public figure is now—to use a word to which I shall return—a figurine. Nevertheless the author is still here, and there, and everywhere, in person. 'Let us praise him' can still be heard, from those who sometimes praise him for seeking to exclude himself from his society, and, as theorists have advised, from his works. Cogent as the reasons for it have often appeared, this talk of exclusion has done harm. It is better to think that all books have in them this doubtful person, and that they also have in them the doubtful polity and community whose claims he is praised for resisting or ignoring. It is better to think that authors can scarcely retreat from view and still be authors—for all the authors now who, in their stories, poems and public statements, pretend to retreat.

The literature of the Thirties in Britain has been seen as ruled by a small group of public-school leftists, Auden and Spender and company. This company has been associated with a public spirit, a feeling for injustice, which might have been expected to reduce the importance assigned to the individual writer: and yet the individual writer went on being admired in the course of the decade, and there were many writers about then, and important then, whom the formula of the engaged writer of the Thirties did not fit. Auden was, in certain circles, a star from the first. The eminence of his eloquence soon set in. But the ethos for which he spoke was unfriendly to stars. As Cyril Connolly reported at the end of the decade, in his auto-biographical *Enemies of Promise*, the message could be heard on the left that theirs was an age which was against individualism. Memories of the First World War had distilled the 'elixir' of 'an equalising philosophy of life'—the words were those of a school friend of Connolly's at Eton. It was felt that a writer should work for the socialist millennium. But it was also felt that he should do so after his own élitist fashion. This reserva-tion helps to explain why there was plenty of room for indi-vidualists on the left, and for fame. After the war, Auden declared: 'In theory, the author of a good book should remain anonymous, for it is to his work, not to himself, that admiration is due. In practice, this seems to be impossible.'[1] And it was impossible in the Thirties too.

Auden and Spender were visible to those who grew up, as I did, in the Thirties and Forties: but I think that the young were more aware of Keats and Shelley. The young, the early dead, of an earlier time, powerful in their powerlessness, were still about. Their spirits walked, and were sometimes to steer the pen which I took up at the age of 15, in 1946, in order to keep a diary. I quoted: 'I fall upon the thorns of life! I bleed!' 'Tame-less and swift and proud . . .'. And I commented: 'Interesting quotations on Shelley's opinion of his own character.' Another of Shelley's opinions was copied out: 'Fame follows those whom she is unworthy to guide.' I was bound to have noticed that the fame which he looked down on had followed the lyric cry which voiced his misfortunes and injuries, but I had very little idea that his poetry had been powerful enough to convert people to a socialist sense of injustice.

Adolescent readers were also to become aware, though, that lyrical romanticism was under a cloud, that the modern had come to put a stop to it. The Modernist regeneration could be welcomed as a form of realism: poetry had returned to the real-ities of what had once been known—in contrast with romance—as 'common life'. These realities, however, did not always include the existence of a public life and of political objectives: where such objectives were plainly inseparable from the daily lives and public pronouncements of the new writers, attempts might be made and would continue to be made to treat them—to treat, for instance, the politics of Pound—as separate from their works of art. Under Modernism, reclusiveness persisted, and so did authorial fame and uniqueness. Boys and girls grew up to a confusing set of signals—to discover if they could that the same author might ebb and flow in his commitment to the *res publica*, that literary scenes rarely capitulate to any one tendency, or school, that schools are formed in order to quarrel and to coexist with other schools, that opposing tendencies can rarely be accurately identified in terms of their favouring, or not favouring, the creation of public works of art, as opposed to the anti-social works of art to which societies attend, and that romance, and a reverential attitude to privacy, may turn a writer to the right as well as to the left. It was difficult for some of us to discover at this time that Romanticism and Modernism were both opposed and allied, rather as Britain and Russia were to be, difficult to think of them as indistinguishable in the poetry, for instance, of Dylan Thomas. It has now become possible to think that they were indistinguishable, too, in their suspicion of the public work of art which they were nevertheless sometimes to tolerate, and even to create.

Turned overnight into soldiers and civilians with the outbreak of war, writers might have been expected to take a new interest in the public interest. Perhaps they did: but it can also be said that a dynamic of privacy took hold—a privacy which was understandable in the circumstances, and which may have been seen both as mildly subversive and as an aspect of the 'freedoms' for which the war was being fought. Much of its literature gave expression to civilian griefs. 'Griefs' was a word which fascinated Dylan Thomas. When he used it in his poems, it was apt to suggest perennial features—'the griefs of the ages', which lovers, in particular, are heir to, even in bed. It was less likely to suggest the consequences of the fire raids on London, though these raids did cross his lips.

The 'griefs of the ages' are mentioned in a poem of Thomas's, 'In my Craft or Sullen Art', which is a transport of privacy. He says there that he writes, not for fame or money, or for a further reason which is harder to grasp, which has to do with 'the strut and trade of charms' on 'the ivory stages' and which sounds like the actor Richard Burton, but for lovers in their sad beds, who are not attending to his sullen art. He is writing for no one that will read him, and it just so happened that he was by then on the way to being widely read.

The Forties are commemorated in a delightful short novel of 1987 by Francis Wyndham, *The Other Garden*. Wyndham read and remembers the little magazines of this time, with their distinctive short stories, including those by the non-combatant and indeed invalid Denton Welch. The book is fragrant with conceptions of the time which can be gathered from such sources. Eventually, the Wyndham-like narrator is called up. But the war is experienced mainly through the troubles of his friend Kay, who goes with American servicemen and ends her days in the arms of a stray Alsatian dog. The story is set in a Home Counties environment lived in by the well-born and their inferiors, the sort of place estate-agents recommend as a paradise. The environment accommodates, moreover, the 'other garden', to which—as the choice of title may tend to overstress—the narrator's father, and the narrator, resort in a spirit of escape: the garden is 'beloved', 'subtly but certainly separate from the house and its bland surrounding lawns'. At the heart of this pastoral tale are its strays. The Second World War rolls over to give them pride of place, and Kay's cold, well-born parents are a graver threat than the Nazis. Kay is a stray, so is her dog, and so is her narrator, whose conscription leads to illness of a non-combatant kind, suffered in a hospital which recalls the notebooks of Denton Welch. The war is present in the story partly as the accentuation of a previous unease and affliction, and Kay is destroyed by that traditional scourge of the innocent, TB. There is death in this Arcadia, but it is not caused by any flying-bomb or shell.

This is a war in which the carnage takes place somewhere over the horizon, rather as, during an earlier war, the Somme bombardments had been listened to by civilians on the English side of the Channel. It was not the only war which was experienced from 1939 to 1945: there was to be a range of very different orders of fiction which described the carnage. But Wyndham's war revives an outlook which meant a great deal to the literature which came about in these years; his novel repeats an experience of the war which was equally the experience of a literary heritage rich in sensitivity, compassion and confession, and which was recorded in the short stories, notebooks and little magazines of the time.

Francis Wyndham's narrator concludes by rejecting the idea of Kay as a 'natural victim'. But the last two sentences are these: 'All the same, as a tribute to her memory, I romantically swore a loyal oath in the other garden that until my own death I would eschew ambition for worldly success and avoid the wielders of influence and power, choosing my friends among the innocently uncompetitive. It is not a vow that I have always been able to keep.' And sure enough, this reclusive work, this innocent tribute to so much in the way of innocent uncompetitiveness, has been awarded a literary prize.

Not long after it appeared, the writer went with friends to revisit the country place where it is set. How quiet it seemed to him. Hardly changed from the days when its dads' army had mounted guard. What was that sound in the distance? Some bird. But it was not a bird. It was the cry of a police car hurrying to Hungerford for the massacre that had taken place there. Here is a short story which is like one of the short stories which were written during the war, like one of those stories in which there was a massacre going on over the horizon, and readers felt with the anxious person who learnt of it, who was free from it and not free, and who had worries of his own. In those tales of the Home Front the war was a form of public life which was both encountered and avoided.

The little magazines of this time were eventually to be mocked in Evelyn Waugh's trilogy *Sword of Honour*, where the writer's war service is enacted by Guy Crouchback, a name that might seem to evoke both a descent from Richard III and the depressed misfit whom we meet on the page. The Waugh-figure is scarcely less ill-at-ease in his uniform than the Wyndham-figure. Evelyn Waugh's three novels make a sense of their own of the biographical reports that the Waugh of this time was a man who loved the Army but did not get on with it, and who did not get on with other people, or with the way of the world: at one point in the hostilities there was even felt to be a risk that his comrades-in-arms might kill him. At the end of the trilogy, however, there are indications that Guy has become popular with the officers and gentlemen with whom he has served.

He says of these friends of his: 'We aren't quite Ludovic's sort of party.' Ludovic is a writer, a romantic word-worshipper, with whom he has also served—a dubious fellow, some knight's homosexual protégé whose notebooks are printed in Everard Spruce's magazine *Survival*, and whose novel *The Death Wish* is rated by a high-born woman as 'tosh'. The allusion to Ludovic's sort of party is uttered in the grateful recesses of Bellamy's club, where one of Crouchback's party then calls out to him: 'Guy, come and play slosh.' This is perhaps the closest he has come to worldly success, the furthest he has come from the closet. The natural victim, fated to fail, goes off and plays what might appear to be some sort of old-fashioned upper-class game. Slosh is or was, in fact, a form of billiards which was to enter the dictionaries with mentions dating from as recently as the late Thirties, and which had been mentioned, not long before this, in the writings of Samuel Beckett.

It may be that, after the war, Waugh was to play his upper-class games chiefly in his imagination. He had moved behind the portcullis of family life, and had fallen out with his peers, some of whom were peers but few of whom can be imagined as readers of his books, keen though he was to distinguish them from Ludovic's sort of book. If we discount the exercise of the profession which earned him his living, such games may by then have been almost his only concession to the communal life of his country in the post-war world. Sooner slosh than the tosh, and worse, that lay all around the Crouchback of Combe Florey. It is worth noting, though, that the egocentricity and special pleading of this romantic work—its derelict's hostility to inferiors, the fantastic politics which called down a curse on allies and enemies alike in the military conflict—did little to alienate his readers, many of whom must have been glad to recognise that his talent had survived not only the war but *Brideshead Revisited*. The trilogy did not fail to win its literary prizes—prizes which are drawn to 'failure' as the moth is to the star.

'The war had raised Spruce, who in the years preceding it had not been the most esteemed of his coterie of youngish, socialist writers, to unrivalled eminence. Those of his friends who had not fled to Ireland or to America had joined the Fire Brigade'—shameful decisions, in which the socialist nature disclosed itself. Spruce is a spite on Connolly, who was to prove, in his eminence, the supreme civilian. He spent the war editing the magazine *Horizon*, which carried a number of the sensitive short stories of the time, and in *Enemies of Promise*, written during the Munich crisis in 1938, he gave his view of the authorial condition. The book was to enjoy a vogue of over twenty years. By post-war undergraduates it was widely taken as a guide to conduct and a literary primer; it was a way, for instance, of being at Oxford or Cambridge, where *Brideshead* was extensively revisited but where the young might also want to become Connollies.

In this book he divides the writings of twentieth-century predecessors into mandarin and realist, fine and colloquial, and in his own writing deftly combines these styles. He seems to hesitate between Romanticism and Modernism, while declaring: 'By the time Eliot and Valéry came to save my generation from the romantic dragon it had already devoured me.' The dragon had not been deterred by his Classical training and prowess at Eton, where the most interesting last third of the book is set. The struggles of golden boys for survival and supremacy, the fever-chart of sentiment and style—this must have done more to charm most readers than the residues of a temporarily attractive socialism and austerity which they may have been conscious of discovering in Parts One and Two. He imparts a leftist opinion, Edmund Wilson's, to the effect that the Modern masters were to blame for their over-emphasis on 'the importance of the individual'. And yet he is intent on the self-portrait of a self-indulgent and self-pitying individualist. This was an act which he was to follow with still more flamboyant displays of weakness: but the notion had already arrived of the man who dared to eat the peach which Prufrock had probably declined. His was to be a famous egotism, which was peculiarly that of an author. It was a performance in which exclusion could be caught, as in the case of those other Irish show-offs Wilde and Shaw, and which was by turns funny, grisly and endearing.

In *Enemies of Promise* he warns of the awfulness of the ephemeral in literature, of the threats which lie in wait for those who hope to compose lasting works. But he himself was to yield in his time to almost all of these threats: to the perils of family life, 'the pram in the hall', to conversation, journalism, drink, sex and success—to almost all except politics. His political commitment was decidedly ephemeral. The dandy of the Left who is evident in parts of the book is more dandy than left. The snob who is evident in parts of the book is a snob, and a subtle connoisseur of privilege. For Connolly, writers are male, and women are enemies of promise. Promise has lots of enemies, and it may be that promise is paranoid. At Eton he sensed in himself a 'persecution mania': and we sense that it helped to make him, as it has helped to make others, a writer. At the end of his time at the school, a time when an equalising philosophy of life was making converts, he took, from the Greek, a motto: 'I hate everything public.' The face of the writer who hates everything public stares in close-up from the cover of the Penguin edition of 1961. There is the hint of a baby seal lifting a forlorn head above the freezing waters of a hard world. Any minute now, you feel, it will be bawling for its peach.

By 1961, it had once again become objectionable to claim that family life was an intrusive or incongruous element in the arrangements writers might make for themselves. The Fifties had put the pram back in the hall. The Movement school of writers conveyed a further disapproval of romantic isolation, and took part in a reinvention of the social conscience of the Thirties; there was some sympathy here with the ideas of Leavis, who made much of the single writer but who also made much of that writer's responsibilities. The Movement is not the only story that can be told of the Fifties, though it is the story that is currently preferred. There were those for whom the Movement writers were upstarts, for whom the new domesticity which had planked its pram in the hall of fame, and the new socially progressive and morally useful tendency to which it was seen to contribute, had to be resisted. There lingered a tenderness for the 'obscurity' of certain poets of the immediate past: for the pleasures of collusion which such displays of privacy were capable of affording, and which had long sustained, in its intermittency, a cult of the inscrutable frowning writer. Connolly had said before the war that religion would never return, but Eliot's authority had assisted it to do so. The religion which had returned could be read as a preoccupation with self-fulfilment and spiritual quests, but it could also argue for social improvements. Eliot's faith showed both faces.

Neither, however, was acceptable to the Movement; Eliot's improvements were not theirs.

Kingsley Amis, Philip Larkin and their friends liked to attack people: but they were inclined to leave Eliot, and Yeats, alone. This set a limit to their iconoclasm, to their rejection of Modernism and Romanticism; and it may also have affected their reputation as progressives, or interventionists. Yeats and Eliot are among the writers of the modern world whose example has been such as to enjoin a marked ambivalence in respect of the public and political endeavours of literary men. Of Yeats, it may be thought in this connection that the poet who observed that poets had 'no gift to set a statesman right' was prepared to become a senator; of Eliot, that he was to arrive at a poetry in which the voice of a statesman could be heard to speak of the futility, and peculiar mortality, of 'statesmen' and 'rulers', 'merchant bankers, eminent men of letters'. Into the dark with them. As it proved, the Movement was itself more ambivalent in this respect than its programme may initially have suggested. What is taken to be an upstart iconoclasm will frequently be taken to be left-wing—as in the case both of the Movement and of Leavis. But the Movement was soon to display a distaste for the left-wing activism of authors.

Throughout the Fifties, a contest between the art which is meant to be socially useful and the art which is socially indifferent, between the artist as citizen, participant or product and the artist as star and free agent, was to encourage, on the part of particular writers, divided loyalties and varieties of ambivalence. Leavis's outlook was one which cherished authors and punished them, which irritated authors but which was intelligible to them. He believed that the good writer made over into something special to himself—while also intimately dependent on the judgement of others—the materials delivered to him from the past. Meanwhile a rival account had started to enter the country from the Movement's abhorred 'abroad'—an account which was to speak of language, not as the precious life-blood of a master spirit, but as an arbitrary system of signs, and which was very much more compelling to intellectuals than it was to authors. In the mid-Fifties, Claude Lévi-Strauss was arguing in France for the existence in literature and folklore of 'mythemes', or recurrent narrative structures. This was an approach which disregarded the factor of historical change, and which also disregarded the factor of authorship.

According to Roland Barthes, whose highly literary freelance version of Structuralism has been singled out for approval by other authors, authors had gone away and been sent away. In a collection of pieces which appeared in 1968, a year in which emancipations were felt to be impending, Barthes reported 'The Death of the Author':

The removal of the Author (one could talk here with Brecht of a veritable 'distancing', the Author diminishing like a figurine at the far end of the literary stage) is not merely an historical fact or an act of writing; it utterly transforms the modern text (or—which is the same thing—the text is henceforth made and read in such a way that at all its levels the author is absent).[2]

Barthes's text insists on a veritable and factual removal. But he himself was to write in such a way as to restore the author who had been removed, to reconstitute the statue which had dwindled to a figurine. And the same thing could be said of the author of Post-Structuralism. Post-Structuralism has held that Lévi-Strauss's structures and mythemes contain a hidden subjectivity, that they are authorial. But Derrida's opinions are authorial too. They do not prevent one from remembering the opinionless, invisible author of the romantic past: but they also recall those authors of the past who were known for the opinions they expressed. Derrida, too, is the kind of author who had been pronounced dead.

'Post-Structuralism' is a name which speaks both of sequence and of severance: 'In place of structuralism we should recognise the interplay of differences among texts.'[3] The resolution of such differences will never come, apparently; there is no truth for authors to aim at or be judged by. And yet Post-Structuralism has itself been telling the truth that licenses a deconstruction of authors. Truth-telling and truth-denying, authorial and sceptical, it can be seen as implicated in a long history, during which authors and their ideas have at times been ejected from their works, but have at all times belonged to a world which admiringly locates them there.

Post-Structuralists have been putting their minds to the question of how this species of philosophical scepticism can be

made politically effective. Derrida has been seen as adversarial
and left-wing, and the activity of deconstruction which has followed his example might almost seem to have been named
accordingly: but it is hard to see how socialism could be served,
rather than leftishly deconstructed, by this scepticism of his.
His ideas entail a refusal of the ideas of other people, and give a
sense of separation—of the separation implicit, for instance, in
the esoteric. The doctrine is separate, in important respects,
from the literature which it consults and expounds. And yet it
resembles much of the literature we are used to, which has, in
relation to politics and public life, its own aversion and inapti-
tude, its own esoteric tendency.

It has become known that Derrida's associate, the late Paul
de Man, was, when he was young, in Belgium during the
war, not so much a socialist as a National Socialist: moved by
conceptions of 'blood and soil' to write articles which extolled
the Germanic tradition and favoured the deportation of aliens.
This has been found interesting, though it can't all be found
utterly different from what a number of respectable European
writers were saying in the years between the wars. It is also
interesting, from the present point of view, to learn that de
Man then went on to write, for a while, essays in which 'poetry
and politics are treated as in some sense antithetical terms',[4] in
which poetry is entrusted with the power to read and to denig-
rate political events and involvements. In later life de Man was
understood to be saying that the author, together with the biographical subject, does not exist. And there are those, now,
who appear to want to understand this as a way of saying that
the author of over a hundred collaborationist articles did not
exist.

A deconstruction of de Man's disgrace has begun. His engagement with the writings of the philosopher Heidegger, a
declared Nazi, comes into the exercise, and one writer[5] has
referred to Derrida's attempt to show that Heidegger's 'repetition of the tradition' which shaped his political adherence
'prepares an opening onto that which is wholly other to the
tradition and which may, as a consequence, displace the political organicism of National Socialist ideology'. This writer
wants us to think, with Derrida, that Heidegger's writings have
us attending to an antithesis of what he must often have wished

to say—if not to someone different from the Heidegger of his actions and declarations. The writer implies that Heidegger's text subverts or retracts itself by preparing opportunities of a kind which other texts may deny. It would be more accurate to claim that such opportunities are commonly discovered by interpreters, who are accustomed to relate them to a main or plain sense of the texts they are examining. If this is an exercise in deconstruction, it is equally a piece of sophistry which seeks to diminish the importance of Heidegger's politics.

We sometimes suppose, in simpler vein, that politics does what literature can't, and that literature does what politics can't. There is an absurdity to the thought of a novelist's coming to power in this country, as in most others, which has to be acknowledged by anyone who tries to assess the ambivalence of authors with regard to public life. Norman Mailer's bid to become mayor of New York acknowledged the absurdity while purporting to dispel it. This was a sort of street theatre, a sort of anti-politics, a holiday from the 'politician politics' despised by the feminist writer Julia Kristeva. Nevertheless, it is also true that some writers have politics, and have been elected, and have governed, and that literature is more political, and the politics of imaginative writers less irrelevant, than our expectations of authors, and than the principles of literary criticism, have made out. Literature and politics, including politician politics, are, moreover, intelligible both as companion texts and as the same text, with politics exhibiting no less than literature does a tension between public and private, collectivism and individualism. Salman Rushdie has suggested, and has had reason to suggest, that they are companions who are certain to keep falling out: 'Writers and politicians are natural rivals. Both try to make the world in their own images; they fight for the same territory.'[6] The ambivalence is mutual.

Under Thatcherism, the British literary culture has held to its low rate of politically-opinionated imaginative works; in response to Mrs Thatcher's success there has been a good deal of silence and dejection; dissent has been sluggish. Meanwhile, with regard to writers stationed somewhere to the right within the literary community, it has been possible to observe a process of recognition. Novelists who had for some years been sympathetic to the Right could now be more clearly seen to be so. Anthony Burgess is a case in point. Having produced a series of brilliant fictions about Anthony Burgess, he had passed into exile from a country which he judged to have been ruined by its welfare state. Now that the country has begun to ruin its welfare state, his exile can be seen as comically mis-timed: but it can also be more easily seen than it once was as politically significant. Equally interesting from this point of view are the careers of the former Movement partners, Larkin and Kingsley Amis.

Larkin's Conservative views were uttered in one or two satir-ical poems and he was occasionally confronted with them in interviews. Asked by an *Observer* journalist in 1979[7] about a poem of his which deplored the withdrawal of British troops from east of Suez, he replied: 'to bring them home simply because we couldn't afford to keep them there seemed a dreadful humili-ation.' But then he went on to say, 'Oh, I adore Mrs Thatcher', and to adore her for restoring the concept that 'if you haven't got the money for something you can't have it'. Teasingly sar-donic though some of these words may appear, their distinction between the kind of thing which Britain can and can't afford was an accurate prediction of the impending Thatcher state. Here was a poet prepared to speak a voter's mind. These are among the sentiments which have enabled her to reign over us. No to a national health service, yes to the Falklands War.

When Larkin's collected poems appeared posthumously in 1988, one reviewer did what we have so often been used to doing with the politics of poets.[8] The reviewer, who was the poet Peter Porter, claimed that Larkin the man was in only a few of the poems, and that there was very little evidence there, either, of the 'caricature persona'—that of 'the bachelor recluse of Tory opinions hating Modernism, "abroad" and the young' —which 'Larkin the poet did nothing to discourage'. Only sometimes can we 'see how the poems belong to the man'. But the poems did belong to the man, and the persona did too. It was his idea, and it is strange to think of discouraging your persona. The man *was* a bachelor, after all, and a Tory; he was not a socialist, or secretly married, or sweet. And the poems show this. They would not have to show it at every turn for it to be plausible to associate this author with his works.

No one imagines, of course, that a writer's politics permit

untroubled inferences as to his art or style. Kingsley Amis started as a socialist and is now, in old age, a Conservative: but this does not tell the story of his art and of the changes it has undergone. On some matters at least, including that of nuclear weapons, he stands to the right of his son, the novelist Martin Amis. At the same time, he is a more public, a more civic writer than Martin Amis is. He has spoken out with the utmost skill on a range of issues which have mattered to fellow citizens who have never read any of his novels, and who might have had trouble finding these issues in the novels even if they *had* read them. They are novels of which it is possible to say that they are written with a view to a concealment of the author who can nevertheless be recognised there. The novels of Martin Amis do not obtrude the opinions of the author any more than his father's do: but they do obtrude the author, as his father's do not.

Money is a *tour de force* of romantic duality, in which the kaleidoscopic impression of a repertoire of Martin Amises is communicated. By Kingsley Amis *Money* is thought to raise a problem of style: it is a fanciful work, a work which concedes too little to the functional element present in such a sentence as 'He finished his drink, got up and left the room.' Kingsley Amis's stylish books have increasingly been such as to suggest that style is the vehicle of a romantic self-engrossment. The difference between the two writers, father and son, is itself kaleidoscopic. In one sense, it is left against right. In another, it is the narcissistic sublime pitted against a concern for decency, rationality and the common reader. Martin Amis is a romantic writer of the Left whose fiction has the élitism inherent in a vividly autobiographical purpose, while his father is a classical writer of the Right whose argumentative élitism has to contend, in his fiction, with a disinterested reticence.

The style which those suspicious of romantic self-engrossment might entitle the victim's friend was not employed by Primo Levi in his two autobiographical books, *If this is a man* and *The Truce*, published in Italy, respectively, in 1958 and 1963: more than that, 'problems of style seemed ridiculous to me'. And yet Levi was certainly a victim. These books—about his time in Auschwitz and his journey home—were written in order to record what had happened to him. It could be said that there is a style here which suits this purpose: but the result is quite incompatible with the romantic literature of alienation and suffering. That is not his style. His books record a determination to survive, and are determined to bear witness. They pay attention to detail and to the functional—to survival routines which have to do with soup bowls, shoes, shirts.

During the months when Levi was in his camp, Samuel Beckett was working on his novel *Watt*, where there are also to be found what we might take to be survival routines, among which the game of slosh figures faintly. Beckett is perhaps the most famous of modern literary recluses, and he is one who has both refused and bestowed access to his private life. Over the decade and a half which preceded this novel, he had been capable of friendship, of the odd companionable routine— billiards, for instance, if not slosh itself: but his attempts to write had gone badly, had appeared to be frustrated by a prevailing literature of social commitment, and he had drifted very near to the point of dereliction, to the end of the world. This suffering was sited for a while, appropriately enough, in the World's End quarter of West London, at a time when Cyril Connolly was to advise him to 'suffer a bit more, perhaps with a job as a dishwasher'. Beckett was engaged in raising 'personal privacy almost to a religious fetish', writes his biographer, Deirdre Bair. Of the time when he was at work on *Watt*, a time of breakdown which sent her for guidance to R. D. Laing's treatise on *The Divided Self*, she writes: 'sanity became analogous with secrecy.' He described himself as a 'baroque solipsist', and had explained in 1935 that for years he had been unhappy, and that 'the misery and solitude and apathy . . . were the elements of an index of superiority'. Deirdre Bair adds: 'he was most certainly unable to put aside thoughts of himself long enough to feel any emotion for another.' Earlier, surrounded in Paris, in his loneliness, by friends who stressed the importance of artistic anonymity, he had been trying to write 'without style', while revealing himself to his biographer, in the Belacqua stories, as 'concerned with style to the detriment of thought and feeling'.[9]

These are episodes in which style was theoretically forsworn and in which it was applied to material drawn from a miserable private life from which his art was theoretically debarred. In the early and middle Beckett, style was a means of securing the privacy he wanted: but it also threatened to expose him to his readers. And the art that resulted was one in which his personal life is apparent, for all his *au contraires*. The stylish name he gave to his character Belacqua was a version of his own surname, as well as an allusion to a slothful someone in Dante. It is hardly untoward that the cover of the *Watt* paperback, like those of other books of his, should be filled with his handsome features—lit so as to seem skull-like and severe judge-like—and with banner words about the Nobel Prize.

At one point in this novel the tramp-like Watt has a stone thrown at him:

Beyond stopping, and laying down his bags, and picking up his hat, and setting it on his head, and picking up his bags, and setting himself, after one or two false starts, again in motion, Watt, faithful to his rule, took no more notice of this aggression than if it had been an accident. This he found was the wisest attitude, to staunch, if necessary, inconspicuously, with the little red sudarium that he always carried in his pocket, the flow of blood, to pick up what had fallen, and to continue, as soon as possible, on his way, or in his station, like a victim of mere mischance. But he deserved no credit for this. For it was an attitude become, with frequent repetition, so part of his being, that there was no more room in his mind for resentment at a spit in the eye, to take a simple example, than if his braces had burst, or a bomb fallen on his bum.[10]

There is a measure of congruence between Levi's text and Beckett's. It might seem to arise from a time of falling bombs, simple examples of cruelty and misfortune, a convergence of accident and design. Phrases from the Beckett might be slipped into Levi's record and not be noticed; some part of what Watt does here is done by Levi. And yet there could be no confusing these texts.

We might say, among other things, that the Beckett passage has style, or that it has the style that is not Levi's, that it has the style that denotes the recluse whom the passage mocks, the style that turns readers away with rare, dandy words, words Martin Amis might use, but not Kingsley. There are readers who would not struggle to ascertain that a sudarium is a cloth, and that it is the cloth with which St Veronica wiped the face of Christ on his way to the Cross. There are readers who would have to struggle, elsewhere in Beckett's novel, to stay with the words which direct a character and his companions out of a place they are in—an exit in style, as it were, and in slow motion, which lasts for two packed pages and which begins: 'and so he rose and rapidly left the hall (as though he could have rapidly left the hall without rising) . . .'. In a manner that seems foreign to the author of *Watt*, Levi is conscious of serving a readership, as well as, to be sure, himself.

Watt depicts not so much survival as a grim persistence, projected, every so often, as comedy. It is a kind of persistence which might not be all that well suited to enabling you to survive, and which can give the impression that human beings do not matter to each other. This is not an impression which is given by the author of *Lear*, another text in which dereliction and isolation appear, and a text in which good people go to the wall. Nor is it given by Levi, who has been there too, and whose concerns are at times the concerns of Shakespeare: what it is to be human, to be a friend or an enemy of other people, what it is to come back from the dead.

There is a mind-set which might prefer to treat these writings of Levi's as a form of journalism, or deposition, and to exclude them from the literary record. They will not be much written about by literary critics. Post-Structuralists will not be enquiring into their availability for deconstruction. But it is difficult to believe that they will cease to be read and valued. He had, and had to have, a robust sense of his own worth: but he also had a subject, and a duty. Carefully characterised, there are people in the books who are not Primo Levi, and there are people outside them to whom he wishes to speak. 'If I had not lived the Auschwitz experience, I probably would never have written anything.' There are authors who might refuse to accept that this is the statement of an author—but who would have to admit that Levi is the author of two books whose every page interests and instructs the reader.

The word 'author' is used to refer to a wide range of functions and expectations. I remember a warning to Scottish schoolboys of the sixteenth century which referred to 'authors of mischief', and I have not forgotten that it has been generally understood since then that the authors of books do things, and make them:

but it is also the case that in modern times we have been conscious of the mischiefs done to authors, and of the things they
can't or don't do, conscious of a general immateriality and
ghostliness. I have just been suggesting that among the expectations we have are those which reveal a taste for the imaginary,
and for the hidden lives of those authors whom we think of as
professors of the imaginary—a taste which might conceivably
make light of Levi's writings. It is unlikely to do the same for
the writings of the American novelist J. D. Salinger, author of
The Catcher in the Rye, who has a hidden life, and who may or
may not—such are the uncertainties of the hidden life—be
another victim of the traumatic events which occurred in the
course of the Second World War. Since the war, Salinger has
wanted to be left alone, and the running drama of his hermit
stance—a stance which belongs to a country notable for its
hermits, and for the publicity which some of them receive—
was recently to reach a crisis.

The crisis began when an English biographer, Ian Hamilton, decided to make an attempt on his life. Salinger wrote
Hamilton a letter which told of his distress that such an attempt
should be intended—a letter virtually suicidal in its implications. He then took to the law, with an involvement of the
Supreme Court, and with the result that Salinger's objection to
the incorporation in the book of brief quotations from letters
of his which are accessible in libraries was sustained. Ian
Hamilton had all along been willing to take his author's distress into account: because of this, and because of the obstacles
which had been placed in his path, the book he published in
1988 is as much about the crisis itself, and the constraints
within which he had to work, as about the early life of Salinger.
As for the later life, that has had to remain little more than the
blank left by Salinger's refusal and retreat, which Hamilton
tentatively relates to an experience of some of the worst fighting
of the war. One irony of the situation is that Salinger's fictions
are not only markedly autobiographical in tendency but have
also been, in later times, markedly expressive of the author's
opinions. No one would call them classically disinterested.
They have come to sympathise with a wisdom of the East, the
wisdom of sages who teach the importance of self-cultivation
and a horror of worldly success. Salinger's imparting of himself

and of his opinions has enabled him to be a successful writer: but he also seeks to refuse all access to his personal life.

It is possible to object to Salinger's objections: to expose them to psychology, to deconstruction, to the knowledge that, in certain circumstances, fame and solitude are congenial states. It is possible to say that a recluse is found in a hut in the woods. He does not write books about living in a hut in the woods, or about anything else. He does not run for mayor. He does not take to the law. And it may appear, to such objectors, that Salinger is only pretending to be a recluse. At the same time, we surely have to concede a good deal to his bitter insistence on the distinction between his private life and what he makes of that life in his art; to concede that if he really does go in fear of the intrusions of publicity, he is entitled to defend himself as best he can; and to concede that there must be plenty of people in the world now for whom their privacy may be a matter of life or death. My concern here is to point out a connection between Salinger's stance and the view of authorship which suggests that a writer's books are continuous with the most private part of him, but which also suggests that his private life, which may well be grievous and which includes his opinions, should be treated as separate from his books, and kept dark.

'The death of the author' is a ploy that tries to outface the facts of an unexpended interest in authors, in many sorts of author, and in their presence between the covers of their books, and it adds to the stock of sometimes incongruous ideas which have concurred in describing an interesting irresponsibility and incapacity, in describing a writer who can't help what he writes and who lives in a world that is crowded and intimidating, a world that has little time for literature. Authors are taken to be inspired, exalted, disturbed, excluded. They are absent-minded, awkward. Their huge wings prevent them from walking about. And they are caused, determined, deceived. According to Freud, they are ill. According to Barthes, dead. These are among the things that we have needed to think of authors, and they have often appeared to indicate what authors undoubtedly suffer from—in their effort and anxiety, in their pursuit of the imaginary. But they are things that are wrong, and right, with other people too. They are not, all of them, peculiar to authors,

who have tended to place an undue trust in restrictive accounts
of their activities. They have abdicated and abstained, while
also figuring on occasion as specialists in the restrictive-
grandiose.

They have told themselves that a writer's opinions and personal life can and should be excluded from his imaginative
works. They have spoken and behaved as if they were exceptional in their suffering and peculiarly cut-off. Writers as far
apart (in their Irish diaspora) as Connolly and Beckett have
concurred in making such statements. Some of the statements
in question will always seem more authentic than others, and it
seems evident that their makers are likely to be drawn both
ways, both away from and towards the people that surround
them. Beckett's biographer explains that he was in that condition when, seeking refuge in the Vaucluse in 1943, he started
work on *Watt*, which stood to the breakdown he was then suffering, Deirdre Bair writes, in the relation of a therapeutic
game. He had just completed a spell of courageous service in
the French Resistance, having spent the years before the war in
an attitude of scornful, and almost preternatural, indifference
to politics. Beckett has himself said that *Watt* was 'only a
game': but there are games and games, and they are all likely
to be more or less therapeutic. What sort of a game is *Watt*? He
was drawn to the notion of solitary games, and went in for his
own form of minimum-contact chess. But literature is less like
that sort of game than it is like slosh. It takes two or more to
play it—and not just the two persons that Beckett had reportedly
become in the Vaucluse, or the chess-playing duo that Martin
Amis becomes in *Money*. *Watt* is literature, though of a most
gruelling kind, and like the literature it is, it may be thought to
be drawn both ways, in the very act of affirming its author's
isolation, and of tallying with the hermit life (and wife) reported
of his time in the Vaucluse.

One way or another, the absent author is never done present-
ing himself, never done quitting his isolation, and in the autumn
of 1987 he did this to startling effect. The feminist publishing-
house Virago, whose list contains female authors from racial
minorities and the Third World, was about to bring out a
book of stories by a reclusive Asian woman which dealt with
generational conflicts within the Asian community in Britain.

It was revealed, however, to be the work of a white man. Rahila Khan was Toby Forward, a real name which looks like a pseudonym. The Toby who came forward proved to be a left-wing, feminist, anti-racist Anglican vicar. He has hereby entered the history of pseudonymy in a line of descent from William Sharp, who in the Nineties devised for himself the alias of Fiona Macleod, a reclusive Hebridean woman of mystical leanings. For this, Forward was condemned by a Virago spokeswoman. 'He pretended to occupy a space that isn't his', she announced, apparently untouched by the thought that this is what novelists are meant to do, and may even succeed in doing.

'To speak with a voice that wasn't mine', Toby Forward has written: 'I had thought that that was the purpose of art.' He says this in an article[11] in which he defends his use of pseudonyms, and which is enlightening about authorship in general. Conversations with publishers and drama producers had suggested to him that all fiction was considered to be, in one sense, autobiographical: a sense which made it wrong of him to call himself Rahila. But before the disclosure he had said to Virago of his Rahila stories: 'in a sense they are all about me and none of them is about me.' In the article, his use of pen-names is aligned with the conviction that

separation, isolation, uncertainty and lack of definition are the common material of humanity. The stories people write are examples of this state that help us to accept it in ourselves. My own alienation was too personal and painful for me to write about, but it gave me a way into the lives and minds of others who for different reasons and in different circumstances felt something of the same things.

The 'image of the isolated writer' is overdone, he thinks, free though he is in the piece with the words which have overdone it; and he thinks that in isolating himself from his stories, in a sense, by employing a pen-name, he was able to express something both of his own isolation and of that of others. Pen-names 'released me from the obligation of being what I seem to be so that I can write as I really am'. This is what he means when he says: 'Rahila Khan was me.' And it may not be very different from what Flaubert meant when he said the same thing of himself and Madame Bovary.

Toby Forward allows us to guess that his reasons for hanging back behind his pseudonyms may in part have been opportunistic: in the media, Rahila's hour had come. And they may also in part have been mischievous: the Rahila manuscript was sent to a house which does not publish men, and the article, too, seemed willing to spread a little discord—among London's publishing sisterhoods, for example. But the reasons he enlarges on in the article are sound enough. He explains that his pseudonyms were fictions, and that they resembled the fictions to which they were applied in requiring to be understood as the expression, rather than the denial, of a personal life.

Virago were worried that, by swallowing an imposture, they might have harmed the Asian community. But the only harm that has been done is the bruise administered to the theory that authors are separate and do not matter. When his cover was blown, Virago decided that the identity of their author mattered very much indeed, and proceeded to make out that there was something the matter with him. It seems to me that there is more reason to feel misgivings about pseudonymy as such than about the behaviour of this particular unknown. We now know that Rahila Khan is Toby Forward. But we would also do well to believe that Toby Forward is Rahila Khan. The space from which the flaming sword of Virago has been raised to exclude him can have no other claimant than this vicarious vicar.

It is now being said that the great days of impersonality are over, when attempts were made to shut down a dimension of knowledge—a knowledge no different from any other, and subject like any other to imperfection and abuse. But it is too soon to be sure. The sad face of the authorial portrait still stares—that of someone who does not belong to his books, and does not belong to, or is pained by, the world that surrounds him. Even those writers who are themselves autobiographical, and who prefer the writers they read to be autobiographical, can be shy of saying so. Not long before his death in 1988 the American writer of stories, Raymond Carver, hesitantly said: 'Writers—the writers I most admire, at any rate—make some use of their own lives.'[12]

Others have been more assertive. Lyndall Gordon, a biographer of the 'unreachable' T. S. Eliot, as she thinks of him, has recently written: 'The idea that Eliot's poetry was rooted in private aspects of his life has now been accepted.' Commenting on this claim,[13] Frank Kermode remarked that Eliot was 'well aware that impersonal poetry was produced by persons: but this doesn't make the impersonality argument bogus . . .'. Nevertheless, as Kermode had observed a few sentences earlier, 'many people have come to think that the impersonality business was nonsense'. The publication in 1988 of the first volume of Eliot's correspondence gave an opportunity to discover what some people have come to think about this business. Valerie Eliot's edition was welcomed and praised, and her decision to publish the letters against her husband's wishes went unchallenged. They were treated as a major cultural event. But there was no impression to be gained from the run of reviews that the letters were either very enlightening or very appealing—so that there was hardly any pressing need for the occasional warning that was issued concerning the ill-effects of allowing them to encourage a biographically-informed reading of Eliot's verse.

It seems that we have started to doubt whether it is right to feed on the life and letters of an important writer while pretending that they are not important for an examination of his work. We have started to disbelieve in one of the authors we have formed for ourselves—an author so sufferingly remote from us that he can't get into his own books. Not long after the publication of Eliot's letters, a leading article in the *Independent* (it was, admittedly, a Saturday) contained the statement: 'common sense and experience tell us that knowledge of the life and times of artists, writers and composers can greatly increase our understanding and enjoyment of their work.'[14] A stultifying hypocrisy has grown tired. But it is certain that we shall go on being told from time to time, and for a long time to come, about the 'authorial intrusions' detectable in some author's text.

For all the philosophical infirmity of its more unctuous formulations, the case for impersonality, for showing and dramatising rather than telling, for a wariness of self-interest and opinion, is never likely to be deficient in impressive instances and applications. Writings are produced by persons, and those persons who are bullying egotists are generally

distrusted. But there is much to be said on the other side, and
I hope that some of it has been said here. It may, for example,
be said that authorship and pain, like readership and pain, go
together, but that the connection has been misjudged, and that
the relief from pain, the escape from emotion, promised,
among other blessings, by doctrines of impersonality was always an illusion. There is reason to discourage the opinionated writer, whose opinions have so often been found wanting,
and there will often be reason to prefer the art that conceals the
artist, or appears to, to the art that in one way or another—
including some specifically modern ways—obtrudes the artist.
We may assume that there will continue to be the various kinds
of author that there have been in the past—the concealing sort,
the obtruding sort, the sort that tells, the sort that is indifferent
to politics—and there is no need for these authors to resemble
each other. But there is a need for them to own up. Those
writers of the present age who were once content to hear that
opinion is a violation of the artist should now attend to the
more sensible opinion that fiction and poetry are forms of
opinion. They should accept that the books they write are
theirs, as well as their readers', as well as the creation of their
language and literature and their time and place. They should
accept this even when they are able to believe that they are
inspired, to believe what Blake did of his designs: a correspondent of his was told that they 'are not Mine' (but of course he
still 'called them Mine', and would have been prepared to share
them with none other than his own angel, or devil, as this letter
of 16 August 1799, with its mention of authorial 'independence',
makes clear).

In the Russia and Eastern Europe of the Stalin years fiction
and poetry were recognised as forms of opinion, and were
punished and destroyed as such. And in setting an example of
resistance to tyranny the authorship of these countries brought
honour to the calling. After the Second World War, Western
authors may be thought to have had a relatively quiet time of
it, and for this they were to pay a price which has been implied
in the criticisms I have expressed of the outlook to which a large
number of them have subscribed. Part of the story must be, I
feel, that they have been the worse for not giving what has not
been required of them. But it may be that this quiet time has

now gone, and that some of them will be required to behave rather more like dissidents. And if they do find themselves learning to be dissidents they will rarely need to be told that their novels and their poems are theirs, and that they are also those of the society to which they are addressed.

More than one of the celebrated poets of this century's English-speaking world have been hostile and miserable people who have stood in serious need of the persuasion that good artists are immune from, their personal deficiencies—which can, indeed, very often seem remote from the best behaviour, as we might think it, embodied in their art. They have been despisers of inferiority and admirers of fascism, and their admirers have forgiven them for it, while also respecting them for it, and perceiving sanctions for it in English literature. It can't in general be supposed that the personal deficiencies and deficient opinions of Western authors have done much to restrict their influence. Nor has their ability to share in the persuasion which has been referred to—to share in the ease-ments and alibis of impersonality. You need be no less famous for being impersonal, and no less influential. Perhaps it could be said that these authors have been both assisted and damaged by a conception of influence which has invited them to set themselves apart from a fan following, to be famous for not being famous, to be the hermit, *exalté*, or atrabilious spiritual leader, who is also an entertainer.

The great authorial crisis of 1989—I am speaking of Salman Rushdie's inflaming of Islam—was occasioned when an influential Western author was sentenced to death, for something he wrote, by an influential Middle Eastern priest. Rushdie's novel *The Satanic Verses* has offended many Moslems, who have been ordered to treat as Western and as diabolic a text that can also be treated as a dualistic fable in which East is West and West East. The two societies are thrust together into a Gothic delirium, by a divided author who belongs to both, and to neither, and who invents a brace of easily confused 'conflicting selves' in order to write about this, to write about fame and madness, orphans and demons. A playful book, which plays with fire. Rushdie's offence may include the breach of a principle of separation spoken of (and breached) by Kipling, and all-important to Khomeini. For diplomatic reasons that can readily be understood, the offence was publicly 'regretted' by the author in the face of Khomeini's anathema, which was not, however, withdrawn. Here was a clash between writers and politicians—a clash, too, between writers and the world; literature has offended the religious fundamentalism which has begun to recover its energies. Rushdie's is a book which most of the world would find difficult to read (Asian children have been turning up at school in Britain with cyclostyled passages), but which has become world-famous. Not that there is anything very strange in that: it is by no means unprecedented in the history of influential authorship, and may even be a part of what we mean now by authorship.

This was and is a bitter business for those who are opposed to murder and to murder threats, and to the burning of books, for those who would like there to be literature, and would like it to be as free as possible to say what it means. And it is all the more bitter, from the present point of view, in that Rushdie is a writer whose playful novels have a political meaning, and have something to say which knows itself to be Rushdie's and no one else's. He wrote them. They are his. He is the author who always has to answer for his work when trouble comes. They are novels, indeed, which have taken courage to write. For several years they have risked the death of the author— which in another sense can scarcely be thought to have occurred when there are those who are threatening his life.

It might be fitting to end what I am saying on a personal note. When I was a boy in Scotland, tending my diary at a fair distance from the centres of influence and self-confidence in the south of the country, I went in awe of the activities of authors. I reviewed their books in that diary. They took part in my excitements and self-pity. They were me. And they were above me. I lifted my eyes to their activities as I did to the Pentland Hills. Then I met some. I met Hugh MacDiarmid—who was living in a cottage not far from the slopes of the Pentlands, and who had been a notable absentee from those centres of influence, as he is now from most accounts of the progressive literature of the British Thirties—and Dylan Thomas, who had returned by then to Wales, to the boat-house in Laugharne, after his colourful stay in London. These, in their humble dwellings, were famous men, whose fame accommodated a degree of estrangement from the life of the nation, and a high degree of difficulty in much of what they wrote—a difficulty relished or ignored by their initiates and worshippers and seldom in the least embarrassing to their critics and ex-pounders. Both men suffered and broke down; both were de-scribed by gossips as mischievous, as egotistical misbehavers. I became aware of such disparagements when I first visited London and talked to a critic of Eliot's poetry, one of the literary moralists then functioning as the profession's inspector-ate. Not all of them could be mistaken for authors, but this one was author enough to branch out later into fiction and film scripts. He asked me, over the wine and olives, whom I liked to read, and I told him. 'Dylan Thomas', said this author, 'is a shit.' From these two shits, Dylan Thomas and Hugh MacDiarmid, I received nothing but kindness.

So much, one could well be inclined to think, for the bio-graphical properties of rumour, and the fascination of the partly true. There can be no doubt that the gossip I'd been listening to is the stuff of which many books about writers are made. But this is not the only meaning which these encounters could be thought to bear. I had discovered that authors were persons, complicated persons, rather than Pentland Hills, at about the time that my university education was inviting me to deny that these are the very persons who write their books; and I had discovered that there is no more injurious judgement than the judgement which one author passes on another.

I am referring to Thomas's despiser in his role of author, and distinguishing between authors and critics—a distinction it has long been convenient to make. But it is now rightly contested among literary theorists, who believe that critics are authors, and there are now few friends for the idea of a barely readable inspectorate which tells writers how to write, and that they are shits. The author whose death has been the subject of exaggerated reports has for the most part been envisaged here as a writer of novels and poems who could be interested in criticism and in public life. But those writers who are temperamentally incapable of publicity, or of criticism, can hardly be excluded from a category which they have at times seemed about to usurp, as exemplars of the privacy of authors which has been held to be imperative; and critics have been thought of too, both those who are and those who are not temperamentally incapable of literature.

There are plenty of authors about in Britain, with more of them in their books than it has been the thing to say. Authorship—its actions and intentions, presence and absence, monologues and dialogues, hostility and authority, portraits and diaries, publishers and readers—has responded for centuries to enduring needs and to a series of new worlds and of new modes and means of expression, and it has now entered a phase associated with the rise to prominence of the electronic media, a phase in which collective responsibility—never an unfamiliar feature of literary practice, though one which writers have frequently impugned and disowned—will be enhanced. It can also be said to have entered a harsher world, in which the authoritarian rule of an entrenched political party prevents legitimate enquiry, and in which protest breaks the law. With this and with other departures from the world of the Fifties a literature which has often come close to the condition of soliloquy will have to deal—in the knowledge that the authorship which enquires, and speaks out, and for itself, may not be wanted by those in a position to refuse it. Publishers and broadcasting chiefs are now less interested in authorship than they were. The new theoretically readable inspectorate of literary theorists has aspired to it, but has also attacked it: the creative writing of the present has been virtually excluded from their agenda, and the authorship of the past has been seen as an aspect of the English literature they profess to dislike. Those who write books are nevertheless tenacious people, and those who read them are tenacious too, and may be slow to settle for the authorial desert of the British films and British television that may be in store for them. If there's a habitable world in a hundred years' time, it is likely to have authors in it.

XV · Literary Journalism

BRITAIN publishes a large number of books, and reviews them in a large number of places. Many of its many publishers are over-producers, and the figure for new books has been put at a rising 60,000 a year. But the proportion of books reviewed to books published is low: very few papers can be discussing more than one in a hundred of those that 'come out'. Together with what appears to be a decline in book advertisements, this means that a painful soundlessness has crept into the utterance of authors. There is a feeling that the country does not read many of the books it publishes. The shops where they are sold have become fewer and fewer, and more and more philist-ine and unfriendly. Libraries are being stinted, and indeed destroyed.

Information of this kind has led to predictions of a collapse. So far as literary journalism is concerned, however, the con-sequences of anything that could be called a collapse have yet to be suffered, though there have certainly been retrenchments, and changes for the worse.

When newspapers are launched in the hope of attracting informed readerships, these newspapers still have book sec-tions: this was the case with the *Independent*, which has had the sense to exploit the news value of books—a resource tradi-tionally underrated in the press—by carrying a daily review. I remember looking at another of the new newspapers of recent times, Robert Maxwell's *Daily News* that once was, and finding that a mid-market London readership was expected to care about the reflections of a man of letters who had been allowed to lavish some hundreds of well-chosen and warmly appreciative words on the work of a writer whom I took to be a friend of his, a friend whose life had accustomed him to battlements and landed estates: no one could claim that the British did not review each other any more, I told myself, or that they had taken to doing so in an entirely new way. This paper was soon to fail: but it can't have been brought down by its rasping innovations.

The paper which I have been editing, and which I shall in future be co-editing, the *London Review of Books*, is about to celebrate its tenth birthday. It began, in 1979, at a time when the luxuriance of British book-reviewing had been trimmed by a lengthy strike at Times Newspapers. It began when Margaret Thatcher began her reign as Conservative prime minister, and when the Social Democratic Party began, and when the rule of the Ayatollah Khomeini began in the Middle East. There must have been those at the time who thought that none of the undertakings in question would last for very long. The SDP has since merged with the Liberals, thereby dissolving in tears the SDP leader who had been understood to support the merger, and the merged party which has succeeded the SDP-Liberal Alliance, the Democrats, is ailing. But Mrs Thatcher and Khomeini went on in their anger to dominate these ten years, both of them holy terrors of a kind, with an air, at times, of the interminable, and the *London Review* is still appearing.

The circulation is getting on for twenty thousand, and its readership is estimated at twice that figure. The books we review are reviewed at a time when the break-even point for academic works is reached with the sale of some two thousand copies, and publishers have seen the paper as a place where academic works are amply discussed. But they have also seen it as a place where the general as well as the specialist reader can be solicited. They don't need to be reminded that our circulation is small compared with that of any daily or Sunday newspaper, but they also know that a high proportion of our readers read books, and they have been willing to advertise with us. Advertising is vital for the paper commercially, as it is for almost all publications. Almost all our advertisers are publishers, and many of them are American university publishers. Circulation is dependent on subscription, and we have as many American as English subscribers. We are read in a large number of countries throughout the world, though we are hard to obtain there except by subscription. The paper, which is privately owned, receives a grant from the Arts Council.

In offering to say something about literary journalism, I shall concentrate on the character and fortunes of the paper I work for, because it is the one I know best, and like best, and also because it is no different from lots of other papers, past and present, in respect of the sorts of thing it finds, and finds difficult, to discuss. I shall be writing about these things, and about the survival from long since of the literary journal which seeks to discuss a wide range of subjects. The paper I work for is one which is reluctant to divide itself up—to hive off or delegate any part of the editorial function—in order to do so. This, too, has its history.

My own experience of journalism has always lain in the field of small papers interested both in politics and in literature, in the behaviour both of rulers and of authors, and it is to this field that I am mainly referring when I use the term 'literary journalism'. The three papers I worked for earlier were all of this kind, and it is a kind which represents the persistence of an ancient strain in British journalism—a strain which preceded the arrival of mass-circulation newspapers and assisted in their creation. This is to hark back to a time when there was a general knowledge, which could be called by the name of literature, and which a journal might hope to publish. There is still a spice of this project in some small papers now—weeklies and fortnight-lies—and it is not altogether missing from politically-active newspapers which concern themselves with books: from the *Observer*, for example, which is personal and authorial in the way that small papers can still be, and which has something of the sense of coterie retained by, and perhaps expected of, small papers. These, however, have usually been more preoccupied than most newspapers have ever been with the struggle to co-ordinate an attention to politics with an attention to literature, and have been exposed to a criterion of consistency in this respect which most journalists now may regard as archaic. This is a preoccupation which also marks them off from the little magazines which continue to appear: a little magazine is likely to specialise, to avoid politics, and to be exempt from the reproach of inconsistency. Over the past twenty years, small papers have moved closer to the margins of journalism. Fissures have opened up between these papers and their customary sources of information and support. But there would seem to be as many of them about as there were twenty years ago.

I've suggested that what we do has been done in the past. At the start of the nineteenth century the *Edinburgh Review* em-barked on an achievement which has not been forgotten in literary journalism, and to which the practice of the old *New Statesman*, for instance, was in certain ways intimately related. Francis Jeffrey's journal can be read and admired to this day for its earnestness and impudence, its politics and letters, its wide spread of subjects on either side of that division, and for its argumentative long articles. These are features which have gone, we'd like to think, to the making of the *London Review*. We have tried to make a book of each issue, which is indeed the length of a book, and we have wanted to carry essays, as opposed to notices, and to be as sparing as we could with the irresponsibility of the opinionated and unsubstantiated short review. This is an approach which appeals to writers who want to make a book of their articles in the paper, and which no doubt looks like a death warrant to many a working journalist.

As I say, it is an approach which commemorates the *Edinburgh Review*. But literary journalists in search of their ancestors might well prefer to begin with an earlier world, which the *Edinburgh Review* supposed itself to have eclipsed: a less reputable founding father can be identified in the Whig Ralph Griffiths, who went to work in the Grub Street of eighteenth-century London. Politics and letters were combined, in his *Monthly Review*, with a keen commercialism, and the journal is said to have been financed from the proceeds of John Cleland's erotic novel *Fanny Hill*. Here, too, there is a precedent for the literary journalism of later times. Journals of review of the kind I'm referring to incorporate a further dual purpose in the form of a participation in the commercial publishing of which they produce a critique. This has caused trouble in its time. But the pursuit of politics and letters has proved on occasion to be as awkward as the exposure to commerce. The *New Statesman* used to deal with its problems in this quarter by having, in effect, two editors, one for the front half and one for the back. The 'pantomime horse' solution, as it used to be called, could, of course, only succeed at the expense of the project of a single expertise, a co-ordinated attention to different subject-matters: but my memory of the matter is that for most of those who were on the paper in the Sixties the project had in some measure survived. On the *London Review* there is just the one consensus, which is literary rather than political, and which has had to be paid for in terms of a remoteness from party-political action and discussion. Perhaps we could do with the political adviser whom we do not want.

During the ten years of our existence a Conservative government has been in power. The country has been experiencing the anxiety of a terrorist war in Northern Ireland and the bitterness of an economic recession. It has also experienced what has come to be called, even by opponents, the Thatcher revolution. The old private enterprise slogans have turned to gold—for some. For others, the signs of the returning prosperity which is now being claimed are hard to read. What they *can* read are their filthy, rutted streets, a conspicuous crime and greed, a country of riot and rot, poison and spillage, the arrival on those streets of beggars and of the privatised mentally ill, the burning to death of commuters in a neglected and squalid major underground station. More people want Margaret Thatcher out than want her to go on with her privateering. But they can hardly be confident that they have the politicians to do it for them. Opposition policy-makers have yet to plan, at any rate in public, for coalition and a hung Parliament, for what could well be their only hope. Each of the Opposition parties is waiting for Mrs Thatcher to retire, while setting out its separate stall and quarrelling internally over the display. It would be good to see political duality restored.

Mrs Thatcher came in with the aim of attacking inflation by reducing public expenditure and accepting an unemployment rate which it was assumed would remain severe. Ten years later both inflation and unemployment have still to be overcome. She has moved on in time to a privatising of the welfare state which has now crossed the threshold of the Health Service. University research has been cut back, university finance has been driven into crisis, and departments have been closed. Freedom of expression and inquiry in broadcasting and the press has been curtailed, and the domination of the press by private interests pledged to Thatcherism has been strengthened. A golden age of British broadcasting—when governments subscribed to an ideal of amusement, instruction and investigation which won a place for broadcasting in the country's intellectual and artistic life—is being brought to an end by government decree, and the savourless huckster sights of the future have already begun to fill our screens. The new, authorised BBC is

likely to be a de-authorised BBC. The Corporation seems set
to become a residual element within a system in which a principle of authorlessness, of dedication to the largest possible
audience, and to the profits to be made by those friends of
government who are awarded the concessions, may impose
a desolation.

Mrs Thatcher is a forthright, powerful and successful politician. But her successes have often been indistinguishable from
failures, and I don't think I am making too much of the public
squalor which has accompanied her ascendancy. Where she
has certainly succeeded is in defeating her enemies, in damaging the confidence of the Left, and in causing it to damage
itself. This has been reflected in the small papers of the
Eighties, which have rarely been for Mrs Thatcher, but which
have been at a loss for something to support and at times for
something to publish. The adversarial leftism which once upon
a time flowed into their columns has dried up in the eeriest way.
The paper I work for would like to see a popular front against
Thatcherism and a left-of-centre coalition government, and
it would like the country to have a decent public life. I don't
believe we have lost the courage of these convictions. But I am
afraid that we have not done enough to make them evident.

The *London Review* saw the point of some of the SDP's early
purposes, but was never an Alliance paper. It is more interested
in democratic socialism than the Alliance was, or than the
Democrats have so far been able to make up their minds to be.
We never felt any urge to go with David Owen, who is now
preaching a kind of benevolent Thatcherism called—but not by
many—the 'social market' philosophy: 'prosperity with fair-
ness', a caring greed. 'Unemployment is socially unacceptable
to the SDP', Owen tells us: but we are also told that he is just
as keen as Mrs Thatcher is on competition. The *London Review*
is best thought of now as a coalitionist paper of the centre-left
whose authorship and readership are characterised by a wide
range of political views, and whose editorial journalists are
agreed that there is much to be hoped for from the rise to
prominence of the Scottish Shadow Ministers, John Smith,
Gordon Brown and Robin Cook. We are not, in fact, greatly
read by politicians. From the standpoint of a small journalist
who remembers the Fifties and who has helped to build a new

paper in the Eighties, the House of Commons appears to have
changed, and to be a poor source at present both of readers and
of writers. The old affinity between MPs and this type of
journalist has receded.

Three matters of general public interest have proved especially sensitive for the paper. First, the Falklands war, whose
fifth anniversary was observed in 1987 on a note of compassion
for the bereaved, and with little or no reference to the fact that
a clear majority of United Nations members was still of the
opinion that the islands should be ceded to Argentina. We
believed at the time that the engagement was rash and prema-
ture, and that the pursuit of a settlement should have been
maintained and intensified. Five years later, the commander
responsible for the San Carlos landing stressed the hazardous-
ness of the Task Force operation: the Argentinian forces were in
a strong position, he was reported as saying, and if they had
'got their act together' they might have won. As it turned out,
the hundreds of men on both sides who were killed may be said
to have lost. It is true that the British victory brought certain
beneficial results—principally, a change of government in Argentina. But we continue to regard this as the unnecessary
war which it was declared to be by a former Labour prime
minister, James Callaghan. At the time, none of the parties,
and no newspaper of any description that I know of, opposed
the war. There were votes, and there were readers, to be
secured by upholding the sovereignty of the Falklands, and by
accepting the decision to risk the Army and Navy in the South
Atlantic.

The second of these matters was the miners' strike of 1984–5.
The paper did not support Arthur Scargill, the Mineworkers'
President, whose strategy could eventually be seen as a predic-
ate of Mrs Thatcher's: so that the miners went down to defeat,
and division, in a war (for that is what it felt like) which had
already divided the Labour movement. Scargill's never seeming in the least to worry about the possibility of these divisions
is a feature which will always remain in the mind. Most of the
correspondence we received on this subject took his side.

Thirdly, the Middle East. We have carried criticisms of Israeli government policy which have not offended the domestic
readership but which have drawn charges of anti-Semitism

in Israel and, more particularly, in America. The course we have followed is one that lies open to misrepresentation as sympathetic or indifferent to hostage-taking and terrorism, and as hostile to the survival of the state of Israel. We are not in favour of terrorism, wherever it originates, and we *are* in favour of the survival of the state of Israel. But we wish it would stop invading its neighbours.

There are matters of more debatable public consequence which have proved no less sensitive for a journal which seeks to treat politics and literature as a single subject-matter, as the one scene. In saying something about these, I shall discuss two very different texts which could each be thought to address the duality of such journals, to deserve consideration there, and to raise questions concerning the discovery of politics in literature. The first of the texts is both literary and political in content. The second, which might seem the more unpromising politically, nevertheless harbours a political meaning. It is a meaning which would encourage no one to believe in that remoteness of literature from politics which has served as a fiction with which to defend and dignify what writers do.

The *London Review* would be beneath the notice, I take it, of many of those who consider themselves literary theorists. For our own part, we notice, and we publish, literary theory. One of the controversies which has recently appeared in our pages, and which appears on an earlier page of the present book, has been about the fascist sentiments expressed during the Second World War by the deconstructor Paul de Man. We are aware that Deconstruction, which has been termed a 'vigilance' rather than a method, belongs to a set of activities in which differences of approach can be identified, in which a dual purpose can be identified, and we think that some of these activities are more vigilant than others. The moment of *Scrutiny*, the prominence of Leavis's ideas in English studies and in schools—this is now over. The contradictions inherent in his approach have been reassessed—by deconstructors and others. But many of the people who were interested in Leavis in the past had been able to take account of these contradictions for themselves, and there is no reason to suppose that nothing of any value will ever be done in Leavis's way again. The deconstruction of Leavis was done in Leavis's way, one might claim:

an entrenched authority has been attacked from a position of moral superiority, by people equipped with a vigilance which can seem to matter more than the method they expound.

There are theorists for whom theory is a millennium, in which former things are passed away, and who might refuse to admit the possibility of a change, let alone of a fresh recourse to any one of the ways in which things used to be done. There are other theorists, though, for whom theory has been hermetic and esoteric, and who wish it to have a voice in the discourse of politics. So it seems that theory has its contradictions too. Theorists are liked for being left-wing, 'radical', just as Leavis once was, before he was discovered to be right-wing. But politicians might retort that theory has so far been an abdication from politics, that its discourse has found no basis for preferring any one form of political commitment to any other, and that the marginality of literary journalism has been repeated at the level of literary theory.

Terry Eagleton has been calling for a politically-engaged literary theory. The first article in the first number of the British journal *Textual Practice*[1] was by him, and it was entitled 'The End of English'. Its last words were these: 'as the material conditions which historically supported the ideology of "English" have been gradually eroded, it is clearer than ever that the only conflict which finally matters is between the internationalism of late capitalist consumerism, and the internationalism of its political antagonist.' The 'only conflict that matters' is like the 'one thing needful' that figured in an eloquence of the past: this is the language of the religious believer that can often be heard in the condemnations and predictions of our late-Christian era. The essay is a work not of theory but of polemical history, though it brings in the theories of the millennial Marx. But my main interest here is in noting that these last words do not specify who or what consumerism's antagonist is, and what weapons are to be used in the conflict. Nor is the article as a whole any more specific in this respect.

We can assume that the antagonist is not democratic socialism, which can be seen by theorists, and is seen by Terry Eagleton, as having been complicit with liberal humanism, expressive realism and English literature in lending assistance to capitalism and imperialism. But Eagleton doesn't say right out that the only thing that matters is that international Communism, or that Russia and its allies, should win the battle of Armageddon—if this is what he has in mind instead. His British readers would not relish being told in so many words that the only thing which should matter to them is that Russia beats America in a war that devastates the world. So the antagonist is left unspecified, and the reader is left in the dark as to how the overthrow of capitalist consumerism is to proceed, just as he is left in the dark as to what Eagleton's sentence may have to do with the present condition of Russia, apparently bent on a measure of accommodation with the West, and on the duality of democracy, or with that of China, which is said to be well on its way to capitalism. It is even possible to wonder whether the conflict he is talking about exists. The gist of Terry Eagleton's sentence might have come from Margaret Thatcher. Both of them would appear to think what all too many people are given to thinking, about states of affairs which may or may not exist: that there are two sides, and that there is only the one thing worth having.

The essay is evidence of a danger that awaits those, including the editors of literary magazines, in whose judgements an attention to politics coexists with an attention to literature. It is quite easy for them to miss both targets. The essay does an injustice to the English literature which it is seeking to end by declaring it obsolete, while the politics contained in the essay are a punitive dream of a kind that has been experienced and approved among the religions.

Tensions between public and private, politics and literature —with literature presumed to be the sphere of a reclusive individualism—can be recognised in certain journals, but are not confined to journals. They are widespread and important. They are important to the poetry of Seamus Heaney, which is important to the *London Review*, as is his feeling for a poetry of transcendence, a quasi-religious world of art, in which politics, among other concerns of everyday life, can sometimes seem to be present on sufferance. He believes that there is a 'gulf' between 'art and life'. Such beliefs have led him to be exercised, and perhaps troubled, by the poetry of his contemporaries in Eastern Europe, where the gulf is apt to disappear. An expression he makes use of, 'the government of the tongue',[2] is intended to signify both the authority of poetry and its repression by systems of doctrine and power, and it relates, as does his conception of an autonomous art, to the history of one subject people in particular, where gulfs were fixed and tongues tied—to that of Catholic Ulster. The poetry he often admires, but does not always write, is one in which public matters tend to be excluded. But he also admires the poetry of the subject peoples of Eastern Europe, in which public matters have been both eluded and embraced.

There can't be many who blame him for failing to put on a hood and pick up a gun on behalf of the Catholics of Northern Ireland, whom the IRA has moved to defend in a terrorist war of attrition. But he should not be praised for being above the battle. This is where he may have wished to be at times: and yet it matters very much to him that he belongs to the 'Irish people' on both sides of the border. It has taken time for his readers in Britain to realise this; some of them may have the impression that he has 'come out' as Irish in the course of the troubles. He holds that the Irish people in Ulster have been and still are oppressed, and that the British Army's presence there is part of the problem rather than part of the solution. He is likely to favour a united Ireland (as does the British Labour Party, whose solution, however, requires the consent of the Northern population which it has no way of knowing how to get). But one might guess that his politics are not otherwise of a kind to please the left-wing literary theorist or Armageddonist. It is necessary for his readers to guess, for they are hard to infer from his prose writings, and harder still to infer from a poetry which can often seem reclusive and contemplative, and which was at one point to make ironic play with a regional saying lately, and less playfully, enjoined on its adherents by the IRA: 'Whatever you say say nothing.' In the same poem he writes:

I incline as much to rosary beads

As to the jottings and analyses
Of politicians and newspapermen . . .

Nevertheless, there are poems by him which do say something political, something which any literary magazine which interested itself in politics would have done well to try to interpret at the time of their appearance. There is a poem by him about the tarring and feathering of girls who went out with British soldiers. As a witness of such atrocities he has 'stood dumb', and

> would connive
> in civilised outrage
> yet understand the exact
> and tribal, intimate revenge.

'Punishment' is a political poem; perhaps there are few poems more expressive of the province of Northern Ireland. What, in the lines I have quoted, is the poet conniving at? Even that doubt is expressive.

I would like to look a little longer at another poem of his, one that could be called unobtrusively political. Written in 1972, 'A Peacock's Feather' celebrates the birth of a sister-in-law's child, and evokes a Gloucestershire country house, contrasting it with the country place in Ulster where he grew up. The house makes him think that he might as well be in Yeats's Coole Park. His poem addresses the child, and the second verse reads:

> Gloucestershire: its prospects lie
> Wooded and misty to my eye
> Whose landscape, as your mother's was,
> Is other than this mellowness
> Of topiary, lawn and brick,
> Possessed, untrespassed, walled, nostalgic.

We know from other texts of his that walls such as these had met his eye when he was a boy in Ulster—an eye that studied them from the outside. The third verse moves through the 'scraggy farm and moss' of that boyhood, towards mention of a government of the tongue which has enabled him to celebrate Daisy's birthday.

> But here, for your sake, I have levelled
> My cart-track voice to garden tones,
> Cobbled the bog with Cotswold stones.

And the last two lines speak of the poem they complete:

> I drop this for you, as I pass,
> Like the peacock's feather on the grass.

The stanzas refer, as I've said, to Yeats, a poet who was also a political activist, and who founded a system of ideas on the tension between public and private. But there is more of Marvell in the poem than there is of Yeats. Marvell was both a public poet and a private one, a poet who wrote about country retreats and about Cromwell's pacification of Ireland. My feeling is that Marvell's 'Horatian Ode upon Cromwell's Return from Ireland' supplies a frame of reference for Heaney's poem, whose four-stress rhyming couplets are present in the Ode, in alternation with two shorter lines. Marvell's poem shows the Pict shrinking beneath his tartan plaid—away from Cromwell's sword. Heaney's poem has the soil of Gloucestershire 'darkened with Celts' and Saxons' blood'. Marvell's poem is triumphal, though not unequivocal. Heaney's poem tacitly dissents from it, in speaking of a contemporary world where tribal and ancestral divisions are deeply involved with divisions of wealth and class.

Heaney is not asking for these walls to be torn down. His poem seems at one point to speak of reconciliation, and it has in it somewhere the patient fatalism which he attributes, elsewhere in his poetry, to working-class Northern Irish Catholics —but which would not be easy to detect among the IRA. The poet is thought to be like a peacock, and the poem could be thought to belong more to an aesthetic than to a political sphere. But it is not preeningly apolitical. It portrays the poet both as a peacock and (less plausibly) as a rough-tongued clod-hopping interloper: a contrast, incidentally, which might be considered relevant to the view taken in Terry Eagleton's essay of the divided loyalties evident in Heaney's language. The poet here is someone only temporarily on the inside of Gloucestershire's walls—the very walls that Nathan Zuckerman was to encounter in Philip Roth's novel *The Counterlife*. Later in the poem the word 'untrespassed' is echoed in 'as I pass': this signals that the poet is a trespasser in relation to these English escarpments and amenities, and contributes to a political meaning. The echo is planted by a famous student of vowels and consonants, and of their tribal significance for Celts and Picts. As it happens, the vowel in 'pass' is one which, in Britain, tends in itself to bestow a class significance on its speaker.

The poem was written at an early point in the current troubles. This was a time when Heaney came under pressure to write public works and to treat the troubles in verse. These urgings were accompanied by allusions to Marvell's Ode, and to uncollected early writings by Heaney which included songs for a Catholic community subject to attack by a sectarian police force. The politics in the present poem are somewhat cryptic, as they are in Marvell's Ode. But it is a poem to which politically-minded literary journalists might have attended in 1972, had it been published at the time it was written,[3] and been persuaded that it spoke, with gentle obliquity, of Cromwell's expulsion from Ireland. It might have induced a little scepticism with regard to the claim made by the Labour leader of the day, Harold Wilson: that the troubles were the work of a few thugs.

Having said as much, I am quite content to admit that one vowel, and a number of supporting suggestions, do not make a political statement, even when they come from Ireland's most important author—who is also, in some residual sense, its tribal bard. The poem exhibits, and indeed acknowledges, the dandyish self-love of the autonomous work of art. It could not be used, as Kipling's poems have been used by Ulster's Protestants, in order to whip up feeling in the service of a political cause. In Kipling's Unionist poems politics and literature are simultaneous. There is a line which says what Hitler was to say: 'One Law, one Land, one Throne.' And another line says: 'We perish if we yield.'[4] The power of such lines is a literary power. At the same time, it is by no means remote from the power praised in Marvell's Ode—that of Cromwell and his army. It would not be true to claim that Heaney has never been as political as that. His ballad about Craig's dragoons is as political as that. But you will not find it in any of his books.

Seamus Heaney's peacock poem counts both as art and as evidence—as evidence of the depth and intractability of these Irish troubles, and of the class divisions which enter into them. And it is a poem which makes it intelligible that there should be papers which set themselves to be both literary and political.

It may be that literary journalism is disappearing, along with English literature: but there is no proof that either of these ends has come. Literary journalism has begun to lose touch with the

political community. It has not succeeded very well in attracting young readers and young writers. The power of television
is formidable, and its investigative capacity in the field of
current affairs, daunted though it is at present, is, so far as
newspapers and periodicals are concerned, the most formidable
aspect of that power. But there is no sign that print has been
defeated, and television could well serve to protect the small
print of small papers. Theirs is a medium which can do what
mass-market moving pictures can't easily accommodate and
television executives have become reluctant to allow. And it is
a medium which stands to benefit, on the whole, from the new
technology which is becoming available to the press. British
literary journalism has always been a precarious business, and
I doubt whether its setbacks and shortcomings, and the interesting times through which it has been living, have caused it to
be more precarious than it was before.

The middle ground between the type of paper I have been
discussing and those papers in which huge sums of money are
invested is very sparsely cultivated in Britain, and it is worth
wondering what would happen if journals of politics and literature, and others like them, were to cease, and if the press were
to become little more than the preserve of a smaller and smaller
group of international magnates. The journals I have been
discussing have tried hard over the years to say things which
newspapers wouldn't say or didn't know, or had to learn by
raiding the journals for ideas and authors. Such raids are an
indication that authors matter, and that authorship, in the
sense which has been defended and desired in the chapters of
this book, is for small papers rather than big ones. Those who
are drawn to the case for an outspoken and responsible authorship, for authorship as a distinctive function exercised by a
succession of different men and women who mean what they
say, would do well to care about the papers where authors can
still be read. The authors who have been read there have been
authors of mischief, but of a great deal else besides. The *New
Statesman* was among the authors of the welfare state and of an
independent India.

What happened to it over the years that led to its recent
merger with another paper was due, as I see it, to misguided
attempts at a change of genre. It was feared that the old idea of

the intellectual weekly—of a magazine written by authors for the general reader, which brings together reporting, politics, poetry, fiction and reflection, and which tries for a single subject-matter and a philosophic overview—had become antiquated. The designers were called in. It lost its looks, and much of its literary content. It was to be like one of the investigative sections that did well for a time in the Sunday papers of the Sixties and Seventies, but was rather more like some American news-magazine short of news and strapped for money. The new style was to have its triumphs. But they would have done better to have left the paper as it was, generically speaking. And I can't help adding: *Time* Magazine it was that died, as an object of emulation, not long after the *New Statesman* was transformed.

Those who claim that there has been a decline in the fortunes of the journals I have been speaking of have sometimes seemed to believe that there is something wrong with them anyway and that they have deserved their fate. The belief is that they are élitist, that they are sites or spaces where the tyranny of the author may be detected and deplored. But if there is something wrong with these journals, there is something wrong with newspapers too. The vacancy and nastiness of so many even of the most celebrated are features which have tended to get worse with the enlargement of readerships and advertising revenues, and with the growth of multiple ownership by representatives of the predatory rich. If this is almost all we are to be left with, there will be good reason to regret the loss of the literary journalism which is now supposed to be in crisis.

NOTES

Publication sources which have been selected for annotation are British except where otherwise stated.

CHAPTER I

1. *The Oxford Book of English Ghost Stories* (1986), chosen by Michael Cox and R. A. Gilbert.
2. *The Ghost Stories of M. R. James* (1986), selected by Michael Cox.
3. *Edmund Spenser: Selected Poetry* (1966), ed. A. C. Hamilton: *Faerie Queene*, Book I, Canto v, ll. 276–9; Canto ii, ll. 284–8.
4. Vernon Lee, *Supernatural Tales* (1987).
5. Jack Matthews, *Ghostly Populations* (Johns Hopkins University Press, 1986).

CHAPTER II

1. By André Deutsch, with a foreword by Carlos Fuentes.
2. *The Life and Adventures of Sir Launcelot Greaves* was reissued by Penguin in 1988, with an introduction and notes by Peter Wagner.
3. Smollett's translation, p. 585.
4. Ibid., p. 582.
5. *The Female Quixote*, published in 1752, was reissued in paperback by Pandora in 1986.

CHAPTER III

1. Edited and introduced by Angus Ross.
2. Lady Louisa Stuart, *Memoire of Frances, Lady Douglas*, edited and introduced by Jill Rubenstein, with a preface by J. Steven Watson (1985).
3. *Clarissa* (1985 edn.), p. 400.
4. *Memoire of Frances, Lady Douglas*, pp. 31–2.
5. Sir Lewis Namier and John Brooke, *Charles Townshend*, with a foreword by Lady Namier (1964).
6. Alexander Pushkin, *Eugene Onegin*, ed. Avrahm Yarmolinsky, trans. Babette Deutsch (1971), p. 62.
7. The 'Introductory Anecdotes' formed part of the edition by Lord Wharncliffe (a nephew of Stuart's) of *The Letters and Works of Lady Mary Wortley Montagu* which was published · (3 vols.) in 1837. See W. Moy Thomas's augmented reissue of 1893 (2 vols.), i. 106–8. Stuart's essay refers at this point both to Fielding and to Richardson: 'If Richardson's inelegancies disturb us less than they did Lady Mary Wortley, it is because we take for old-fashioned much that our fathers and mothers knew to be vulgar, or even

ridiculous.' Lady Mary served as Louisa Stuart's godmother—see Robert Halsband's *Lady Mary Wortley Montagu* (1956), p. 266—and sent her good wishes to her daughter: 'may she be as meritorious in your eyes as you are in mine!'

8. Johnson says this in his life of Pope, in the course of a discussion of Pope's 'Elegy to the Memory of an Unfortunate Lady'. The lady, Johnson writes, had been 'about to disparage herself by marriage with an inferior', and the poem had attracted attention by exhibiting 'the illaudable singularity of treating suicide with respect'.

9. *Memoire of Frances, Lady Douglas*, pp. 87–101.

10. *Charles Townshend*, pp. 1, 2, 78–104, 166. *Memoire of Frances, Lady Douglas*, p. 39.

11. Louisa Stuart's further posthumously published writings are as follows: *Gleanings from an Old Portfolio* (ed. Mrs Godfrey Clark, 3 vols., 1895, 1896, 1898)—these volumes (1778–1813) contain letters by various hands, besides her own, and are interesting for the picture they give of the affairs of the Stuartry during the first half of her life, and, in particular, of her relations with her sisters Lady Portarlington and Lady Macartney; *Lady Louisa Stuart: Selections from her Manuscripts* (ed. James Home, 1899)—this has the memoir entitled 'Some Account of John, Duke of Argyll and his Family', together with a number of her letters; *Letters of Lady Louisa Stuart to Miss Louisa Clinton* (ed. James Home, 2 vols., 1901, 1903)—a correspondence of several years' duration which concludes in 1834; *The Letters of Lady Louisa Stuart* (1926)—a selection edited and introduced by R. Brimley Johnson; *Notes by Lady Louisa Stuart on 'George Selwyn and his Contemporaries' by John Heneage Jesse* (ed. W. S. Lewis, 1928). Susan Buchan's *Lady Louisa Stuart: Her Memories and Portraits* (1932) is a brief biography based on extracts from the published writings.

12. 'Introductory Anecdotes', *Letters and Works of Lady Mary Wortley Montagu*, ed. W. Moy Thomas, i. 111–12. *Letters to Louisa Clinton*, ii. 354.

13. *Lady Louisa Stuart: Selections from her Manuscripts*, pp. 58–79.

14. Ibid., pp. 61, 141–9.

15. Ibid., pp. 138–40.

16. Samuel Johnson, *The Rambler*, no. 97, 19 Feb. 1751.

17. *Lady Louisa Stuart: Selections from her Manuscripts*, pp. 30–1.

18. *Gleanings* has an appendix (iii. 325–34) which gives a number of short poems attributed to Stuart. A note by her, dated 1800, explains that 'The Cinder King' had been published in ignorance of her authorship.

19. R. Brimley Johnson's *Letters of Louisa Stuart*, pp. 243–4.

20. The description comes from an article in the *Edinburgh Review* (Oct. 1833): see *Horace Walpole*, ed. Peter Sabor (1987), p. 312. Sabor's 'Critical Heritage' volume has a passage from Stuart's 'Introductory Anecdotes' on the private life of Sir Robert Walpole, which is followed by a 'Supplement' in which she absolves her grandmother, and her grandmother's diary, for most (though not, it would seem, all) of the responsibility for the treatment in the 'Anecdotes' of 'Lady Walpole's amours, of Sir Robert's indifference', and of what she took to be the open secret of Horace Walpole's paternity (pp. 327–30).

21. *Letters to Louisa Clinton*, ii. 351.

22. Ibid., pp. 246–56.

23. An unappealing poem attributed to her, 'On the Death of Miss Brougham', muses that the politician's only child may have lived long enough to have become 'an humble instrument' for the correction of the great: 'To curb ambition, to make genius bow' (*Gleanings*, iii. 329).

24. See R. Brimley Johnson's *Letters of Louisa Stuart*, p. 226, and Susan Buchan's biography, pp. 252, 258.

25. *Letters to Louisa Clinton*, i. 265, *Lady Louisa Stuart: Selections from her Manuscripts*, p. 244, and James Hogg's *Memoir of the Author's Life* and *Familiar Anecdotes of Sir Walter Scott* (ed. Douglas Mack, 1972), p. 95.

26. *Lady Louisa Stuart: Selections from her Manuscripts*, pp. 156–9.

CHAPTER IV

1. Paul Theroux, *Sunrise with Sea Monsters* (1986), p. 94.

2. *A Bend in the River* (1979), pp. 77–8.

3. Ibid., pp. 22–3.

4. Ibid., p. 69; cf. p. 171.

CHAPTER V

1. Published in 1979.

2. *Growing up in the Gorbals* (1986), pp. 74–5.

3. Ibid., p. 78.

4. Published in 1988.

CHAPTER VI

1. *Lud Heat: A Book of the Dead Hamlets* is dated on the title-page 'May 1974 to April 1975', and was published in 1986.

2. Louisa Stuart's contemporary opinion of Chatterton and his suicide consisted of two opinions. She felt that Horace Walpole should have been ashamed for treating him as an impostor, and for playing a part in depriving the world 'of such extraordinary genius'. But then Chatterton 'seems to have been but a profligate boy, notwithstanding his astonishing talents'. A profligate, but also, as he was to be for Ackroyd's Wilde, a prodigal prodigy. See *Gleanings from an Old Portfolio*, i. 35–6.

CHAPTER VII

1. From Philip Roth's 'Afterword: A Talk with the Author' to Kundera's *The Book of Laughter and Forgetting* (1983), p. 234.

2. *Life is elsewhere* (1986), pp. 59–60, 192–3.

3. *My First Loves* (1986), translated by Ewald Osers, pp. 138–42.

CHAPTER VIII

1. *New Left Review*, no. 158, July / Aug. 1986.
2. Translations of the three books by Kapuscinski which are discussed in this chapter were published in Britain over a period of four years: *The Emperor* (1983), *Shah of Shahs* (1985) and *Another Day of Life* (1987). The second book was translated by William Brand, the other two by William Brand and Katarzyna Mroczkowska-Brand.
3. *The Emperor*, pp. 15, 119–20.
4. *Shah of Shahs*, pp. 134–9.
5. *Another Day of Life*, pp. 13–15.

CHAPTER IX

1. Published in 1988.
2. Mikhail Lermontov, *A Hero of Our Time*, trans. Philip Longworth (New English Library, 1962), pp. 9, 82, 113.
3. V. G. Kiernan, *The Duel* (1988), pp. 285–7.

CHAPTER X

1. *London Review of Books*, 7 June 1984.
2. *Difficulties with girls* (1988), pp. 16, 112, 179. See also Amis's collection of essays, *What became of Jane Austen?* (Penguin, 1981), p. 103: the remark about Jewish jokes begins an unamused discussion of Philip Roth's novel, *Portnoy's Complaint*.
3. *Difficulties with girls*, pp. 107, 256.
4. Ibid., pp. 158–9.
5. *Take a girl like you* (Penguin, 1962), pp. 171, 302.
6. *London Review of Books*, 20 Sept. 1984.
7. Ibid. 10 Nov. 1988. Hugh Kenner's fantasy is communicated in *A Sinking Island: The Modern English Writers* (1988).

CHAPTER XI

1. *The Facts* (1989), p. 99.
2. *The Counterlife* (1987), pp. 323–4.
3. See *Reading Myself and Others* (Penguin, 1985), p. 128. This collection of articles and interviews is dedicated 'To Saul Bellow, the "other" I have read with the deepest pleasure and admiration'.

CHAPTER XII

1. Quotations are taken from the following editions of English translations of Levi's books: *The Periodic Table* (translated by Raymond Rosenthal, Abacus, 1986), *If this is a man* and *The Truce* (translated by Stuart Woolf, Abacus, 1987), *Moments of Reprieve* (translated by Ruth Feldman, Abacus, 1987), *If not now, when?* (translated by William Weaver, Abacus, 1987), *The*

Wrench (translated by William Weaver, Abacus, 1988) and *The Drowned and the Saved* (translated by Raymond Rosenthal, Michael Joseph, 1988).

2. *London Review of Books*, 23 Oct. 1986.

3. *The Periodic Table*, pp. 151–3.

CHAPTER XIII

1. *A Disaffection* (1989), pp. 276–7.

2. *The Book of Sandy Stewart*, ed. Roger Leitch (1988), p. 3.

CHAPTER XIV

1. W. H. Auden, *Selected Essays* (1964), p. 22.

2. From Barthes's 'The Death of the Author', reprinted in *Modern Criticism and Theory* (ed. David Lodge, 1988), p. 167.

3. See Robert Con Davis's commentaries for his anthology *Contemporary Literary Criticism* (1986), p. 298.

4. Christopher Norris in 'Paul de Man's Past': *London Review of Books*, 4 Feb. 1988.

5. Simon Critchley, in a letter to the *London Review of Books* (31 Mar. 1988) on matters arising from Norris's article of the previous month.

6. Quoted in an *Observer* editorial of 19 Feb. 1989.

7. The interview, with Miriam Gross, was reprinted in *Required Writing: Miscellaneous Pieces 1955–1982* (1983), p. 52. The title of the collection gives us the recluse who might well have refused to be interviewed: it is as if we are meant to think that he did not want to write these pieces, or that they have something in common with completed income-tax forms.

8. *Independent*, 8 Oct. 1988.

9. See Deirdre Bair, *Samuel Beckett* (Picador, 1980), pp. 132, 145, 157, 172–3, 205, 279.

10. *Watt* (Picador, 1988), pp. 30–1.

11. *London Review of Books*, 4 Feb. 1988.

12. Ibid. 15 Sept. 1988. Raymond Carver made this remark in the course of an interview with Kasia Boddy.

13. Ibid. 29 Sept. 1988.

14. *Independent*, 1 Oct. 1988.

CHAPTER XV

1. Spring 1987.

2. These words supply the title of a volume of critical writings published in 1988: see pp. 92–3, 96, 121.

3. It was published in the collection of 1987, *The Haw Lantern*.

4. The lines come from the poem 'Ulster: 1912'.

INDEX

Gothic novel, the 85, 88
Grange, Lord 43
Greene, Graham 117
Griffiths, Ralph 195
Guardian 109, 125

Haddington, Lord 57
Haile Selassie, Emperor 105–6
Hamilton, Ian 133, 181
Hawthorne, Nathaniel 60
  The Blithedale Romance 60
Hayter, Sir George 41
Hayter, John 41
Heaney, Seamus 101, 201–5
  'A Peacock's Feather' 203–5
Heidegger, Martin 174–5
Hemingway, Ernest 108
Herling, Gustav:
  A World Apart 147
Hitler, Adolf 205
Hogg, James 37, 53, 55
  Confessions of a Justified Sinner 40
Home, Lord 23
Horizon 170
Hugo, Victor 99
Hume, David 51
Hungerford 168
Hunt, Leigh 47

Independent 125, 186, 192
India 65, 206
IRA 202, 204
Iran 106–7
Israel 134, 136, 139, 146, 199

Jacobson, Dan 150
Jamal, Hakim 59
James, Henry 2, 5–7, 9
  'The Friends of the Friends' 8
  'The Jolly Corner' 9
  The Spoils of Poynton 7
  The Turn of the Screw 5–9
James, M. R. 2
James, P. D.:
  A Taste for Death 87
Jaruzelski, General 110
Jeffrey, Francis 195
Jewish life and literature 79, 122–3,
  134–7, 139, 144–7, 150–1, 152–5
Johnson, R. Brimley 50
Johnson, Samuel 36, 49, 106
  The Rambler 47, 48
  Rasselas 106, 107
Joseph II, Emperor 46

Joyce, James:
  Ulysses 19
Jung, Carl Gustav 37

Kafka, Franz 105–6, 160
Kalandra, Zavis 98
Kapuscinski, Ryszard 104–5, 109–10
  Another Day of Life 108–9
  The Emperor 105–6, 107
  Shah of Shahs 106–8
Keats, John 95, 165
Kelman, James 156
  A Disaffection 156–60, 161
  Greyhound for Breakfast 156, 160
Kennedy, Bobby 137
Kenner, Hugh 129, 130
Kermode, Frank 129, 186
Khan, Rahila. *See* Forward, Toby
Khomeini, Ayatollah 188–9, 193
Kiernan, V. G. 115–16
Kipling, Rudyard 188, 205
Klima, Ivan 96, 97, 101–2, 103
  My First Loves 96, 98, 101–3
Kristeva, Julia 175
Kundera, Milan 19, 96–8, 103
  The Farewell Party 96
  The Joke 98
  Life is elsewhere 96, 97, 98–101
  The Lyric Age 98
  The Unbearable Lightness of Being 97
Kunstler, William 59
Kussi, Peter 98

Labour Party 111, 202
Laing, R. D.:
  The Divided Self 178
Larkin, Philip 127–9, 130, 131, 172,
  176–7
  'Letter to a Friend about Girls'
  126–8
Leavis, F. R. 6–7, 93, 171, 172,
  199–200
Lee, Vernon 11
  Supernatural Tales 10–11
Lennox, Charlotte:
  The Female Quixote 21–2
Lermontov, Mikhail 115–16
  A Hero of our Time 115–16
Levi, Primo 133, 137, 144–6, 147–55,
  177–8, 179, 180
  The Drowned and the Saved 145–6,
  153–4
  If not now, when? 149, 150, 154
  If this is a man 144, 145, 149, 177–8

OXFORD

MORE OXFORD PAPERBACKS

Details of a selection of other Oxford Paperbacks follow. A complete list of Oxford Paperbacks, including The World's Classics, Twentieth-Century Classics, OPUS, Past Masters, Oxford Authors, Oxford Shakespeare, and Oxford Paperback Reference, is available in the UK from the General Publicity Department, Oxford University Press (RS), Walton Street, Oxford, OX2 6DP.

In the USA, complete lists are available from the Paperbacks Marketing Manager, Oxford University Press, 200 Madison Avenue, New York, NY 10016.

Oxford Paperbacks are available from all good bookshops. In case of difficulty, customers in the UK can order direct from Oxford University Press Bookshop, 116 High Street, Oxford, Freepost, OX1 4BR, enclosing full payment. Please add 10 per cent of the published price for postage and packing.

DEPRESSION AFTER CHILDBIRTH

Katharina Dalton

Second Edition

With a foreword by Esther Rantzen

Using many case histories to emphasize her belief, Dr Dalton attacks the popular idea that postnatal depression is caused by a combination of sleeplessness, lack of outside contacts, and loss of independence, and argues that a cure will only be achieved when it is recognized for what it is—a hormonal change that occurs in a woman's body after childbirth. Along with the vivid descriptions of the effects of postnatal depression are the hopes for the future given by women who have been cured through hormone therapy.

For anyone, male or female, concerned with postnatal depression, this book will give a greater understanding of the suffering that it causes, and above all it will help mothers to recognize their own symptoms and seek the correct treatment.

THE A–Z OF WOMEN'S HEALTH

Derek Llewellyn-Jones

Every woman needs to know the facts about herself. *The A–Z of Women's Health* puts these facts at her fingertips. Alphabetically arranged for easy reference and complemented by many diagrams and photographs, this is an indispensable guide to female life and health.

'His understanding and compassion are as evident as his sense and expertise.' *Times Educational Supplement*

'sensible and authoritative' *Journal of Obstetrics and Gynaecology*

Oxford Reference

THE REPRODUCTION REVOLUTION
New Ways of Making Babies
Peter Singer and Deane Wells

'It is a delight to welcome *The Reproduction Revolution* a lucid, sensitive, up-do-date account of just what has been achieved, what has *not* been achieved, and what might be achieved in applying bioscience to human procreation . . . the book is far and away the clearest guide yet published to the techniques of artificial fertilisation, surrogate motherhood and sex selection; futuristic possibilities such as cloning and genetic manipulation; and the ethical issues which are with us today or likely to arise in the future . . . this must be one of the best buys of the year.' *New Society*

'more valuable than hordes of specialist committees are books like this which discuss the issues, opening them up for the interested but ethically inexpert' *Hospital Doctor*

WHY ARE WE WAITING?
An Analysis of Hospital Waiting-lists
John Yates

This book sets out to challenge British complacency about hospital waiting-lists, and rejects the assumption that a large proportion of British citizens must inevitably have to wait long periods of time for simple surgical procedures.

The book is aimed at two audiences—those within and those outside the NHS. For those outside it reveals the most enormous variations in the provision and use of resources between the hundreds of health authorities throughout the length and breadth of Britain. With those who work in the NHS it may not be popular—it expresses openly some of the inefficiencies of the current system. In so doing it runs the risk of bringing some criticism to the large number of surgeons and managers who are devoting time and attention to improving the situation.

MEN AND WOMEN
How different are they?

John Nicholson

Dr Nicholson considers that it is high time that some of our civilization's many myths about the differences between the attitude and behaviour of the two sexes were quashed. In this revised and expanded edition of his popular and successful book, *A Question of Sex,* he brings us more startling conclusions about the real similarities and differences between the sexes.

'An invaluable book for any woman (or man), it deserves an immediate place on the book shelf of home, clinic, or women's centre.' *Journal of the Institute of Health Education*

'*Men and Women* is a mine of useful one-liners with which to trump most suggestions of male superiority . . . As a review of research on sex difference, the book is lucid, and admirable for the caution it advises in interpreting the results of psychological research.' *New Scientist*

MORAL DILEMMAS IN MODERN MEDICINE

Edited by Michael Lockwood

Test-tube babies, surrogate mothers, the prescribing of contraceptive pills to girls under sixteen—these are some of the moral dilemmas in medicine that have recently hit the headlines, and will continue to do so for some time. Mary Warnock, Bernard Williams, and R. M. Hare are among those who tackle the ethical problems in modern medical practice from the standpoints of philosophy, medicine, and the law. Other contributors are: Michael Lockwood, Ian Kennedy, J. A. Muir Gray, Raanan Gillon, and Roger Higgs.

ARISTOTLE TO ZOOS

A Philosophical Dictionary of Biology

Peter & Jean Medawar

In this book Peter and Jean Medawar have compiled their personal A–Z of the life sciences. In some two hundred short essays on a wide variety of biological topics of general interest they offer both an introduction for the layman and a source of new insight for the specialist. The book provides a blend of fact, literary allusion, historical anecdote, and mythical and folk tradition.

'One of the most delightful, and delightfully eccentric, dictionaries I have ever encountered.' *New York Times Book Review*

'beautifully written . . . a thoroughly incisive and level-headed treatment of how practising biological scientists think and what they think about' *Times Higher Education Supplement*

THE STANDING OF PSYCHOANALYSIS

B. A. Farrell

Psychoanalysis is a notoriously controversial and confusing subject. What are we to make of it? In this book, B. A. Farrell addresses the two central problems psychoanalysis raises. How believable is it as a doctrine? And how effective is it as a therapy?

Mr Farrell's book offers a view of what Freud's 'discoveries' amount to, and what psychoanalysis has achieved. It places the subject on our contemporary map of knowledge and belief by showing where it stands in relation to science, history, psychiatry, objective psychology, and common sense. And by clarifying the controversy that surrounds the subject, it dispels some of the confusions which perplex experts and laymen alike.

An OPUS book

THE MORAL STATUS OF ANIMALS

Stephen R. L. Clark

Most of us exploit animals for our own purposes. The moral status of animals has long been a subject of heated debate. According to the great philosophers, morality has nothing to say about our relations with non-humans. Modern liberals, though, have allowed that animals should at least be spared unnecessary pain.

In his lively and controversial book Stephen Clark argues that this liberal principle is powerful enough in itself to require most of us to be vegetarian. He discusses the arguments and rationalizations offered in defence of our behaviour in farms, in laboratories, and at home, and reveals their roots in neurotic fantasy.

'an erudite, intriguing, provocative, disturbing book which deserves close attention' *Month*

THE OXFORD COMPANION TO ANIMAL BEHAVIOUR

Revised impression

Edited by David McFarland

* Over 200 authoritative articles, written by specialists and arranged alphabetically for easy reference
* Find out how different animals select their partners, bring up their young, organize their societies, and much more—
* NEW in this revised impression: a detailed subject and animal index for quick access to a wealth of information in the *Companion*

'indispensable for understanding how and why animals do such fascinating things' *Times Educational Supplement*

Oxford Reference